Quakernomics

Quakernomics

An Ethical Capitalism

Mike King

ANTHEM PRESS
LONDON · NEW YORK · DELHI

Anthem Press
An imprint of Wimbledon Publishing Company
www.anthempress.com

This edition first published in UK and USA 2014
by ANTHEM PRESS
75–76 Blackfriars Road, London SE1 8HA, UK
or PO Box 9779, London SW19 7ZG, UK
and
244 Madison Ave #116, New York, NY 10016, USA

Copyright © Mike King 2014

The author asserts the moral right to be identified as the author of this work.

British Library Cataloguing-in-Publication Data
A catalogue record for this book is available from the British Library.

Library of Congress Cataloging-in-Publication Data
A catalog record for this book has been requested.

ISBN-13: 978 0 85728 112 8 (Pbk)
ISBN-10: 0 85728 112 7 (Pbk)

Cover photo: FotoSergio/Shutterstock.com

This title is also available as an ebook.

CONTENTS

Illustrations: QUAKER TRACES IN LONDON

Part III: QUAKERS, SOCIETY AND SOCIAL JUSTICE

FOREWORD

Mike King sets Quakernomics in its historical context. He explains the central role which Quaker firms played in the development of industrial capitalism. He defines enterprises as capitalistic if they produce a return beyond that which is required for their survival. Such firms are able to provide capital for investment in the future. What is remarkable about the contribution of Quaker businesses to the Industrial Revolution is how far the members of a small religious society dominated the economic canvas of their day. Their early success as bankers and shopkeepers was because they were trusted. They were the first to put fixed prices on their goods for sale. Customers said that they could send their children into Quaker shops, knowing that they would be treated as if they had gone there themselves. King attributes their success to hard work and thrift, supported by their religious beliefs. They believed in equality between women and men and in the worth of every individual.

The author illustrates their business methods and approach through brief histories of a wide range of successful Quaker enterprises. There were occasional lapses, but one of their strengths was their common concern for the Quaker reputation. This led to a degree of supervision by fellow members of the Quaker Meetings to which they belonged. They also benefited from having ready access to an active and widespread Quaker network. The author's history of Quaker firms, beginning with the Darbys of Coalbrookdale, brings out another attribute of their success: their capacity for innovation. It may be that those who were prepared to think for themselves in matters of religion questioned accepted practice in their trades. They sought improvement and looked for better methods and processes of achieving their commercial aims. King cites the example of Robert Ransome, a manufacturer of agricultural machinery who, around 1800, devised a process for chilling steel and used interchangeable parts to build his implements, paving the way for modern manufacturing methods. In another example of their application of science to industry, the Quaker historian Raistrick writes: 'In strict proportion to their numbers, Friends have secured something like forty times their due proportion of fellows of the Royal Society during its long history'.

After making such an extraordinary contribution to the founding of a market economy in Britain, why did Quaker enterprises then seem to lose their distinctive management style with its ethical dimension? This is perhaps connected to two of the characteristics common to the firms described by King. First, they were notably family firms. Family ownership builds in an incentive to take a long-term view, to maintain the firm for subsequent generations. That is reflected in the way those companies invested in the future. That sense of continuity offers security to all who work in such companies, leading to their length of service and to the value of investment in training. Equally families running businesses have a direct interest in their own personal reputations and wish to see their ethical values perpetuated. But the family line may run out and the ownership of their enterprises may change.

Second, the working relationships which were typical of the early Quaker firms were well suited to owner-managers taking a personal interest in the wellbeing of their employees. However the economic scale of banking, for example, inevitably resulted in the amalgamation of the Quaker country banks into larger units which could not be managed in the same personal way. The Quaker ethical approach to ownership and management became less practical and possible as companies became larger in order to harvest the advantages that came with size.

Against the background of individual enterprises, King turns to how Quakernomics might fit within mainstream economic theory from Adam Smith to John Maynard Keynes. Economists drew on the way enterprises were managed; Adam Smith did so, for example, on the division of labour. This was however to derive overall theories on the development of market capitalism and the economy. Even where Milton Friedman wrote at company level in order to expound his egregious theory of social responsibility, he was basing his analysis on the publicly quoted shareholder-owned company model, responding to a changing pattern of investors. This is far removed from the ownership pattern of the pioneering Quaker firms. King therefore understandably concludes that the history of the Quaker enterprises has not found a place in any generalised theory of economics, yet its ethics remain an inspiration. At its heart, he writes, Quakernomics is the enthusiastic pursuit of economic activity as a social good. That is an aim which it is valuable to retain and to champion as this book does.

Sir Adrian Cadbury
June 2013

ACKNOWLEDGEMENTS

I am grateful to the bloggers at the Quakernomics blog (www.quakerweb. org.uk/blog), in particular Tony Weekes whose early encouragement and pointers .to sources were invaluable. As shown, however, by the varied comments and views on the Quakernomics blog, there are differing interpretations of what 'Quakernomics' might be. The views set out in this book are entirely mine and are not necessarily endorsed by or constitute official positions of Quaker Peace and Social Witness or the Religious Society of Friends in Britain.

I would also like to thank Dunkin Shultz, the librarian at Ipswich Meeting House, for leaving a legacy of marvellous books that helped me in my initial researches, and the librarians at Friends House in London for their assistance. Thanks go too to many other people who encouraged me in this project, above all to my beloved wife Heather Bruce for putting up with – of all topics – economics.

INTRODUCTION

This is a book about economics, or capitalism, which is more or less the same thing. It is about the way the Quakers ran their businesses, and the ethical implications of their business practice for capitalism. We shall examine these businesses, mostly in a historical period that may seem rather remote to us. We shall then review the history of economic thought from the perspective of those Quaker enterprises, asking to what extent the question of ethical capitalism – as informed by the Quaker example – has formed part of that discourse. Some may think that the political debate of left vs. right has been made obsolete by the politics of the middle ground. Some may think that the economic debate of socialism vs. capitalism has long been futile. But early economic thought can be clearly divided between left and right, between those polemicists wary of the free market and those advocating it. What remains true today of these divisions is that economists of the right want to see government reduced, while those of the left want to see the state expand its regulatory powers over unbridled capitalism. Whatever apparent convergence there may be in economics and politics, the reality is that the debate over the regulation of capitalism is as vital today as a hundred years ago. This book is intended as a contribution to that debate.

The 2012 Olympics opening ceremony, created by film director Danny Boyle, received universal critical acclaim. It was a reprise of British history including a spectacular visualisation of the bursting forth of the Industrial Revolution from under a rural idyll, and in Boyle's statement of intent for the show he wrote:

> In 1709 Abraham Darby smelted iron in a blast furnace, using coke. And so began the Industrial Revolution. Out of Abraham's Shropshire furnace flowed molten metal. Out of his genius flowed the mills, looms, engines, weapons, railways, ships, cities, conflicts and prosperity that built the world we live in.[1]

Boyle didn't mention that Abraham Darby was a Quaker, and that his genius was no one-off but a characteristic of generations of Darby ironmasters; a genius also found in the many other Quakers who helped shape the Industrial Revolution. In fact the unique role of the Quaker Darbys has often been commented on. For example, in an American environmentalist novel called *The Iron Bridge* the heroine time-travels into the eighteenth century in order to stop the Darbys powering up the Industrial Revolution.[2] We will also time-travel to the same location, that of the Quaker ironmasters in Shropshire, but with an eye for the economics of the business. It turns out that not much has really changed in economics since then, only that the fundamentals are regularly forgotten. For example the crash of Lehman Brothers in 2008 marked what is known as the Credit Crunch or Great Recession, while in 1866 a few foolish Quaker financiers created a parallel disaster in the crash of Overend & Gurney, causing a mini-recession and the bankruptcy of a further two hundred firms. These Quakers turn out to be the exception to the rule of economic competence more regularly exhibited by the group as a whole – a tiny handful of investment bankers forgot the fundamentals of economic life in 1866, just as the derivatives traders did in 2008.

So who are the Quakers? They leave their traces everywhere, but only if one knows where to look. For example, if coming into London from the east by train, one passes the 2012 Olympic Games site in Stratford where the triumph of Abraham Darby I was celebrated in such style. Less than a mile south of the track is West Ham Park, where the Quaker botanist, physician and philanthropist, John Fothergill, left his botanical collection to the nation. In the heart of Stratford itself, just out of sight from the train, is an obelisk dedicated to the Quaker banker and philanthropist Samuel Gurney. He was brother of the famous prison reformer Elizabeth Fry, and wise director of Overend & Gurney, whose immediate descendents managed to ruin the company. Should you spend a £5 note in the Starbucks coffee-shop just by the obelisk, then on the rear of the note you will see Elizabeth Fry herself, with another Quaker in the background, Thomas Buxton.[3] His name is associated with a brewery that was the largest in London in its day. It would also be poignant to have a copy of Herman Melville's *Moby-Dick* with you, should you want something to read, as it opens in Nantucket, a Quaker whaling community of the mid-nineteenth century. The connections multiply, however: the two academics who founded the coffee chain named it after the first mate on the whaling ship in Melville's story. The first mate's name was in turn taken from a Quaker family in Nantucket called Starbuck. If one returns to the train then after passing the Olympic site one sees to the right the impressive architecture of the Bryant & May match factory, now flats. This was built by Quakers, one of the largest match factories in the world. Still looking north one may spot the sign 'Allen & Hanburys' on an old factory in Bethnal Green. This too was founded by Quakers, in its time one of the largest pharmaceutical companies in the world. And when one crosses the great foyer of Liverpool Street station and out of the Liverpool Street exit, one passes not one but two tributes to Quaker activism: sculptures commemorating the 'Kindertransport' which rescued nearly ten thousand Jewish children from Nazi Europe – my mother being one of them. The Quakers played a prominent role in this operation: in its funding, in persuading government to relax immigration requirements and in accompanying the children, often traumatised by the separation from their parents and even siblings.

Some people may either have a friend who is a Quaker, or may have spotted a Quaker Meeting House in their town, or may know that Cadbury's (of chocolate fame) was a business run by Quakers. But beyond that there is little awareness of their origins or the remarkable place they have in the history of industrial capitalism. In 2012 Melvyn Bragg devoted one of his *In Our Time* broadcasts to the Quakers, starting with the assertion that it was the biggest and most powerful force in Puritanism in the wake of the execution of Charles I and the dismantling of the Church of England's power. The Quakers, we learn, became a substantial movement that survived harsh persecution in a time of religious ferment. The programme commented on the Quaker habits of literacy, prolific letter writing and knowledge of legislation, the all-important 'Peace Testimony', and the idea that they had an influence quite out of proportion to their numbers, including perhaps the hastening of the Restoration. The latter period saw the real backlash against them. But only towards the end of the programme did Bragg mention their success as traders – selling drinking chocolate as an alternative to alcohol. Their lasting impact on the English-speaking world, it was suggested, lies in the principle of equality and the force of personal conviction, which has contributed to the British tradition of equality and toleration in public life.[4]

In this book I will show that in addition, the lasting impact of the Quakers was through the central role they played in the development of industrial capitalism. It sought to be a moral and philanthropic form of business. This is however an idea that is rather out of favour today. For example, Zoe Williams of the *Guardian* says philanthropic capitalism gives her the 'heebie-jeebies'.[5] Her objection could be – and many might agree – that wealthy capitalists probably get rich by charging too much for their products, paying too little to their workers or avoiding costly environmental safeguards (even if they do not break the law). Or perhaps we simply object to outdated paternalism. The Quaker philanthropic capitalists we shall consider in this book might stand thus accused, as do the other wealthy philanthropists of the Industrial Revolution. Of course even the word 'capitalism' gives the heebie-jeebies to many on the left, possibly including the majority of *Guardian* readers, despite their shares and properties. For the far left, the essence of capitalism is private ownership and the exploitation of those without capital and who are forced to work for a wage. For them, no amount of regulation could check the inherent evil of capitalism: it has to be abolished. A recent expression of this view comes from Michael Moore, the American documentary filmmaker. In his movie, *Capitalism: A Love Story*, he documents some of the poverty to be found in America after the shocks of Hurricane Katrina and the 2008 banking crisis. He concludes by saying that capitalism is an evil, and you can't regulate an evil, you have to eliminate it. (His proposed alternative, rather naively, is 'democracy'.) Similarly, in a 2010 article on Ralph Miliband, the *Independent* pointed out that unlike his sons – the Labour politicians Ed and David – Ralph was a Marxist who believed not in the reform of capitalism, but its overthrow.[6]

But perhaps capitalism is not an evil per se; perhaps its overthrow makes no sense; and perhaps philanthropy is what humanises it and needs to be restored in some modern innovative manner. The Quaker industrialists and financiers we shall examine here show us a capitalism in the service of the community, regulated effectively by religious morality and suggesting, despite the very different world of today, many positive steps we could take to better regulate our global contemporary capitalism, one that has been drastically *deregulated* in the last thirty years. But the Quaker example does not necessarily lead us to either an argument for religion or an argument for traditional socialist solutions, to the old-style 'big government' of the post-war nationalised industries. Instead, the Quaker example seems to suggest a genuine middle way – one that I am calling 'Quakernomics'.

As indicated above, this is a book of two halves. Chapters 1 through 13 deal with the Quakers, while Chapters 14 through 23 deal with economic thinkers from the perspective of ethical capitalism. In doing so the politics of much economic thought has inevitably been laid bare, and that politics is quite clearly divided between left and right. We should not be dismayed by this: after all the early term for the discipline of economics was 'political economy'.

A Note on Sources

We will see that Quakernomics is about a business ethos, and therefore about a whole way of thinking, or in other words a *philosophy* of economics. When it comes to the disciplines of economics, political economy and philosophy I will draw on well-known writers going back to Adam Smith, all the way up to contemporary Nobel Prize–winning economists of today. But I draw on more obscure sources for the history of the Quaker enterprises, so I will introduce them now. The first comprehensive study of Quaker businesses was by Paul Emden, in a book called *Quakers in Commerce*, published in the 1930s. According to Sir Montague Burton, who wrote the foreword to Emden's book, Emden himself was an authority on the history of European finance.[7] Given this fact and that he was not a Quaker I believe that his work is both likely to be sound on questions of money and likely to be impartial. I will cross-reference Emden's account with some more recent ones, including *The Quaker Enterprise* (1980) by David Burns Windsor, who is also not a Quaker as far as I can tell, and James Walvin's *The Quakers: Money and Morals* (1997). Walvin, again not a Quaker, became interested in the Quaker businesses during research for his main academic pursuit, the history of slavery. Walvin draws on neither Emden nor Windsor, but does rely on a Quaker writer of industrial history: Arthur Raistrick, who wrote three books in all, one on Quakers in science and industry, one on the Darbys of Coalbrookdale, and one on the Quaker Lead Company. Raistrick was not born a Quaker, but became one, drawn to the Society of Friends – as they are known – because of its pacifism. By cross-referencing the general accounts from these four key authors, reinforced by more specialist volumes and other sources dealing with individual Quaker companies or industrialists, I hope to give a reliable historical picture of Quaker business practice and the sheer scale of it.

Part I

BACKGROUND

Chapter 1

QUAKERS AND COMMERCE

There are many excellent books on the early Quakers, which naturally focus on their religious beliefs, the religious and political turmoil of the period, and the emergence of George Fox as the preacher who founded the movement. Here I will simply draw out the key characteristics which were to shape the Quakers as ethical and highly successful industrialists and financiers (with occasional exceptions: they were, after all, only human).

The personality of George Fox (1624–1691) is no doubt the key to these characteristics. Fox was born into a Protestant family that had known persecution. His father was a weaver. George was taught to read and write and was apprenticed to a shoemaker and trader in sheep. His father did well and left Fox some money, so we can say that he had a rounded background as an artisan, a husbandman, a man used to ordinary people and also to trade and the proper investment of money. He has been described as 'more prosperous than all but a handful of his contemporaries' – perhaps an exaggeration, but indicative at least that he was no stranger to money and its ways.[1] As the movement he founded became a force in British religious and political life, so too it became persecuted. The key problem for the Quakers lay in Fox's insistence that all are equal before God and that priests and churches make religiously unacceptable claims on the people – in particular the claim to deference and the claim for tithes. Under Cromwell the Quakers were protected to some degree, but with the Restoration in 1660, which brought both the monarchy and the Church of England back to power, persecution was brutal. Fox himself was often imprisoned, and his astonishing and robust vitality finally broken in Launceston Castle in 1656, even before the worst of persecutions visited on his followers.

To this day Quakers have a standing executive called 'Meeting for Sufferings', a name going back to that period of the seventeenth century when Quakers would meet to record in minute detail the persecution of their members and the action they would take to support those beaten and imprisoned and their families. Their solidarity and record keeping – initiated by Fox and Margaret Fell – were crucial to their initial survival and growth as a movement, and later became central to their business success. Margaret Fell, wife of Justice Thomas Fell, was 'convinced' (the Quaker term for conversion) early on by Fox, wrote many important Quaker tracts (one of which is believed to have been translated into Latin by Spinoza), and brought to the movement her husband's knowledge of the law. She married Fox after the death of Fell. This keen interest in the law – and the abiding by it – was also an important element in Quaker business success, and also, of course, in their efforts to change or introduce laws such as those that led to the abolition of slavery.

The scattering of Quakers across the country, away from large centres like London, prompted much letter-writing, including by Fox, whose lengthy journal includes extracts from much of his voluminous correspondence. Quakers also had a keen interest in science and the emerging patterns of thought now termed the Enlightenment, which fed in turn into an interest in education and the creation of Quaker schools round the country and abroad. To this day many prominent non-Quakers speak of their exceptional education in Quaker schools, and it is notable, for example, that the eminent Palestinian peace-maker and negotiator for the PLO, Hanan Ashrawi, was educated at the Quaker school in Ramallah. Edmund Burke, the Irish statesman and philosopher, was also educated at a Quaker school, in a pattern typical of many outstanding individuals who were not themselves Quakers.

The refusal of Quakers to swear oaths, and the many other characteristics that placed them beyond the Church of England – more so than almost any other sect – led to them facing obstacles to many livelihoods and positions of public office. The Corporation Act of 1661 for example prevented their election to any position in local government or corporations. They were thus excluded, not just from the professions, but also from the universities. In so-called corporate towns it was not possible to carry on most trades without being a freeman of the corporation, as it was known, and to do that one had to swear oaths of loyalty. Hence Quakers flocked to non-corporate towns like Birmingham. Of course non-conformists of all stripes experienced the same problems, so Birmingham attracted such men as Priestley, Watt, Boulton, Keir and Wedgwood, which group created the Lunar Society for scientific and philosophical discussion and exchange of information: a 'college' of intellectuals operating outside of the conventional system. Quakers were very much involved with groups like this.

Quakers rejected priests and churches, hymn-books and ritual. Their meetings for worship had no structure other than silence and the 'ministries' of those moved in that silence to speak of the inner light, as they called it. 'Meeting' with a capital 'M' became the term for the community at different levels, a structure later formalised as Local Meeting, Monthly Meeting (now Area Meeting) and Yearly Meeting. Meeting Houses were built, an expression of the Puritan rejection of art and icon, and in time the grand Meeting House in Euston, London was built as the UK centre for the Quaker movement.

James Walvin, in his book on the Quakers and their business ethics, tells us, 'Of all the heirs of the Puritan Revolution who survived into the eighteenth century, the Quakers were perhaps the most conspicuous.'[2] While many non-conformists played a significant role in the Industrial Revolution, we will see that there is no single group as large or as consistent in its contribution – or indeed as conspicuous. Quakers *looked* different, and did not take their hats off. That alone led to countless attacks in the early days of their persecution. The characteristics that made them flourish included literacy, education, solidarity, equality and the yeoman instinct for hard work, thrift, husbandry … and growth. The Quaker Business Method – a method for reaching decisions that has nothing to do with commerce – and the insistence on the acting out of conscience gave both the ethical background and a powerful group dynamic to Quaker enterprises. The ethics of the Quakers are summed up in their four 'Testimonies': Peace, Equality, Truth and Simplicity. These derive directly from George Fox's teachings, but they are also those of the Christian tradition of Christ and St Paul. However, as I hope to establish, no other single identifiable religious group in history has applied these so extensively to economic activity.

Economic Activity, Social Justice and Capitalism

In the vast literature on economics the nature of economic activity itself sometimes gets lost, or its characteristics taken for granted. By exploring the history of the Quaker enterprises we gain a vivid insight into the very nature of economic activity, that fundamental exchange of goods and services between people most often mediated through money. I define 'Quakernomics' here to be the economic activity of the Quakers, a well-documented practice of commerce, rather than a theoretical system.

However, as we investigate this practice, we can test it against existing economic theories. Crucially, we are looking at how Quakernomics embodies principles of social justice, or more specifically, economic justice. We will see that the Quakers were at the heart of developments in industrial capitalism, a system that in its early days produced some spectacular and appalling examples of social injustice. To what extent were Quakers responsible for this or to what extent did they mitigate the worst effects of the Industrial Revolution, or even use it for progressive social ends?

I am using the term 'industrial capitalism' here to indicate that capitalism in a broader sense had been around a long time before the Industrial Revolution, and that its character was greatly changed by industry, meaning such things as factories, steam power and modern transport and communications. Early Quakers were often merchants, who are capitalists without necessarily requiring the methods of industrial production as the background to their trading. What they do need is capital. The work ethic of the Quakers and their simplicity of speech and life quickly led to prosperity and property, and that property soon included ownership of the industrial base of factories and transport and their financial underpinnings through banking. In other words, despite the almost otherworldliness of their conscience and spiritual practices, the Quakers were instinctive capitalists. To some sensitive ears, perhaps inclined to romantic or socialist literature, the term 'capitalism' is vaguely offensive, and cannot be associated with any good in the world. We need then some definition of capitalism as a starting point for the consideration of the Quaker businesses. In examining the various definitions put forward I prefer to start with this bare minimum:

Capitalism is the investment of a surplus for a return.

Socialists might insist that one insert the word 'private' before the word 'return', to indicate that profits accrue to individuals – capitalists – and not the community, and clearly this will be a central issue in Quakernomics. But this basic definition of capitalism can be adapted to cover major variants, such as the Soviet system, and the European post-war nationalised industries. In the Soviet economy capital – a surplus – had to be found just as in Western economies, in order to build the factories necessary for industrial production. This capital was extracted from the social order by central planning, and devoted to projects chosen by central planning, and the returns so created distributed to the people through central planning. The nationalised industries in post-war capitalist Europe were in principle not much different. In each case an existing surplus has to be taken from hoarding or circulation and devoted to buildings, machinery, stock, wages and distribution in order to produce goods for consumption.

In Quakernomics the existing surplus, or capital, was privately raised by Quakers, was privately invested in privately owned factories or banks, and the resulting returns privately held. There was nothing recognisably socialist in any of this. It was classical capitalism. So where was the economic justice in it? Where is the ethics in it?

Perhaps one of the most useful terms introduced or made popular by Marx in relation to economic justice is 'means of production'. It indicates the necessary natural or man-made resources whereby a person can sustain life and support a family, and it is of course a central Marxist contention that these means of production should be 'returned' to the worker. In considering the nature of the means of production, and who has control over them, we get to the heart of many issues in economics. We will see that as the Quakers moved from a predominantly farming background, in which they clearly owned their means of production as pre-industrial smallholders, to the position of traders and industrialists, they become the owners of the means of production for thousands, and collectively hundreds of thousands, of dependent workers.

When people own their own means of production, whether in the most basic form in a smallholding producing the bulk of food requirements for a family, or in small cottage industries, they are clearly more politically free than when their entire labour is expended via the means of production owned by an industrialist, such as in a factory. The history of economic development is that of this mass movement from self-reliant control over one's immediate means of production to the indebted reliance on the factory or land owner. The ethics of this are clear: once it is impossible for a family to own their immediate means of production, the owners of such means have various ethical obligations to their workers. The history of Quaker businesses demonstrates the keen sense of that obligation.

Thomas Paine, in his 1795 pamphlet *Agrarian Justice*, pointed out that the Native American knew nothing of the wretchedness experienced by a whole swath of humanity under so-called civilisation – the part generally called the working poor. Those who lived by hunting and gathering didn't know affluence either, but the issue was that the agricultural methods of civilisation could support ten times the population of the hunter-gatherer ... but only some of them in great affluence. One could not reverse civilisation in the pursuit of an end to wretchedness, but one could compensate the ordinary person for the loss of their birthright, that is land. Paine says:

> It is a position not to be controverted that the earth, in its natural uncultivated state was, and ever would have continued to be, *the common property of the human race*. In that state every man would have been born to property. He would have been a joint life proprietor with the rest in the property of the soil, and in all its natural productions, vegetable and animal.[3]

With the Enclosures Acts, colonisation and other means whereby the ordinary person is deprived of access to land an injustice is created. On this basis Paine believed that every owner of cultivated land 'owes to the community a *groundrent*'.[4] No original right to property can be discerned in history: land was always cultivated by collective human labour. He says however: 'The value of the improvement so far exceeded the value of the natural earth, at that time, as to absorb it; till, in the end, the common right of all became confounded into the cultivated right of the individual.'[5] Hence the system of landed property throws everybody else 'out of their natural inheritance.'[6] The unlanded person has no immediate means of production. Paine's solution to this injustice? To pay every person, at the age of 21, the sum of £15, to be taken from a national fund.

Paine's solution has never been attempted, but his arguments identify a source of economic injustice. In the days of their persecution the Quakers suffered the 'distrainment' of their lands and goods as a punishment that often deprived them of their means of production. Quakers who were farmers were driven off, not by Enclosures Acts, but because they refused to pay tithes. In other cases magistrates punished Quakers by confiscating workmen's tools.[7] Hence Quakers found themselves in the position of the majority under what Paine calls 'civilisation' – without a livelihood. Like so many others this meant a drift into towns and cities where employment was offered, but in the case of Quakers, they rapidly became the employers. Quakers, as originally merchants and yeomen, were used to being 'landed', that is to having private property, and, as they became wealthy industrialists and bankers, the extent of that property raises this question of economic injustice for their employees. Crucial to this, particularly as the Industrial Revolution was underway, is the problem of low or subsistence wages. We shall later use this issue as a touchstone for exploring the ideas of key economists from the eighteenth century to now.

The Protestant Work Ethic: Weber and Tawney

This is a book about economics, not religion. Ethically practiced economics is not just the preserve of the religious, and neither is unethically practiced economics the preserve of the godless. If the ideas of Quakernomics are not transferable to non-religious groups then there is little point to this book. But, in considering the history of Quaker businesses, we have to consider the role of religion from time to time, especially as it may have had a formative role in the Industrial Revolution itself.

Most thinkers in the fields of economics naturally ignore the role of religion. Two important exceptions exist however in the thought of R. H. Tawney and Max Weber. These writers appear to have independently come to similar conclusions: that the Industrial Revolution had a great deal to do with religion, specifically Protestantism or Puritanism. At the very least they point out that non-conformists like Quakers were barred from universities, professions and public office and so turned to trading and industry instead. More controversially the thesis of the 'Protestant work ethic' suggests that wealth was sought as a sign from God of righteousness.

Max Weber published his famous work *The Protestant Ethic and the Spirit of Capitalism* in 1905 in German, and the first English translation appeared in 1930. Weber does not associate capitalism with any intrinsic greed, in contrast to Marx. Weber says: 'Unlimited greed for gain is not in the least identical with capitalism, and is still less its spirit.'[8] Its 'spirit' or ethos is however influenced by certain religious ideas. He continues: 'In this case we are dealing with the connection of the spirit of modern economic life with the rational ethic of ascetic Protestantism.'[9] In Weber's thesis the origins of this lay in the Reformation and the replacement of the priestly assurance of God's grace with temporal signs, including self-confidence. This in turn was assured through the assiduous pursuit of a vocation, the success of which affirmed virtue, and also brought wealth. However, the asceticism of Protestantism demanded that this wealth be saved, so it became capital accumulated for investment or good works. Paul Emden reminds us of John Wesley's teaching: 'Make all you can,

save all you can, give all you can.'[10] The historian of banking, Noble
Foster Hoggson, chose to use the fuller version of Wesley's dictum to
introduce a chapter on the Amsterdam bourse:

> Get all you can without hurting your soul, your body, or your
> neighbour. Save all you can, cutting off every needless expense.
> Give all you can. Be glad to give, and ready to distribute; laying up
> in store for yourselves a good foundation against the time to come,
> that ye may attain eternal life.[11]

Weber himself comments: 'Even more striking […] is the connection of
a religious way of life with the most intensive development of business
acumen among those sects whose otherworldliness is as proverbial as
their wealth, especially the Quakers and the Mennonites.'[12] He identifies
the first movement towards this business acumen in the injunctions of
Luther who rejected monasticism as selfish. Weber says of him: 'In
contrast, labour in a calling appears to him as the outward expression
of brotherly love […] every legitimate calling has exactly the same
worth in the sight of God.'[13] It is Calvin who cements the association
between faith and industry, through the doctrine of the 'elect': these
are chosen by God for salvation, but it is impossible to ascertain who
they are. Instead it is an absolute duty to consider oneself 'chosen', as
any lack of such self-confidence must be the temptation of the devil. To
bolster this self-confidence intense worldly activity is the recommended
route.[14]

   But this part of Weber's thesis does not apply to the Quakers, who
utterly rejected the idea of the 'elect', insisting instead on 'that of God'
in everyone – total equality in the eyes of God. Hence for Quakers
prosperity was not a sign of salvation at all, but more often a troubling
eventuality that could lead them astray. But it was certainly true that hard
work and thrift came close to being religious ideals for the Quakers; the
laziness and luxury of the spendthrift, along with debt, were anathema
to them. The idea of 'good works' united all Protestants, however, and
the Quakers saw their industries as a means to pursue good works. Weber
makes clear that in Wesley's Methodism 'works are not the cause but
only the means of knowing one's state of grace.'[15] This was a doctrine
not held by the Quakers: they did not pursue good works to discover or
confirm their state of grace; that was a question of the inner light, and
that was cultivated in silent worship. Hence David Burns Windsor, in
commenting on the paternalism of the Quaker Crosfield family in their

soap factory, considers that it 'contained none of the Calvinistic notions of predestined superiority often associated with successful Protestant entrepreneurs.'[16]

Arthur Raistrick points out that George Fox and other early Quaker leaders often emphasised that 'trade and other occupations show forth truth to the world, and that traders must be scrupulous to keep all their dealings in the spirit of truth.'[17] In other words business activity and subsequent success did not show a state of grace or otherwise, but rather it tested one's capacity to adhere to the truth in one's actions. Nowhere was this as hard as when wealth went down the generations – as the Quakers were to discover.

Richard Tawney published his *Religion and the Rise of Capitalism* in 1926. Essentially it is a polemic against the divorce of commerce from social morality – put in his memorable words as against 'the abdication of the Christian Churches from departments of economic conduct and social theory long claimed as their province […]'.[18] The origins of this decline lies, as for Weber, with the Protestant Reformation. But Tawney thinks the Quakers an exception to this abdication: 'The Society of Friends, in an age when the divorce between religion and social ethics was almost complete, met the prevalent doctrine that it was permissible to take such gain as the market offered, by insisting on the obligation of good conscience and forbearance in economic transactions, and on the duty to make the honourable maintenance of the brother in distress a common charge.'[19] This is as good a summary of Quaker business ethics as any.

But why should we take the Quakers amongst all the Protestant sects to be capitalists of an exceptional sort? Or, more widely, amongst groups from other religions also noted as successful in business? For example a parallel has been drawn between the Quakers and the Jains of India (a religious sect originating in a similar fashion to Buddhism but much earlier).[20] A third and more obvious group is the Jews. However the Jains tended to specialise in trading, import–export, wholesaling and retailing,[21] while the Jews tended to specialise in retailing and finance. In contrast the Quakers included all these activities but also a strong manufacturing base. Where the Quakers have perhaps more in common with the Jains than the Jews is in their pacifism, but all three groups in different ways suffered from exclusions from public life, and are tiny minorities. All three groups became wealthy.

Geoffrey Elliott, in a book on the Quaker banking disaster of Overend & Gurney, compares Quakers and Jews as close-knit, small communities, quoting a writer of 1844: 'The clannish spirit kept alive in the tribe enables the wealthier members to command in their often daring speculations the assistance of the modest funds of their less wealthy brethren […]'.[22] Emden suggests of the Quakers: 'Together with two other vital types, the Jews and the Parsees, they invented and introduced "indebtedness by book-keeping" credit, that mighty instrument on which modern commerce is founded.'[23] (The Parsees are the Indian community of Zoroastrians, a religious group originally from Iran.) Are Quakers significantly different then from other Protestants, including Mennonites and Methodists, and significantly different from Jews, Jains and Parsees? I hope to demonstrate that the answer to this question is yes. We will see that the Quakers share the pacifism of the Mennonites, the industry and philanthropy of the Methodists, the financial genius of the Jews, the industrialism of the Jains and the trading nous of the Parsees. But I hope to show that what makes them stand out is that they were significant drivers of the Industrial Revolution not just in their innovations but also in their reach. I suggest that no other single group operated on such a huge scale in furthering industrial capitalism; no other group collectively pursued what I will call 'total capitalism' – that is a penetration of almost every aspect of industrialisation and its capital base.

Weber and Tawney stress the origins of capitalism in the religious doctrines of Protestantism, and there is no doubt that Quaker ethics as they applied them to business have a religious source. But I don't want to make the arguments in this book about economics and social justice stand or fall on religion. Tawney was a Christian whose thoughtful views on ethical economics were very influential in his time, but he is now completely forgotten. Contemporary thinkers of the left, often casting wide for radical ideas on the economy, ignore him today: I think it is because he is so overtly Christian. However, while religion has largely retreated to the private sphere, ethics has not; indeed it cannot. Hence I suggest that an atheist, socialist, humanist or otherwise non-religious ethics is equally applicable to economics.

Quakers and Class in Britain

Quakers were originally drawn from all walks of life, but one group is perhaps larger than the rest: those who farmed the land as 'husbandmen' or 'yeomen', terms whose meaning and significance are rather forgotten today. These were traditionally higher-ranking than peasants and either owned or leased land of anything from ten to a hundred acres. The wealthiest of the yeomen employed labourers and servants and approached minor landed gentry in their holdings, but the key element perhaps was in their status as free men. The equivalent class in Stalinist Russia were the so-called *kulaks* who largely resisted the collectivisation of farms and who were targeted for class destruction by Stalin because of their property-owning and employer status.[24] Their deaths through execution, purges, and famine are estimated anywhere between 600,000 to 60 million. In Britain of course no such fate befell the equivalent minor smallholders, but Quakers in this class were persecuted, as we saw, for an entirely different reason: they refused to pay tithes to support the local clergy.

Today the term 'yeoman' has lost its meaning as a free person owning perhaps a little land or a workshop such as a forge and engaging in as much trade as necessary with their goods in order to have a rounded set of life's necessities. Today we have such terms as the 'self-employed', 'farmer', or 'businessman' if we hold them in relative esteem, or 'peasant' to denigrate them as mere toilers of the soil. Yet the qualities of the yeoman are the key to understanding the mindset and success of the Quakers. People of this mindset, as Weber points out, are industrious yet not greedy; are self-reliant and dubious of state intervention; and above all are deeply cognisant of the *practical* bond between land, resources and flourishing. They are the antithesis of what the economist John Maynard Keynes and the journalist Will Hutton lambast as the *rentier* class: land- or stock-owners who get rich through the labours of others. Yet today anyone encountering a group of Quakers would instantly label them middle-class. Historically it is true that they were not of the proletariat, having arisen before that term had meaning, though in fact many Quakers have been and still are drawn from the ranks of the working class. It is also true that a significant number of Quakers were in fact gentry, for example the Gurneys of Norfolk who had originally arrived in England with William the Conqueror. Quakers who gained affluence became members of the middle class by default: they held the middle-class respect for industriousness, education and sobriety, though they mostly spurned the artistic trappings or minor luxuries of the lifestyle. Walvin, in considering the Quakers in the second half of the nineteenth century, puts it like this: 'The meetings did have their share of humble Friends, but they rarely got in the way of the middle-class-oriented local and national organisation that became the Society's distinguishing feature.'[25] Despite this I would say that the Quakers' origins as a persecuted group mean that they have one psychological trait normally lacking amongst the middle classes: their sense of being *outsiders*. This means that they took little for granted, did not in the first instance expect that the Establishment would help them when in difficulty, and feared debt because that would make them vulnerable.

Chapter 2

INDUSTRIAL CAPITALISM

Economic activity has always carried ethical implications. For example conservative politicians have declared at times that unemployment is a price worth paying for their favoured economic goal: a famous example being that of the British Chancellor in 1991, Norman Lamont, for whom reducing inflation was the top priority, and the price in unemployment 'well worth paying.'[1] But the unemployed, through no fault of their own, suffer for this goal, while the wealthy do not. This is a form of economic injustice. It appears that economic thinking is almost never divorced from political thinking, and it is the economics of the left that is generally more concerned with social justice. At the extreme of right-wing economics, in the thinking of people like Ayn Rand and Milton Friedman, there simply is no such thing as society (as Margaret Thatcher famously insisted, adding: 'There are individual men and women, and there are families'), and any interest in social justice is perfunctory or non-existent. Or, bizarrely, social justice means justice for the *wealthy*.

It is clear that working people in the factories and businesses of the early Industrial Revolution often faced appalling conditions, very long hours and miserable pay. The essential economic issue for the workers lay in the question of subsistence wages. Early economists thought that capitalist competition would inexorably drive down profits, which would drive down wages to subsistence level, meaning just enough for a working family to survive on and bring enough children into productive labour to keep the system going. The very language used by these economists is chilling: it suggests that people are like rats or other animals whose usefulness is measured by work and by the offspring they produce for more work. Indeed complaints were often made that animals were better treated.

A short extract epitomises both the fears of the workers and the solemn conviction of the early economists in contemplating industrial capitalism:

WHAT is competition, from the point of view of the workman? It is work put up to auction. A contractor wants a workman; three present themselves.

'How much for your work?'

'Half a crown; I have a wife and children.'

'Well; and how much for yours?'

'Two shillings; I have no children, but I have a wife.'

'Very well; and now how much for yours?'

'One and eightpence are enough for me; I am single.'

'Then you shall have the work.'

It is done; the bargain is struck. And what are the other two workmen to do? It is to be hoped they will quietly die of hunger. But what if they take to thieving? Never fear; we have the police. To murder? We have the hangman. As for the lucky one, his triumph is only temporary. Let a fourth workman make his appearance, strong enough to fast every other day, and his price will run down still lower; there will be a new outcast, perhaps a new recruit for the prison. Who would be blind enough not to see that under the reign of free competition the continuous decline of wages necessarily becomes a general law with no exception whatsoever?[2]

This extract from *The Organization of Labor* by Louis Blanc (an early French socialist) helps us pose one of the central ethical problems that Quakernomics in its early days had to address: subsistence wages under competitive capitalism. In Britain after the Credit Crunch in 2008 there was a rise in malnourishment amongst poor families, reports of adult starvation, and efforts by charities to increase provisions such as soup kitchens and food banks. But the scale of the problem is small compared to what poor people faced under the Industrial Revolution and in times such as the Great Depression, right up to the post-war period. We now have universal welfare rights, and a total prosperity that allows charities substantial funding from the conscientious well-off. But I would argue that the astronomical rise in income disparity now takes the place in questions of economic injustice that subsistence wages did in the heyday of Quakernomics in the nineteenth century.

The dividing line between the rich and the poor now is precisely an issue of capitalism: the person on the minimum wage – or below it in industries not bound by it – never earns enough to accumulate *capital*. Most professional people, on the other hand, do. 'Capital' here may mean not much more than owning a house, having a decent non-government pension, and having savings, perhaps some bonds or stocks, but that already separates Western society into two deeply divided communities. And when wealth climbs beyond this basic position of ownership, savings and pension, it rapidly becomes an obscenity when its owners compare their lives to those of the low-paid who work long hours and late into life with no prospect of savings. Why should the life-long labour of the poor become *more* burdensome with age and hold out no prospect of respite, while the labour of the other group leads to early retirement and savings that permit leisure pursuits and the best of medical attention? Why should those with high wages be able to save, invest their surplus, and live idly off the return, when those with low wages barely live off their labour? An economics that addresses this disparity is broadly left-wing, while an economics that welcomes it is broadly right-wing.

The issue of subsistence wages is not the only question of economic injustice of course. As Tawney puts it, the Quakers believed in 'the duty to make the honourable maintenance of the brother in distress a common charge.'[3] They held that the person in distress, whether through orphanage, sickness, disability or even just extreme youth or age, calls for 'honourable maintenance' from the rest of us as an obligation.

Quakernomics as a Microcosm of Industrial Capitalism

In Part II of this book we will examine the Quaker enterprises from the eighteenth to the twentieth centuries as examples of industrial capitalism. I claim that not only were the Quakers clear pioneers in some aspects of this – whether in technology, trading or finance – but that collectively they drove forward a significant sector of the entire Industrial Revolution. I am suggesting therefore that the Quaker enterprises can be seen as a microcosm of industrial capitalism and that Quakers effectively practised what I call 'total capitalism' – that is they drove into every niche of finance and production that goes to create an industrialised society. Nearly all, one should say, because they largely avoided spirits and the arms trade. Their habit of meticulous record keeping makes all of this history available to us in great detail, though I draw on secondary rather than primary sources.

But what would it take for this collective record to stand as a microcosm of economic activity that would be entirely relevant today? Surely *everything* has changed since the times of Victorian Britain? I would say no, and justify it by drawing attention to economic writings since the Credit Crunch. 'The Return of Marx!' 'The Return of Keynes!' Newspapers have been full of such headlines: a whole publishing industry has arisen with books like David Harvey's *The Enigma of Capital* and Robert Skidelsky's *Keynes: The Return of the Master*. Economists bewailing the unpreparedness of their discipline to predict the Credit Crunch are trawling through the history of their discipline and resurrecting many earlier thinkers; debates on the Great Depression are re-opened; and the Tea Party flock to the film version of Ayn Rand's *Atlas Shrugged* which promotes a free market utopia envisioned back in the 1950s. Perhaps it is not that economics has changed that much – though electronic banking, the Internet and securitisation are admittedly new – but that it has been imperfectly understood from the beginning. Hence I suggest that the relative antiquity of the thinker makes little difference: Adam Smith may be trawled for useful insights as much as Amyarta Sen. With this in mind I would argue that Quakernomics, of an average vintage of that of Marx, is no more outdated than any other dataset of economic activity, at least in its broad principles. It may tell us nothing specific about derivatives but everything about the necessity of banking regulation; it may tell us nothing specific about the exact minimum wage but everything about the economic injustice of wages that never permit a worker to share in the better things of life granted to the middle classes.

Chapter 3

CONTRASTING CULTURES IN 1845

In suggesting that the economics of the right is less interested in questions of social justice than the economics of the left I am not implying that Quakernomics necessarily draws on socialist thinking. In general Quakers were politically inclined to the Liberals rather than the socialists. But the common ground with socialists, the shared passion for social justice, suggests that we need to understand what actually divides the Quakers from the socialists. I will use two iconic events of 1845 to illustrate the difference: firstly the founding by the Irish Quaker industrialist John Grubb Richardson of the model workers' village of Bessbrook in Northern Ireland, and secondly the publication by Friedrich Engels of his influential book *The Condition of the Working Class in England.* A third event, the publication of Benjamin Disraeli's novel, *Sybil,* in the same year, will provide further contrast.

First let us consider the concept of the 'model workers' village'. Soviet Russia and Maoist China were full of 'model villages', and Hitler turned Terezin in what is now the Czech Republic into Theresienstadt, a model village for Jews and showcase to the world that between visits by the Red Cross and other concerned dignitaries slaughtered its inmates. We are suspicious of model villages. Yet, at the dawn of the industrial age, when industrialism by necessity implied the creation of new residential areas close to the factory gate, what were the alternatives? Market forces led to early forms of Rachmanism (speculative building), overcrowding and unsanitary conditions with the threat of fire. Unplanned conurbations sprouted across industrial England in which the working classes experienced not only the deprivation due to the loss of the means of production, but also the ills of dense urban life away from the country. So what is not to like about a planned garden city, where workers have space to grow vegetables and perhaps keep poultry and a pig; where amenities are planned to cater for life's necessities; and where a school and pharmacy are included?

This is what John Grubb Richardson provided for the workers of his linen mill at Bessbrook. It anticipated the better known model village of Bournville, and followed Robert Owen's earlier efforts at New Lanark in 1816, and also Quaker experiments in town planning in various colonial settlements. Richardson was a wealthy Quaker linen merchant whose father had so prospered in this business as to be one of the wealthiest in Ireland. John Grubb Richardson turned down a baronetcy from David Lloyd George – a recognition of his good works – due to his belief in equality (a pattern we will observe in other Quakers). Incidentally, he attended the same Quaker school in County Kildare as did Edmund Burke.

Bessbrook was a substantial venture: it was built to house four thousand workers, and, true to Richardson's Quaker values, had neither a public house nor a pawnbroker. He had been most directly influenced by the urban planning ideas of the Quaker William Penn, founder of Pennsylvania.[1] To build Bessbrook was not in itself an investment of a surplus for a return: it was the investment of a surplus to fulfil what Quakers thought of as their obligation. To some extent it was enlightened self-interest, perhaps: no doubt the men and women of Bessbrook were a fine workforce. But in monetary terms it made no sense at all: why not allow the market to provide the usual unsanitary hovels on the edge of a conurbation, live with ten per cent less productivity, say, from a restive workforce, and pocket the difference? If profit were the *only* motive, then Bessbrook would not have been built. But this was not socialism, neither was it ogre capitalism: rather it conformed to Weber's idea of capitalism in the first instance as not being solely about profit.

Engels and the Conditions of the Working Class

But what could workers expect in a typical urban setting where factories sprouted, housing development followed in hotchpotch fashion and workers had to face hard-nosed entrepreneurs, including publicans, determined to part them from their wages? And when their meagre wages ran out, forced them to turn to the loan shark? Engels' book, *The Condition of the Working Class in England*, tells the story. His father owned a thread mill in Manchester, to which the young Engels was dispatched, and in which town he researched the conditions of the working classes. Quite simply, the book portrays life on subsistence wages unmitigated by industrial philanthropy of the kind practiced by the Quakers at Bessbrook.

Engels was only 24 at the time of writing, and was apprenticed into the family firm, starting in Bremen and then in Manchester. But his intellectual development followed a continental turn: critical of religion, he came under the sway of Hegel and then Marx. In Manchester Engels was inducted into the lives of the working class through an illiterate Irish serving girl that he had a relationship with. All in all his was not a conventional life but we have to take seriously his acquaintance with the working poor of Manchester. The book that came out of his precocious research was first published in Germany in 1845, and did not see an English translation until 1892. This means that it appeared in Britain after a similar work by Charles Booth in 1889, *Life and Labour of the People, Vol. 1.* A third such endeavour was completed in 1901 with *Poverty: A Study of Town Life* by the Quaker Benjamin Seebohm Rowntree, and we shall examine the influence of these reports later on.

There can be no denying the realistic detail of Engels' writings, including his account of the Irish population and their habits: 'He builds a pigsty against the house wall as he did at home, and if he was prevented from doing this, he lets the pig sleep in the room with himself.'[2] Because, Engels argues, the Irish in their poverty would accept worse working conditions than the English, 'the degrading position of the English workers, engendered by our modern history, and its immediate consequences, has been still more degraded by the presence of Irish competition.'[3] Disregarding the possible prejudice in this – perhaps the English workers he encountered vented their frustrations by elaborating on such stories as the pig – the point is valid: it reinforces the scenario put forward earlier in the extract from Louis Blanc about competition between workers. In other words Engels both witnesses the impact of subsistence wages and also deduces the mechanism which drives these wages ever downwards. Engels agrees with the thesis of Thomas Malthus (who we consider later), that workers are destined forever to this downward cycle, and that it is little better than the slavery of old:

The only difference as compared with the old, outspoken slavery is this, that the worker of today seems to be free because he is not sold once for all, but piecemeal by the day, the week, the year, and because no one owner sells him to another, but he is forced to sell himself in this way instead, being the slave of no particular person, but of the whole property-holding class. For him the matter is unchanged at bottom, and if this semblance of liberty necessarily gives him some real freedom on the one hand, it entails on the other the disadvantage that no one guarantees him a subsistence, he is in danger of being repudiated at any moment by his master, the bourgeoisie, and left to die of starvation, if the bourgeoisie ceases to have an interest in his employment, his existence.[4]

This is the socialist position in a nutshell, one could say. The language of it may belong to the socialists, but the ethics of it to us all, and in particular it belongs to Quakernomics. Let us return to the question of the means of production and recall Paine's idea that originally the land belonged to everyone, and now that it was cultivated (or enclosed), 'the common right of all became confounded into the cultivated right of the individual.' Those driven off the land who find themselves on the job market cannot hope for the compensation that Paine recommended, but worse still they find that they have no redress at all if the property owner 'repudiates' them. If the businessman has no job to offer, then the worker can go and starve. Yet if the industrialist elsewhere makes a fortune, then his wealth stares indifferently at the worker who vainly offers his labour but has nothing himself to work on as a last resort. If he is even denied a pig – or a chicken or a small plot of land, or tools, or woodland to gather nuts, berries or mushrooms in, or to gather firewood in to sell as faggots – then he stares at wealth with rage. This is social injustice, and Engels' passage above is as good a summary of it as any.

The Marxist scholar David McLellan, who wrote the introduction to the Oxford edition of *The Condition of the Working Class*, points out that Engels has a 'ludicrously idyllic picture of pre-industrial England at the beginning of the book [...]'.[5] Engels does indeed begin with a rosy picture of the English worker before the Industrial Revolution as in full ownership of their means of production – a small plot of land, a cottage industry, and so on. There is no doubt that one can romanticise this situation, and forget that industrialisation brought in fact for many working people at many times higher standards of living than could be hoped for in earlier times. But industrial capitalism was, and still is, a clunky machine, and in its early days it also created poverty on a scale that cried out for redress.

Symbolically, Engels' youthful work stands as the point of departure for Quakernomics from socialism. It points to a solution no Quaker could possibly hold to: class war and revolution. Although Engels had a pacifist streak in him, his Malthusian pessimism drove his theorising to predict violent revolution. For Quakers all are equal in the sight of God, but are granted different capacities. Those with the capacity to enter a town like Manchester and rise to the position of a capitalist are under the obligation never to 'repudiate' the working person, but to strive to their utmost to provide 'the honourable maintenance of the brother in distress', as Tawney put it. The best 'maintenance' lies in good wages and good working conditions. But revolution? Quakers as a group were formed in a revolutionary period, and knew immense hardship, but they believed in the basic conventional structures of society. These structures were for reforming, not overthrow.

Disraeli's *Sybil* and One Nation Conservatism

The novelist who lent his name as a description for the appalling conditions faced by the Victorian working classes was of course Dickens. It is a perfectly useful shorthand to talk about 'Dickensian conditions', but in Disraeli's novel, *Sybil*, we actually find a more uncompromisingly realistic account than in Dickens, often matching that of Engels. Perhaps Disraeli as a Jew had more of an outsider's mentality than Dickens. In any case Disraeli indirectly contributed another term to the English language: 'One Nation Conservatism' (borrowed in 2012 by the British Labour leader as 'One Nation Labour'), which arises from the subtitle of *Sybil* alluding to 'The Two Nations'. These are those of the rich and the poor, and Disraeli's interest in showing how the Industrial Revolution and other modern ills had led to the poverty of the working classes stands in a long line of concerned Conservatives, the last British politician in that line being perhaps Edward Heath.

Unfortunately *Sybil* as a literary work does not compare with Dickens: it is the pulp fiction of its day, heavily larded with romantic clichés. But it dares to go where Dickens hesitates: it spells out working class poverty where Dickens merely alludes to it. One of the characters in *Sybil* mentions that Queen Victoria reigns over the greatest nation that ever existed. 'Which nation?' asks another, 'for she reigns over two.' He pauses and then explains: 'Yes. Two nations; between whom there is no intercourse and no sympathy; who are as ignorant of each other's habits, thoughts, and feelings, as if they were dwellers in different zones, or inhabitants of different planets; who are formed by a different breeding, are fed by a different food, are ordered by different manners, and are not governed by the same laws.' 'You speak of—,' says the first, hesitatingly: 'THE RICH AND THE POOR.'[6]

In Chapter 7 of Engels' book he discusses the iron district of Staffordshire, in particular the dreadful conditions for working children.

Both Engels and Disraeli seemed to have drawn on the same government reports into the district, and it has been suggested that Disraeli's fictional name, 'Wemsbury', is a reference perhaps to Wednesbury and 'Wodgate' to Wednesfield, both parts of historic Staffordshire. But Disraeli's solution is naturally different to Engels': he proposes that what is needed is a restoration of the ancient monastic orders that provided a moral basis for society.

If Engels looked into the future and saw socialist revolution and Disraeli looked into the past to restore ancient values, then the Quakers took an entirely different route again. They saw a future of prosperity and equality, made possible by industrial capitalism, and looked back only in the sense of retaining the religious impulse deriving from Christ and St Paul and modified by George Fox. If Disraeli was a 'high' Romantic and Engels a Romantic of the German Idealist tradition, then in contrast it has to be said that Quakers had not a shred of any Romanticism in them. I would suggest that the modern world has taken shape much more in the Quaker image than that of either Disraeli or Engels, however. And it began, as Danny Boyle visualised for the entire world, in the Shropshire forge of the Quaker Abraham Darby.

Part II

THE QUAKER ENTERPRISES

Chapter 4

THE DARBYS OF COALBROOKDALE

In David Morse's novel, *The Iron Bridge*, mentioned in the Introduction, a young woman called Maggie Foster time-travels to Coalbrookdale in the Severn Valley in order to undermine the Industrial Revolution. Following the convention established in the *Terminator* films that requires one to time-travel naked, Maggie arrives in this fashion in the midst of iron-smelting Shropshire during an earthquake. In the confusion of this rare event Maggie manages to find clothes and gradually joins the community with a trumped-up story as a New England traveller waylaid by highwaymen. Her task is to enter service in the Quaker family of Abraham Darby III. She is to subtly alter his plans for the Iron Bridge that he built, and which stands today as a monument to iron as the key material of the Industrial Revolution. By the reasonings of the futuristic environmental group she belonged to, if Maggie could get Abraham to adopt a more fanciful design, then she could introduce weaknesses that would cause the bridge to collapse. This would discredit cast iron and turn the world away from industrialisation.

Was Morse right to pick on this Quaker enterprise as the key moment in the march to modern industrialism? It is unlikely that the collapse of a single bridge would have slowed down industrial progress very much, but as a symbol I think it is excellent. It also suggests that a survey of Quaker businesses and their place in the Industrial Revolution could do worse than start with Coalbrookdale and the Darby family.

For now we too will time-travel to the early Darby ironmasters and attempt to enter that world as if it were our own. Our twenty-first-century entrepreneurs may operate in the digital revolution, but the basic economics of what they do is little changed from the iron revolution that the Darbys initiated. The digital world may seem so virtual, but then perhaps the architectural iron castings produced at Coalbrookdale, with their ornate patterning, struck the Victorians too as rather virtual. Software can be instantly replicated and transmitted over the Internet, but iron casting used the same idea of replication: the mass production of iron goods from a pattern – literally a wooden 'pattern' as it was called – was a revolution at the time, and the sand casting of iron was a Darby innovation. Above all goods, in any form, have to be valued by a market, payments must be received, and out of that running costs have to be met – wages, premises, materials – and loans repaid with interest. More important still: entrepreneurial creative genius is required. Quakers had the odd fortune to have both the creative genius and the ability to raise capital, all under one roof as it were. But Bristol in 1700 is a city more than three hundred years away – and it is there that the story of the Darby ironmasters begins.

By 1700 the Quakers as a movement were barely more than fifty years old but had already come through the times of persecution to hold many trading positions round the country. Bristol and Liverpool were particularly important merchant cities because of the wealth brought by the colonies and slavery. Wealth meant *capital* – then as now. Merchant capital was ever interested in new ventures that would provide a good return, and Abraham Darby in 1700 wanted to move up from brass to iron. Over the next two hundred years the Quaker family business in iron that he founded, spanning five generations of the Darbys, became nothing short of a microcosm of the Industrial Revolution. Its product range in iron became so extensive that multi-volume catalogues were printed in Victorian times, but, more than the extent of the product range, what is striking is the extent of allied activities that went into the business: activities that required an all-round *ecology* of economic activity. The Darbys had to source iron ore, coal, water power, horses, farms for grazing and hay for the horses and food for their workers; they had to develop brickfields for the bricks for their workers' cottages; they made essential components for steam engines, rails and wheels for railways; they built railways and canals, and used all of those in turn in their business; and finally they had to raise capital through friends and family who became their bankers. In modern business terms this is 'vertical integration', and for Quakers this could also include loans to clients to enable them to purchase their products. This is a microcosm of economic activity, or an example of 'total capitalism' as I call it, even though it is centred on a single key product: iron.

Iron *was* the key material of the early Industrial Revolution, quickly giving way to steel, a material at the heart of the twenty-first-century global economy. Steel may not have the glamour of smart-phones or high-definition TVs; it may seem remote from coffee bars, our working day, or a flight to a holiday resort in another country. It might appear to have little relevance to social networking, music downloads and contemporary furniture. But steel, and iron before it, is the hidden basis of every single economic activity: it is hidden in the infrastructure of our buildings, networks, transport and machinery that *delivers* our twenty-first-century life to us. Everything that we would fear to abandon: hot and cold running water, electricity, computers, hospitals, the family car, abundant food; all these things rest on iron and steel, and so we owe it to the ironmasters of the eighteenth century to understand a little about their role in the economy of their time, the period in which our current lifestyle began to take shape.

Quaker fortunes were made in the early days of iron – and devoted to philanthropy in typical Quaker fashion. But Morse makes much of a Quaker lapse in his novel: the production of arms for a short period, contrary to Quaker principles. The cannon produced at Coalbrookdale are a blot on the Quaker record, it is true, but we shall consider other such exceptions and find that we have to take them into account for a rounded picture of Quakernomics. 'Otherworldly' the Quakers might have been in their spiritual life, but in the real world they could be drawn into commercial temptation like any other people.

Coalbrookdale in the early eighteenth century is part of the larger picture of small ironworks scattered on the Welsh borders, where the combination of iron ore, forests for charcoal, and water power made these industries viable. The ironworks owned by the Darby family dynasty were fully capitalist, became fully mechanised, and belched fire and smoke into the pristine surrounding fields and forests; but did they demean their workers or the nature of their labour? A Darby daughter described the scene in 1753: 'the stupendous Bellows whose alternate roars, like the foaming billows, is awful to hear; the mighty Cylinders, the wheels that carry so many different Branches of the work, is curious to observe' – an image that invokes both Blake's 'dark satanic mills' and Charlie Chaplin's factory in *Modern Times*. An American Quaker who visited the works in the same year said 'we are presented with all the horrors that Pandemonium could shew.'[1] In Marx's terms, as the business grew, it was a fully capitalist one. The records of course confirm the concentration of the means of production into the hands of the owners, but suggest in contradiction to Marx that the 'abundant means' now possible through the industrial form of production was shared as much as possible with the workers.

Can I *prove* that the workers at Coalbrookdale – and in the other Quaker enterprises – were not exploited and that the nature of their work was not demeaning? Is it really the case that, where Ruskin believed wealth to arise only through the taxing of the labour of others, the Quakers are an exception? All I can do is to put forward what evidence I have found in the following account, which traces the history of the company through the generations of the Darbys. I attempt to do two things here: firstly to make the 'microcosm' case, that Coalbrookdale is truly significant in the scale and scope of its activity; and secondly – which is perhaps more difficult – to make the ethical case, that the dark satanic mills of this venture coexisted with, and provided for, human flourishing and the fair treatment of workers.

Abraham Darby I

David Burns Windsor says: 'Abraham Darby was an innovative genius whose ideas were fundamental to the creation of an Industrial Revolution. It is scarcely surprising that Quakers came to dominate the iron and steel industry.'[2] This first iron-making Darby was a malt mill maker and then a partner in a Bristol brass works whose family, typically, came from yeoman stock. Another Quaker company called the Bristol Brass Wire Company was then in operation, showing that Quakers were already established in the metal industries of Bristol, and indeed developed a near monopoly on brass domestic goods in the region.[3] The entire capital for Darby's new venture came from local merchants, and is estimated at a total of £3,500[4] – perhaps between £200,000 and £350,000 in today's money. Further capital came from partnerships and mortgages: a typical mix for entrepreneurs then and now. Many a businessman has mortgaged his home to fund his business; many have lost both. Socialists rarely recognise the risks that entrepreneurs take, and the legion of the disappointed.

In 1709 Darby moved his operations from Bristol to Coalbrookdale in Shropshire, where for a long time iron had been smelted using charcoal from the local forests. His move was prompted by the lack of interest shown by his partners, or some disagreement with them, over the patent he had taken out the previous year for casting in sand, a technique he learned in Holland, and perfected by a Quaker in his employment. An industrial historian has commented: 'There, his competitive advantage in the form of the patent on sand casting for iron, permitted him to succeed beyond expectation.'[5] The problem of deforestation at the dawn of the Industrial Revolution was so acute that the production of iron in Britain was 'coming within an ace of what might have become a national calamity', according to Emden.[6] Raistrick confirms that by the middle of the seventeenth century iron production was in decline.[7] Darby, building on his first innovation of sand casting, then perfected the coke smelting of iron, and this development was crucial for the entire Industrial Revolution. Coal itself had too high a sulphur content, which made the iron brittle, while coke had additional advantages of withstanding a greater load of iron in a furnace than charcoal could support. Darby perfected iron smelting with coke in 1710, and in 1717 followed it with yet another breakthrough: by eliminating the effect of sulphur on iron he was also able to use coal in smelting. Windsor tells us that Darby would have learned about coking during his apprenticeship in the malt trade;[8] just one of many industrial processes that he would have mastered, all by the age of 29 when he made his major breakthrough.

These are the technical glories of the Darby legacy, but the core of the Coalbrookdale Company business was rather mundane: the production of cast-iron domestic wares such as pots and grates at low prices made possible by these innovations of sand casting and coke and coal smelting. The company sold these products direct to markets in the region, and to this day the name Coalbrookdale lives on in a range of cast-iron stoves produced by descendent companies which also make the Aga range of stoves.

Abraham Darby II and Richard Reynolds

In 1732, some fifteen years after the death of the first Darby ironmaster, his son Abraham Darby II joined the management of the firm. It was in this period that arms – cannon – were cast during the war with Spain in 1739.[9] Later on, during the American War of Independence from 1775–1781, all government orders for arms were declined by the Darbys.[10] Walvin tells us that from the time Abraham Darby II took over the firm he wound down the production of armaments, adding that the Quaker Galtons of Birmingham were disowned in this period for refusing to give up the trade.[11] Abraham Darby II took his father's innovation of coke pig iron as foundry feedstock and adapted it for use as forge feedstock, 'giving fresh impetus to the whole iron industry of England'.[12] Where he differed was in the refusal to patent the process, believing instead that the public should generally benefit from the innovation.

Windsor tells us that this Darby experimented further: 'An account of that period preserves the tradition that Darby spent six days and nights without sleep at the furnace until he finally produced iron of the desired quality. Tradition has it that he had to be carried home asleep by his workmen.'[13] It is in the period of 1740 to 1780 that the Industrial Revolution was fully underway according to the industrial historian Peter Mathias,[14] and Abraham Darby II is in many ways a quintessential figure of that revolution. An iconic move on his part might confirm it: his adoption of the 'fire engine', or steam engine as we now know it. Water power for the bellows was one reason for choosing the location of the works, but in summer it was irregular and furnaces had to remain idle in the driest periods. To solve this problem horse power was used to pump water from the lower pools to the upper pools in order to keep water flowing, but the replacement of horses with steam power enabled year-round blowing.[15]

Another important Bristol Quaker, Richard Reynolds, then joined the company and in 1763 became the head of the firm. His Quaker convictions led him to suspend production on Sundays, risking the solidification of iron in the furnaces. Enormous profits however were made after a patent was taken out for a process called puddling: clearly not all commercial advantages were sacrificed in the Quaker tradition. Reynolds also oversaw further innovations in iron making: the use of iron instead of wood for rails.[16] The directors of Coalbrookdale became closely connected with James Watt and Matthew Boulton, and had been amongst the first to install a Newcomen pumping engine at their works. This adoption of steam power to iron manufacture was a first, as was the use of their own railways for transporting materials for iron working.[17] In 1738 Coalbrookdale began production of iron wheels, and in 1768 production of cast-iron rails, possibly the first used on any railway.[18] Raistrick records of Reynolds:

> His relations with the workpeople continued the policy of the Darbys, complete friendliness and care for their well-being [...] In all the property that he acquired he laid out walks and made access to the woods and hills and encouraged their fullest use by the workpeople. The policy of the Darbys in providing housing for the workpeople was continued by him [...].[19]

Reynolds represents for us one of the early Quaker industrialists whose wealth derived solely from his business, and whose philanthropy on retirement was extensive. He was against the idea of making charitable bequests by will – perhaps he was conscious of how easily trustees could alter the terms of a bequest – and so he hired four almoners to assist him in dispersing his wealth before he died. The chief mourners at his death in 1816, apparently, were the poor of Bristol.[20]

Abraham Darby III

We now come to Abraham Darby III, the Quaker ironmaster fictionalised in the novel *The Iron Bridge*. Much of the detail in the novel appears to be historically justified – and therefore provides a fascinating insight into Coalbrookdale in that period – but the emotional constitution of this Abraham is a literary invention, necessitated by the relationship with the imaginary Maggie Foster. This period in the firm saw one project that was iconic of Coalbrookdale: the construction in 1780 of the famous Iron Bridge, just a few miles from the factory (it took nearly four hundred tons of iron castings to build).

But what was the real legacy of the Iron Bridge for the Industrial Revolution? It certainly led to other bridges being made of cast-iron elements, in which Coalbrookdale was involved. The wider use of cast iron as an architectural material appeared in the early nineteenth century with the construction of an iron-framed mill at Derby, copied widely by other mill owners because it reduced the damage done by fire. In 1810 Coalbrookdale cast the structural members for its own Liverpool Warehouse, and also a half-domed roof designed by John Nash for the picture gallery at Attingham Hall.[21] But it is in popular language that we keep finding Iron Bridge, or the town Ironbridge, referred to as the 'birthplace of industry', the 'birthplace of the Industrial Revolution' and so on. Darby died in 1789 at the age of 39, by which time engineers from all over Europe flocked to Coalbrookdale to study the techniques employed there.[22] Royalty was not immune to the attraction either: on 12 August 1796 the Prince and Princess of Orange toured the works.[23]

Further Generations

From 1803 Edmund Darby (1782–1810) took charge of the works, and led it again to the forefront of technological progress, including further production for iron bridge building: an entire 52 ton bridge was exported to Jamaica in 1807.[24] The company built many steam engines under licence from James Watt, and constructed the first steam locomotive to run on the works railway in 1796. Steam engines were now being produced to many designs, including by Boulton & Watt, Newcomen and Trevithick. In 1839 the company produced 800 tons of wrought iron plate for the hull of Brunel's great steamship, the S.S. Great Britain.[25] Francis Darby (1783–1850) was the eldest son of Abraham Darby III and eventually became a partner in the firm, but the role he played was a little obscure. He was an art lover and it is generally believed that he was responsible for involving the company in the manufacture of art castings, having introduced artists and designers from France to the company. He was however criticised as a Quaker who did not dress plainly and loved high art.[26] Just after his death the Great Exhibition in 1851 brought the company more fame than any other event apart from the construction of the Iron Bridge. The ornamental gates at the northern end of the Crystal Palace were cast by the company, and a towering thirty-foot-high cast-iron dome was the centrepiece of their exhibition, along with an ornamental fountain, a cast-iron altar rail and various items of garden furniture.[27] Abraham Darby IV was asked to re-erect the ornamental gates at the entrance to Kensington Gardens, where they remain today, known as the 'Coalbrookdale Gate'.

Five generations of Quaker Darbys had been involved with Coalbrookdale. John, the father of Abraham Darby I, had been a farmer and blacksmith, running a small forge, and entirely owning his own means of production.[28] He was a typical Quaker of yeoman ancestry whose type could be found across the world in all cultures since the dawn of the Iron Age, and whose working life had not changed that drastically since then. But five generations on, the proportion of people who possessed their own means of production had drastically declined. This is the legacy of the Industrial Revolution, and Quakers were at the centre of it. From John Darby's forge which would have worked a small fraction of a ton a week, to twenty tons a week under Abraham Darby II, to two thousand tons a week under Abraham Darby IV, Coalbrookdale became for a while the largest foundry in the world.

A Personal Digression on Foundries

People might readily agree that iron and steel were a core part of the Industrial Revolution: the Lawrencian image of the coal miner stripped to his waist, revealing muscles shining with sweat, transfers readily to the ironworks, the satanic mills. Few however have personal experience that would give them direct insight into the workings and significance of foundries. I was however fortunate to grow up with high-temperature workings from both sides of my family: my father's home-built bronze foundry and my grandmother's pottery kiln. However, like most teenagers in the late 1960s and early 1970s, I acted out the generation gap, given cultural sanction through the Monty Python TV series and films and the music of Jimmy Hendrix. But despite this hippy background of the rejection of my parents' values, and the certainty that we were not like the previous generation, I built a foundry. My father had died when I was five, so this was a curious acting out of his own obsessions under the bemused gaze of my science teacher, brought to an end only when the intense heat melted the strip light covers in the project lab – risk assessments had not been heard of in those days. I also occasionally tended our family kiln in overnight firings, sleeping on a camp bed in the small pottery room as it filled with noxious fumes from the glazes melting at high temperatures. Again, no health and safety measures!

These experiences no doubt give me an instinctive sympathy for the Darbys and for the other Quaker steel- and ironmasters we shall discover. It is a sympathy clearly missing in Marx, who is more likely to have been immersed in Hegel in his late teens. In contrast I would avidly turn the pages of the Foseco catalogue, which listed crucibles, tongs, refractory linings and casting sands. What this background gives me is the insight into the crucial role played by foundries in the Industrial Revolution, not just in the huge tonnage of cast-iron products that literally changed the landscape, but in the mass production methods now emerging. A skilled carpenter makes a wooden pattern – whether plain or covered with floral motifs makes no difference to the later processes – which is used thousands of times to make the impression in the upper and lower sand casting boxes. As the molten metal flows from the crucible along the ducts into the mould and reaches the venting holes it takes the exact shape of the wooden pattern, with just a tiny shrinkage: it's a highly dramatic moment. A design, a *thought*, can be turned into a durable good of almost any conceivable shape. And to pour the molten metal, wait for the mould to cool and then tap the sand off the article is an immensely satisfying experience: it is a giving-birth. And thousands of almost identical copies can be made, whether cooking pots for the kitchens of Victorian England, cast-iron columns for domestic and civic architecture, or the parts for lathes, sewing machines, steam engines, railways, ships and locomotives.

I am not pretending of course that the thousandth copy is especially thrilling to the workpeople involved, but *something* of the satisfaction of this peculiar human creativity accompanies all productive work.

The wooden patterns for cast-iron products could also include those for making cannons and guns, against Quaker principles, but which were turned out for a brief period at Coalbrookdale. The technology is morally neutral. Leaving the question of pacifism aside for the moment it is clear that within this highly skilled and labour-intensive industry the first giant leaps were taken into factory mass production of the infrastructure of modern life. Automation in weaving may have changed production methods and the lives of working people in a similarly iconic way, but iron and steel built the deeper fabric of modernity. Danny Boyle was right to say, as we saw, that out of the genius of Abraham Darby flowed the mills, looms, engines, weapons and so on of the modern world. In fact Boyle's opening statement points out that, while nations experience revolutions that change them, the United Kingdom's Industrial Revolution 'changed the whole of human existence.' His opening ceremony for the London Olympic Games included an imaginary furnace from which poured molten metal into the shape of giant ring, to be forged ready to be assembled into the Olympic logo. It may have mixed up the casting of iron with the forging of iron for dramatic purposes, but the image was perfect as the moment our modern world took shape.

But what strange passion is this? My father cast bronze as a sculptor – at one time he was an assistant to Sir Henry Moore[29] – and my grandmother's pottery made fine art pieces in Depression-era Vienna. The Darbys, like Quakers in general, were not artistically inclined, apart from Francis, who was lambasted for it. The love of kilns and furnaces and mills, all hazardous to the health and to the environment, all dangerous and dirty places within which to work, is not the love of *artistic* creativity, at least, not in the first instance, and neither was it about profit per se. The passion for these places was not so much money driven as arising from some Vulcan instinct in the human mind. It incidentally led to affordable goods for millions, but through a Faustian compact that we are only beginning to see the price of. But to truly understand capitalism one needs to truly understand this instinct, whether it is for foundries, for chemical plants or for the antiseptic world of the software developer (I trained in that field too, and know its own rather abstracted preoccupations). It is the mindset of the dwarves under the mountain in Tolkien's *Lord of the Rings*; it is the mindset – dare I say it – far more of men than of women; it is a mindset bordering on the autistic; and it is the mindset that gives us the supreme comforts, luxuries, and opportunities of modern living. I would argue that industrial capitalism is driven by it first and foremost, and only secondarily by profit. The derivatives traders give everything away with the term 'derivatives': they are financial transactions derived from other financial transactions, derived ultimately from *making* things, where all wealth begins.

Whether one has sympathy for the obsessive Darby types who built the foundries, is indifferent to them, or loathes every aspect of their dark satanic mills, they are here to stay. Can they be run on an ethical basis? That is the question that the Quaker history poses so starkly, a challenge that makes equal demands on the Marxists as it does on the extreme free-marketeers.

Quakers, Non-human Energies and the Capitalism of Metals

Most analysis of early industrial capitalism focusses naturally enough on weaving: the transition from cottage industry to factory production in this field holds in train all the potential evils heaped on the worker. But the metal industries are more foundational, I would argue, for four reasons: the jump from family forge to industrial complexes like at Coalbrookdale is a much bigger leap than from family loom to factory loom; its capital requirements are correspondingly much larger; the goods produced are needed in all other branches of industry; and these goods are central to the *harnessing of non-human energies*.

At Coalbrookdale all of these factors are apparent, in particular the last one: the issue of non-human energies. The location was chosen in the first place because of abundant water power for the bellows and hammers; this was augmented by horse power in the dry season (to pump water to higher pools); and – in the crucial development for the Industrial Revolution – replaced by steam power. If the bellows and hammers had to be operated by human labour, as in family forges, production is severely limited, a typical economic horizon of the pre-modern world. Water, wind and animal power increase production, but only by small steps, and tie one to land and rivers. Steam power on the other hand begins the real divorce from ancient ways of life, and Coalbrookdale, both in its purchasing of early Newcomen engines for pumping, and in its key role in making the major components of steam engines for the great entrepreneurs of this industry – Boulton, Watt and Trevithick – led the world.

I don't believe that economics as a discipline pays sufficient attention to the use of non-human energies, which now include oil, gas, nuclear and renewables alongside coal, in wealth creation. Yet clearly, just as in the affordable pots and pans turned out by Coalbrookdale, we are seeing the co-mingling of human labour and non-human energies in the production of goods – a step-change in the history of human economic activity. Throughout Marx's three volumes of *Capital* he studiously avoids using the term 'goods' to describe the output from factories (apart from the occasional lapse which makes his usage the more apparent). Instead they are loathsome things called 'commodities'. Yet in both English and the German equivalent the term 'good' clearly implies that something is good about the product, that it furthers human flourishing even if only in some basic way. The iron pots and pans produced at Coalbrookdale can be taken to epitomise such a basic 'good'. The innovation of Abraham Darby I in coke and coal smelting and sand casting combined to allow him the production of these domestic goods at a fraction of the cost of brass and copper equivalents. Raistrick tells us that the market for his wares was 'almost insatiable'.[30] For a working-class household to cook meals was an essential, and affordable domestic wares a key to basic survival. Why should capitalist production be an inherent evil if it provides such things? Earlier copper and brass wares were so expensive that they were named in wills and used for generations. What if you were not the lucky one to inherit such basic items? Now every family could afford them. And in all of this it was the harnessing of non-human energies that began the drive to mass production that brought affordable goods – good things – to ordinary people.

Coalbrookdale as Ethical Capitalism

From the various sources I have drawn on we have been able to construct Coalbrookdale as a microcosm of capitalism in the Industrial Revolution and beyond. What of the question of its *ethics* however? I have no authoritative sources beyond those already cited, that focus exclusively on that question. But scattered through these works are various pieces of evidence, which I now draw together.

Raistrick tells us that 'the friendliness and fellowship of the meeting would be carried forward into the works.'[31] ('Meeting' here means the Quaker religious service.) Walvin adds: 'the Friends in charge gave generously to a wide range of charitable causes, though often anonymously to avoid any acclaim for their benevolence.'[32] Later on Raistrick comments: 'It is not possible in this first century of the Company, to separate, in any of its leaders, their character and habit as Friends from their outlook and actions as employers and works managers. There was a striking unity and simplicity of life, which was their strength.'[33]

In 1792 the company built forty workmen's houses near Ketley,[34] but by the 1830s the firm was employing more than two thousand men, the most pressing social problem thus created being that of housing. Many cottages were built of local clay, requiring the construction of a new brickfield. All of this was carried out under Alfred Darby, as were improvements to transport including the quartering of around a hundred horses – in itself a substantial operation. This allowed for the company to hire its own men to work this horse-drawn transport and 'many of the difficulties and abuses that had crept in through the great amount of hired labour and horse teams formerly needed, were now corrected.'[35] Raistrick does not elaborate, which is a pity, but the implication is clear: when they subcontracted to other employers workers (and possibly the horses) were not treated well, but when they had control over their own horse teams they could correct this.

Richard Reynolds and Abraham Darby III had built small schools for the miners' children in earlier years, and in 1846 Alfred Darby built a large school to serve seven hundred boys and girls – another huge undertaking. Later the company financed the Coalbrookdale Literary and Scientific Institution and also contributed to a 'School of Art'. In another move typical of the Quakers not only Quaker Meeting Houses were built by the owners of the company, but gifts of money, material and land were donated for chapels and use by the Church of England.[36] The latter was also the recipient of a peal of bells, designed and cast in iron at the works. This is remarkable, considering the Protestant tradition which generally frowned on bells, and considering the Quaker tradition which entirely avoided them. Indeed we find that in the famous journal of Quakerism's founder, George Fox, even the sight of the 'steeplehouse' set him in a rage against the established church, let alone the hearing of bells.

We see in all these activities a paternalism at work which we now assume the state to largely manage, at least in most European nations, and to a more grudging extent in the USA. Sickness insurance for the workers and schools for their children were provided by the Quaker capitalists at Coalbrookdale on an entirely voluntary basis. There was no obligation to undertake such expenditures, or even assist in their organisation, other than a moral one.

In 1756 there were food riots around Coalbrookdale. Raistrick reproduces a letter from Hannah Darby describing and deploring the action of desperate people in breaking into businesses and houses, including that of a baker. She tells us that 'the mob gave themselves the title of levellers' and that the company took steps to provide them with drink and bread, though bread was hard to find throughout the county. Four workmen from the company were amongst those subsequently arrested and Abraham Darby II had to plead with the king by letter for their lives, vouching for their good character up to this time.[37] (Raistrick is uncertain as to their fate.) In 1795 and 1796 financial instability caused food shortages again and high prices when it was available. Richard Reynolds and the company initially contributed a hundred guineas each for the relief of the local poor (this figure should be multiplied by a factor between fifty and eighty to arrive at today's money in pounds sterling), and the company subsequently bought in stocks of rice and corn to be sold to workers at three-quarters of cost price – all of which helped avoid the food riots common elsewhere.[38] Reynolds also offered allotments on his property so workers could grow some of their own food. Raistrick comments that 'Houses for workpeople, roads, canals, schools and public amenities have been their gift to the district.'[39]

The Coalbrookdale story is hence an interesting microcosm of industrialisation, which at heart is a story of human flourishing made possible by industry. An environmentalist ethics that demands that such an industry – which tears at the bowels of the earth, burns fossil fuels, and belches smoke into the air – should not exist, would deny a flourishing made possible in that way. A Marxist ethics which demands that the company be owned by the workers, while more attractive in theory, has shown in the Soviet system and other communist countries to be possible only in a police state, and reliant on borrowed capitalist technologies. It is the entrepreneur who develops those, and the Quaker – in this instance – who mitigates against exploitation. In defiance of both the rejection of industrialisation by the extreme environmentalist and the rejection of capitalism by the extreme socialist, we can propose that Coalbrookdale created human flourishing through industrial capitalism.

Chapter 5

QUAKERS IN LIGHT AND HEAVY INDUSTRY

We turn now from the history of a single Quaker dynasty of ironmasters to the bigger world of Quaker iron and steel. Emden states: 'in relation to the iron industry, it may be said without fear of contradiction, that its early history can be written without going outside of the Society of Friends.'[1] James Walvin quotes US historian Charles K. Hyde: 'Quakers owned or managed between half and three-quarters of the ironworks in operation' in the early eighteenth century.[2] But what more can we learn about the Quakernomics of iron by going beyond the Darbys? First of all the question of scale alluded to by Emden and Walvin is important: it is in *iron*, not chocolate, that the claim for Quakernomics as a microcosm of industrial capitalism is most borne out. And the Darbys of Coalbrookdale have a historical position in iron making substantially augmented by other Quaker enterprises including the Fell–Rawlinson group in the Lake District, the Lloyds businesses in Wales, Birmingham and Bristol, and Reynolds, Getley & Co. in their South Wales ironworks.

One of the key partners of the Fell–Rawlinson group in the iron trade was Sarah Fell, daughter of Margaret and Judge Fell. This couple played a central role in the early recognition, protection and patronage of George Fox, and in the life of Sarah we can see the close relationship between the Quaker tradition and the iron trade,[3] and between religion and commerce in general. Margaret Fell had made Swarthmoor Hall, her family home near Ulverston in Cumbria, a kind of hub for Quaker hospitality, activity and relief, and after she married George Fox it became Sarah's role to manage its estates and accounting. From her unusually detailed and extensive accounts, published in 1920, we learn much about the mixed economy of farming and business typical of the era, particularly prevalent away from the centres of power in the south of England. Sarah's trading extended to ventures involving shipping, using both conventional money sales and barter (or 'trucking').[4]

The picture of economic integration in the Fell business ventures is important: it mirrors that of Coalbrookdale, and in this case it is in the direct service of 'Quaker Central', as it were. It is a reminder that the Quakers were deeply networked, and that was to be one of their great competitive advantages in the early days of industrial capitalism. It is also a reminder that Quaker women played prominent roles in the history of the religion and of the enterprises.

Walvin tells us that Richard Reynolds, who ran Coalbrookdale between the time of Abraham Darby I and II, effectively became the firm's banker. This does not mean that he went into banking proper, though his son Joseph did set up a bank in Wellington and thus became Coalbrookdale's banker in the conventional sense.[5] But Reynolds senior was able, due to his own growing wealth, to participate in a common Quaker practice: lending to other Quaker concerns at below the market rate.[6] Clearly this gave the Quakers collectively a further competitive edge, but it was not just philanthropy: they knew that the risk level for their capital was lower than average because of the reliability of those who borrowed.

While the story of the Lloyds as ironmasters is a more modest one than that of the Darbys, involving little by way of technological innovation, they typify another feature of business life rather well: the gradual movement from merchandising into banking; from the real to the virtual economy. The first Lloyd in our story is Charles, who took over a forge in 1697 in Pool Quay, mid-Wales, with water-powered bellows and hammer, using charcoal from local forests.[7] Other Lloyds were iron merchants having given up working on the land to enter that trade. Charles Lloyd also ran a mixed farm as well as the forge – in a pattern we are now familiar with – and persistently refused to pay tithes on it to the local clergy.[8] In 1727 Charles Lloyd's business failed and he was broke, owing more than he had in assets. What follows next is instructive of early Quakernomics. He failed to raise capital at the Yearly Meeting in Marlborough and his position in his Local Meeting was compromised. He was eventually disowned by the Society of Friends, the guiding principle of which was: 'that none trade beyond their ability nor stretch beyond their compass [...] and that they keep their word in all things.'[9] He even went to Parliament at one point to sort out mistakes in accounting, as part of his efforts to rehabilitate his reputation. In 1760 Charles junior was disowned by the society for even less responsible behaviour, but his father was re-admitted in 1742 after 'a proper acknowledgment of his sincere repentance for his misconduct therein.'

This was not a promising start for the Quaker Lloyds dynasty, but another family were doing rather better. Ambrose Crowley, son of a Quaker, became partner to Sampson Lloyd, Charles' younger brother, in Birmingham, and was also active in Bristol amongst the Quakers there (who had been badly persecuted in that town).[10] In turn Crowley's son, Ambrose Crowley III, became a leading seventeenth-century ironmonger and sheriff of London. Although born into a Quaker family, he later became an Anglican which opened the path to him becoming a Tory MP and receiving a knighthood.[11] In the middle-late period of the eighteenth century four of the five sons of Sampson Lloyd II became partners in banking concerns and both his daughters married bankers.[12] The Lloyds banking story begins with their creation of Birmingham's first bank, and from here the Lloyds as a banking dynasty grew, with its twenty-first-century legacy still visible in the high street. But iron making continued in other branches, as did a wide variety of businesses pursued by the Quaker Lloyds, for example, Lloyds, Foster and Co. was a huge concern which in 1866 was a manufacturer of railway rolling stock with three thousand employees. In 1862, along with a Sheffield company, they were the first licensees of the new Bessemer steel-making process.[13] Where the Quakers did not innovate themselves they were quick to adopt the innovations of others.

Samuel Lloyd ran the firm from 1837, a strict Quaker whose dress and ways led to him being known simply as 'Quaker Lloyd'. It is said that 'he used a Quaker approach in his labour relations which made for loyalty among the workmen and contributed to the prosperity of the firm.' He also took pride in personally buying key items stocked in the 'truck shop' or 'tommy shop', which was a provisions shop or company store run by employers, a common practice of the day, but eventually made illegal through such measures as the Truck Act of 1887. Quaker Lloyd ran the shop honourably with low prices, sometimes lower than in regular shops. It also had the reputation for the best butcher's meat in Wednesbury.[14] The 'truck' or 'tommy' system, where workers were paid in kind rather than in cash, was extensively abused by other employers, and the injustices of it highlighted in a lengthy passage in Disraeli's *Sybil* where one of the workers describes how they are 'tommied to death', to general agreement from his workmates.[15]

Like so many Lloyds this Samuel attended the Bull Street Meeting in Birmingham with his family. His wife was the founder of the Ladies' Negro Friend Society offering support to slave women wherever slavery had not yet been abolished. Five years after Quaker Lloyd's death in 1862 saw the end of the company, sunk by crippling losses on the manufacture of the ironworks for Blackfriars Bridge. The bridge itself was opened in 1869 by Queen Victoria and is still in use today.[16]

Two Quaker ironworks in South Wales are worth mentioning. In 1720 the Hanburys started the manufacture of tinplate in Pontypool. Capel Hanbury had founded these ironworks in 1565, and it was his grandson Richard who met George Fox and became a Quaker. Their descendents married into the Lloyds and the Barclays and also the Gurneys, giving rise to links to various Quaker banking dynasties, into Quaker brewing via Truman, Hanbury & Buxton, and also into pharmaceuticals via Allen & Hanburys.[17] (When one begins to see the extent of Quaker links by marriage one is rather glad that they didn't use their 'mob-like' connections for organised crime!)

Towards the end of the eighteenth century the tinplate works at Melingriffith run by the Bristol Quaker firm of Reynolds, Getley & Co. were the largest of their kind in the world. The owners also pursued a typical Quaker interest in their workers by setting up a benefit club in 1786, and setting up schools for children and some housing, though not on the scale at Coalbrookdale.[18]

Benjamin Huntsman and Cast Steel

Cast iron is perhaps a quaint material to our twenty-first-century eyes, and to the extent that we are aware of it we may have a picture of an old lamp-post or set of ornamental railings – probably cracked. It was indeed a brittle material, and often cast in irredeemably Victorian floral taste in its ornamentation. It's so century-before-last. Hence the development from iron working to steel working becomes an essential transition from early industrialism to the modern world. In our minds a 'man of steel' rings more contemporary than 'a man of iron', perhaps. But the essential processes involved in the development of steel working from iron working were innovations from outside the Quaker tradition, with one exception: the cast steel of Benjamin Huntsman.

Huntsman was a clock-maker – a not uncommon profession amongst Quakers – who had difficulty obtaining quality steel for springs. In his quest for steel of the right grade he experimented in tempering the steel, and moved to Handsworth near Sheffield in 1740 in order to obtain the necessary fuel. Far more than perfecting steel for springs, his experiments led to the discovery of crucible steel or steel casting.[19] This became the hardest steel then available in Britain, but the Sheffield manufacturers were not interested in it and Huntsman's entire production landed up being exported to France. There is a great British tradition of course of innovation that is originally spurned in its country of origin, for example the jet engine of Frank Whittle and the cordless kettle, which also found its first take-up in France.

In fact the steel used by the Sheffield manufacturers had derived from the process invented by the Quaker Ambrose Crowley, using iron from Sweden. This so-called 'blister steel' was considered hard enough for their needs, but when Huntsman's superior steel later returned as French cutlery the Sheffield cutlers attempted to obtain an import ban. It was only when that failed that they decided that Huntsman's steel was, after all, just what they wanted. It was harder to work, but the results were better. Huntsman, like Abraham Darby II, had refused to take out a patent on his process, and the story is that a Sheffield cutler, Walker of Grenoside, posed as a starving beggar to get into Huntsman's works for warmth, and thus discovered the secret.[20] Thereafter Walker set up a rival concern, but this did not impact on Huntsman's reputation or success. The firm was continued by his son William, and then Francis, and survived long into the twentieth century.

Huntsman was a typical Quaker: he lived simply and little is known of him beyond his refusal either to accept fellowship to the Royal Society or to have his portrait painted. He was a man clearly absorbed in his work, as were the Darby innovators, and made countless test firings in the pursuit of perfect steel. This is deduced from the hundredweights of assayed – tested – steel samples found buried in the fields around his factory.[21]

The Quaker Lead Company

We now turn away from iron and steel to look at two more metals that have an interesting role in the economy: lead and silver. Both come from the same ore, mined extensively in Britain since Roman times. The Quaker Lead Company, which mined and smelted lead, copper and silver, was 'a dominant influence in mining' in Britain for two centuries according to Raistrick.[22] As with iron the smelting of these metals had traditionally depended on charcoal, and with the decline of forests the industry had lagged behind demand until a method of smelting lead with coal had been invented using reverberatory furnace technology. It was the Quaker Edward Wright who developed this innovation, one that transformed the industry, and which paralleled the Darby discovery.[23] John Freame (1669–1745) was a notable Quaker partner in the Quaker Lead Company, along with Edward Wright, and was a goldsmith banker in Lombard Street, whose operation eventually evolved into Barclays Bank – it was he who originally bought the sign of the spread eagle, the symbol still in use today. The connection between Quaker metals, Quaker goldsmithing, Quaker banking and Lombard Street is another small microcosm of emerging British capitalism which we will explore later on, including the role of the goldsmith banker. Freame's story is typically Quaker: he had moved to tolerant London from persecutory Gloucester, and there did exceedingly well. As Reynolds did for the Darbys, Freame did for the Quaker Lead Company: he provided capital.

The Quaker Lead Company's venture became well established in Wales with early smelting operations in 1703, though the lead produced had to transported by sea to London at risk of storms and French privateers. As usual the Quaker gift for technological innovation saw rapid improvements to traditional methods, and the Welsh works were considered the most efficient in the country. Raistrick tells us that:

> The needs of the workmen were not forgotten in this development. [...] Usually the smelt mills worked very irregular times with the variation in the amounts of ore produced in their related mines, and smelters had often to suffer long spells of unemployment and no pay. The Quaker Company always either accumulated ores onto stock in good periods, or bought heavily in the outside market, so that they always had a sufficient ore on hand to keep the smelt mills in perfectly regular work. This enabled them to get the best workers, as there was complete security of employment. The wages also were related to the cost of living, and by the standards of the country generally were generous. Reports frequently stress the contentment of the workmen, even in contrast with the unrest and strife in the immediate neighbourhood.[24]

In return for these good conditions workers were required to abstain from alcohol and swearing. In 1728 there was a scarcity of corn which made the wages of the smelters of low real value, so the Quakers, to avoid pay rises that would be awkward to rescind after the shortages passed, decided instead to buy corn. Cargos of wheat and other foodstuffs were made available so that the miners were assured of food prices appropriate to their wages. There were also distress funds and funds for social purposes.[25]

In 1753 in their Teesdale operation the company further accepted responsibility for the welfare of their men, and introduced training and education, and later on a school. Mining is historically a dangerous pursuit, and the Quakers did their best to improve ventilation and drainage. As in Coalbrookdale they organised sick clubs and made their own donations in the form of annual grants to the Workmen's Fund. In the 1750s there were riots in Cumberland amongst miners, at the same time as unrest hit Coalbrookdale. Just as on the Welsh border, the Quaker employees of the company had such good working conditions that they refrained from participating.[26] The Quakers universally ran the 'company store' or 'truck shop' system to the benefit of their workers, and in Cumberland used their shops to drive out the moneylenders or predatory practices described in novels such as Disraeli's *Sybil*, Zola's *Germinal* and Steinbeck's *Grapes of Wrath*. But the Quakers never restricted their honest dealings to their own workforce, and opened these shops to all residents of the area.

A by-product of working with lead is silver, in much smaller quantities. The refinements to the reverberatory furnace for lead smelting made by the Quakers enabled them to dominate silver refining in the country, and substantial amounts of their silver entered the coinage of the realm. Their pre-eminence in silver production coincided with the tenure at the Royal Mint of Sir Isaac Newton, under whose direction the entire Quaker Lead Company's output was sent to the mint.[27] This led to the term 'Quaker Shilling' to apply to the resulting batch of new coinage, which bore a distinguishing mark identifying its Quaker origins.

In 1737 the price paid by the mint for silver to the Quaker Lead Company was below the market price and the company ceased supply, which was argued over but finally accepted by the mint solicitor. In fact the company had long supplied silver to the mint at below market prices through a sense of public responsibility, but in 1737 control of the company was less in the hands of Quakers. The Quaker majority was re-established in 1750, and Raistrick implies that the company turned again to selling the mint silver at the low price.[28] For a people that had historically suffered distrainment of wealth and property at the hands of the Crown, this was indeed highly public spirited.

So far this account of the Quaker Lead Company presents a
Quakernomics of integrated finance and industry, of care for workers
rising well above what could be expected of the raw capitalism of the
day, and of profitability. But mining is a dangerous occupation, and lead
is a toxic substance. Lead poisoning is one of the oldest known work
and environmental hazards, and it is now accepted that no levels of
lead are too low to not represent a risk to health. The industrial-scale
mining and refining of lead, made possible by the development of the
Quaker Edward Wright and the entrepreneurial savvy of the company,
take us straight to the charge in Morse's novel: that Quakers brought
about all the ills of industrialisation. The fumes from lead smelting must
have been a serious pollutant and health hazard to those nearby, let
alone the workers. Hence it is of interest to see that water condensers
and horizontal flues were experimented with to reduce the nuisance of
flue smoke, and universally adopted within the company and then the
industry as a whole.[29]

In contemplating the economics of the Quaker Lead Company,
finance once again takes a central role. Wright's innovation in lead
smelting, like Darby's innovation in iron smelting, led to the company
being called one of 'Britain's largest, most successful and long-standing
industrial operations' and 'a prime exemplar of increased output
for industrial development, stimulated by the seventeenth-century
commercial revolution.'[30] We saw that John Freame's bank was directly
involved in this financing, and in his later years Freame joined the
company's 'court' or board of directors. But it turned out that Edward
Wright, who effectively ran the Quaker Lead Company in the 1720s had,
along with other Quakers, misappropriated company funds in unwise
speculation during the South Sea Bubble of 1720. It was a substantial
fraud. This only emerged on the death of Wright in 1728, after which
Freame took over as company governor and prosecuted the surviving
fraudsters. Freame helped revive the company and its reputation after
this scandal.[31]

The 'total capitalism' of the Quakers was not, it seems, without
temptations that could corrupt. But the role of the Meeting in this
is interesting: warnings from the London and Middlesex Quarterly
Meeting about the South Sea Bubble may have arrived too late to
prevent the abuse, but what was the response from the Meeting to the
scandal? We are seeing perhaps the first signs that the growth in the
complexity of industrial capitalism and its financial services would
eventually outpace the ability of the Meeting to understand and oversee

their ethics, though the real end of Meeting intervention in business affairs came perhaps a century and a half later.

Agricultural Equipment: Robert Ransome

Before we leave the world of metal mining, smelting and working we look briefly at a Quaker whose foundry in Suffolk turned out innovative ploughs: a vital boost for a largely agricultural region. Richard Ransome was 'convinced' in 1676 and in 1685 was imprisoned for nearly fifteen years in Norwich Castle for refusing to pay tithes – a terrible punishment. His descendents included Robert Ransome, apprenticed as an ironmonger in Norwich, learning much about the manufacture of ploughs. He devoted himself to researching improvements to the cast-iron ploughshare, which was the most expensive part and wore away quickly, requiring costly rebuilding of the whole plough. In 1789 he moved to Ipswich and set up a foundry with a single workman in a disused malting house. His business soon expanded onto a forty acre site in which he pursued his research into the casting of the plough, culminating in a chilling process patented in 1803 that produced the definitive method of making plough shares used to this day.[32] Like most good inventions it came out of an accident: he spilled molten iron on the foundry floor, and where the iron made contact it cooled more quickly and was harder than the rest. He also introduced a design for the plough as a whole in which the share was a replaceable component, amongst others, allowing its quick replacement. Because of these developments, Ransomes became the largest plough and agricultural equipment manufacturer in Britain, and its products used on farms the world over.

Railways and Canals

While we have shown that Quakers were heavily involved in the core iron and steel industries of the Industrial Revolution, and also in lead mining and smelting, it is important to show that their genius was applied to a much larger spectrum of economic activity. In the following sections we look at railways and canals, cotton, wool and textiles, shoes and matches. This is a more rapid survey which rounds off the general picture of Quakers in light and heavy industry, on the lookout as usual for anything that adds to the picture of Quakernomics as a capitalism determined to be socially useful. We are also now able to construct a bigger picture of what a rounded economy requires, starting with a key essential: transport.

First, we turn to railways, where Quakers made as significant a contribution to the national picture as they did in iron and steel making, and in lead and silver mining. Once again the Quaker connections were central to the financing of their railway ventures. A single project stands out here: the Stockton & Darlington Railway, also known in its day as 'The Quaker Line'. Originally intended by the Quaker Edward Pease, a wealthy wool merchant, as a conventional horse-drawn line, George Stephenson persuaded Pease to work it at least partly by steam. In fact Quakers were responsible between them for building the Stockton & Darlington, the London & Birmingham, the York & North Midland, the Leicester & Swannington and the Liverpool & Manchester lines, and had seats on the boards of many other railways.[33] Charles May, a Quaker engineer at Ransomes, patented an essential device for fastening rails to sleepers.[34] In addition a Quaker called George Bradshaw, an engraver and printer of maps, invented the *Bradshaw's Railway Times*, the essential national guide to train journeys. The first edition came out in 1839, went through numerous changes as the railways were much later nationalised, and ceased publication only in 1961. It was also a Quaker, Thomas Edmonson, who designed the railway ticket and the ticketing machines for those early ventures.[35]

Railways were in the air of course, and in their horse-drawn versions were widely used both by Quaker industrialists and others. In Coalbrookdale in 1749 the first major railway line to supply an ironworks was built, though then it was horse-drawn.[36] Only later, in 1796, did the Darbys build a steam locomotive for this line, though we saw that Coalbrookdale had already made the essential innovation of iron rails and wheels. Indeed, although a Sheffield engineer is credited with being the originator of the iron tramway in 1774, Raistrick believes that Darby and Reynolds had beaten him to it by about six years.[37]

Returning to the Stockton & Darlington Railway, it was the world's first steam passenger railway, and for many years also the longest. It was a typical Quaker triumph. In its inaugural journey in 1825 Stephenson's 'Locomotion' engine pulled 33 wagons with sufficient space for seven hundred passengers, which figure caused the greatest astonishment in its day. When it arrived in Stockton the train was met by a crowd of forty thousand people and a 21 gun salute. What the Quakers brought to the emergence of the national steam-driven railways was not so much technical innovation as its organisation and finance. History had been made, but without the determination of Edward Pease it is doubtful that the venture would have begun. It was he, in combination with two Quaker bankers, Jonathan Backhouse and Thomas Richardson, who raised the money for the venture by issuing a 'prospectus' to the public – and which method became the standard way to raise finance for railways.[38]

By this stage in Quaker history the Society of Friends had become a significant force in Britain, their persecution long abandoned. Pease and his colleagues had to approach Parliament for the appropriate Railway Act for permission to build the line, which was initially opposed by the Earl of Darlington on the grounds that it would interfere with his fox hunting. However in Parliament only 13 voted against the bill. An experienced MP apparently commented: 'if the Quakers in these times, when nobody knows anything about the railways, can raise such a phalanx in their support I should recommend the county gentlemen to be very wary how to oppose them in future.' Pease drove the bill through both Houses and in 1821 it received Royal Assent.[39] Raistrick concludes, on Pease's decision to use Stephenson's locomotive instead of horses: 'It was by this daring experiment that the Stockton & Darlington Railway initiated the railway era in Britain, under Quaker auspices.'[40] It also created Pease's reputation as 'Father of the Railways'.

Edward Pease came from a prominent and wealthy Quaker family. It was another Pease, Edward Reynolds Pease, who was to become a founding member of the Fabian Society, and by extension, the London School of Economics (LSE). To his sons Edward Pease gave this advice: that a business is not an estate, and it seems they acted well upon it.

The Quakers were also involved in the other major innovation in transport of the day: canals. Both the Coalbrookdale Company and the Quaker Lead Company were involved in the building of canals; in the former case it was Reynolds and his son William. The latter invented a method for passing boats between canals at different levels involving a double railway on a short incline, an innovation that impressed the great Thomas Telford enough to write about it in detail.[41] Needless to say, Coalbrookdale cast many of the iron parts needed for the building of their canals, and the wider Quaker community put up capital for such projects. Another Quaker wool-stapler (dealer in wool), John Hustler, was the driving force behind the Leeds & Liverpool Canal. He is also considered to have played a leading role in transforming Bradford from a village to a prosperous industrial town. On this theme one can add that it was a group of Quaker investors – most of them from the same group of families which had invested in the Stockton & Darlington Railway – which transformed Middlesbrough from a hamlet of 154 people in the 1830s to an industrial landscape of blast furnaces and docks with a population some years later of six thousand.[42] This was mainly due to the coal port that Joseph Pease, son of Edward Pease, established there, and is another example of how the industrial capitalism of the Quakers created flourishing communities along the lines of Coalbrookdale (through the Darbys) or Middleton (through the Quaker Lead Company). Of course some, including perhaps the fictional Maggie and the real-world Marx, might deny that one can 'flourish' in the shadow of blast furnaces.

Cotton, Wool and Textiles

Many theorists of the Industrial Revolution pay great attention to weavers and the changes brought about by the mechanisation of that industry. Quakers in these and related wool and textile industries were as usual in the forefront of these developments, and we saw in the Introduction that Bessbrook became the archetypal Quaker settlement combining a huge linen mill with a model town for four thousand workers. Wool was central to the economic life of Britain at the time when the Quakers emerged, and one of the trade's principal concentrations was around Kendal in the Lake District, very much Quaker country. We saw that the Pease family were wool-staplers, while another concentration of the trade was in Norfolk, in which area the Gurney family became rich. John Gurney of Norwich joined the Friends in 1683, suffered three years in prison for refusing to take an oath, and left a son John who became known as the 'Weavers' Friend'.[43] He defended Norwich weavers in 1720 before a parliamentary committee, resulting in the banning of the wearing of garments made from foreign calico (white, unbleached cotton) imported from India, which helped save St Augustine's weavers from ruin. In turn it was his son Henry who founded the Gurney bank in 1770; we pick up that thread a little later. The combination of wool and banking allowed for a significant proportion of East Anglian wealth to remain controlled by this Quaker family.

The interventions made by cotton, wool and textile merchants in Parliament to protect their trades, or to press for related legislation, is a key part of early industrial capitalism. Returning to the canal builder, John Hustler: he gave evidence in 1752 before a parliamentary committee on false practices in wool growing, and pressed for legislation against the closed shop for textile workers. He was also elected to a Yorkshire committee policing fraud and embezzlement in the industry. Once again we see that Quakers, despite having been persecuted by the mainstream, were by now actively involved in securing and implementing legislation that met their principles.

In this connection John Bright, the cotton manufacturer and political Radical, has to be introduced. He was the fourth Quaker to sit in Parliament, and was best known for his oratory and for his role in the Anti–Corn Law movement. In a series of Punch cartoons in 1878, Bright featured alongside Disraeli and Gladstone as among the most influential politicians of the age. Although Bright's Radical Party was a precursor to the Liberals, his politics has appeal across the spectrum, as a recent biography by the Conservative MP Bill Cash demonstrates. John's father, Jacob, had set up a cotton-spinning factory with £6,000 of Quaker capital, and in 1809 the first steam-engine began to power the works.[44] This was the classic textile factory of socialist horror stories, in theory at least, but in Quaker practice most likely as good a place to work as was then available.

We have seen however that not all Quakers met the ethical standards of the Society of Friends. I have not been able to confirm or repudiate Marx's claim in Chapter 10 of the first volume of *Capital* that Quaker mill owners in Batley, Yorkshire, were fined £20 for forcing children to work in appalling conditions, but it gave Marx the opportunity to deride George Fox as a hypocrite, deliberately misquoting some lines from Dryden:

Fox full fraught in seeming sanctity,
That feared an oath, but like the devil would lie,
That look'd like Lent, and had the holy leer,
And durst not sin! before he said his prayer![45]

The original poem (a translation of Chaucer) has 'A fox', not 'Fox', and makes reference to John Foxe, author of the *Book of Martyrs*, not to George Fox. We see here the instincts in the Marxist tradition to mock religion and deny the very possibility of decent capitalists.

Marx was not the only one hostile to industrial capitalism of course (though perhaps one of the more muddled). Luddites did not so much object to the capitalism part as the industrialism part, and, as Quakers were at the forefront of the introduction of machinery and steam engines into the textiles industry, their factories also came under attack.

In 1812 Luddites smashed a Quaker-owned factory at a place called Low Mill in Yorkshire in the same year that Parliament passed the Frame Breaking Act and the Malicious Damage Act, making such vandalism a hanging offence. Lord Byron was one of the few defenders of the Luddite movement, emblematic of the long-standing romantic objection to industrialisation.

Shoes

Clarks, the Somerset shoemakers, was perhaps the firm held longest in Quaker family hands, and appears to be as successful in the twenty-first century as it was in the nineteenth. Their outlets are still found on most high streets, and for some reason their products are very popular in Jamaica. Emden introduces the Clarks in this way:

> For many and most diverse achievements – manufacturing slippers and galoshes and declining government orders, constructing a machine for turning out hexameter verse which scanned and the making of cloth waterproof – the Clarks of Street have become famous.[46]

Like the Darbys they benefited from the Great Exhibition, but in the Crimean War not long afterwards they declined substantial orders for sheepskin coats – sheepskin being the original basis of their business. It was subsequently argued that the soldiers would die of cold without the coats, and on that basis Clarks agreed to supply them, but put the profit from these sales aside to build a new school. The ethics of this are complex, as one discovers in the subsequent severe criticism they came under from the Bristol Quarterly Meeting, that they were 'killing Russians by keeping alive soldiers to do the killing'.[47] In times of war, almost any industry can be co-opted into the supply chain, and Quakers always collectively agonised in this fashion. We note here that the Local Meeting was fully apprised of the Clarks' business activities, and didn't hesitate to criticise if they felt that standards had slipped.

In 1855, John Bright (whose daughter married one of the Clarks) was called upon to open a workers' college built by the Clarks containing 'a library, billiard, lecture and reading rooms, a gymnasium, and even a geological museum'. We see again a common Quaker pattern, found in Bessbrook, Coalbrookdale, Middleton, Street and in many other locations, most famously in Bournville – all of them 'dry', it has to be added.

At the time of the college's opening Clarks employed about eight hundred workers, smaller than the other operations just listed, but destined for longevity.[48]

And the machine for turning out hexameters? This was down to a member of the family called John, a far better poet than businessman, because it was also he who invented the method of making waterproof cloth, but sold the process to a man named Charles Macintosh for a tiny fee. It was a loss to Quakernomics, but on the other hand taking a handy 'Clark' with you in case it rains doesn't have quite the proper ring to it.

Matches

William Bryant and Francis May were two Quakers who founded a merchandising company in 1843 and soon began importing large quantities of Swedish matches. Ten years later they were selling over eight million boxes of matches a year, and in 1861 they took over a site in Bow, East London, for their own production of the article. The factory they built there was a model factory, now apartments overlooking the canal and main rail artery into London, as mentioned in the Introduction. Their aim was to make only safety matches, and along the way to reduce the incidence of phossy jaw, a dreadful disease caused by white phosphorus. However, commercial pressures led them to also produce traditional, more dangerous 'Lucifer' matches and to continue in the use of white phosphorus.

In 1884 Bryant & May was reshaped as a limited company with a capital of £300,000 in a flotation involving sixty thousand preference shares of £5.[49] In modern terms this translates into a capital injection of around £15 million – a substantial sum even by today's standards. The company was then in the hands of Wilberforce Bryant who wanted the newly capitalised company to have something of a co-operative nature, so he allotted some proportion of the shares to heads of department, long-serving employees and travelling salesmen. Increasing mechanisation helped the necessary downward drive of costs in order to meet foreign competition. The company later merged with various other match makers to become the British Match Corporation and in 1929 took over part of another Quaker company, Albright & Wilson. Eventually it merged with Wilkinson Sword.

The paternalism within the company is thought to have derived more from Francis May, who died in 1885, but whatever the cause, it was under William Bryant's son, Wilberforce Bryant, that the infamous Matchgirls'

Strike took place in 1888. The controversy over the Matchgirls' Strike is an important one in the history of industrial relations, and quite possibly tarnishes the company's record, but the contribution of Bryant & May is recorded by Paul Emden as a 'great social benefit to England'.[50] Why? Because the safety match, which strikes only on the special surface on the box, must have saved *countless* lives. It had been invented in Sweden, and shown at the Great Exhibition of 1851, but it was only when Bryant & May bought a license for the patent that it was universally sold in Britain. Older forms of matches were a fire hazard because they only had to rub together to ignite, and there was also enough white phosphorous in a pack to kill a person – eating match heads even became a common method of committing suicide. The traditional 'Lucifer' matches were so dangerous that, for example, in 1874 the Australian government considered banning them.[51] Hence no less a thinker than the Victorian English philosopher Herbert Spencer (whose father had taken up Quakerism) praised the safety match as 'the greatest boon and blessing to come to mankind in the nineteenth century.'

With this in mind the Matchgirls' Strike makes for a startling contrast to the reputation of the firm for good working conditions, and its legacy of contribution to society at large. In fact the strike of 1888 is a key moment in the history of industrial relations and provides us with material for considering many aspects of paternalist industrialism and economic justice. The strike was sparked by a talk on the working conditions at Bryant & May given at a Fabian Society meeting in London where Annie Besant, a feminist and occultist, was in attendance. She then interviewed employees at Bryant & May and discovered that pay was low, workers were liable to receive substantial fines for a range of petty offences, and that phossy jaw still plagued the workforce. At this time in economic history America and Sweden had banned the use of white phosphorus in match making, but the British government had refused to ban the import of matches made that way, saying it was an infringement of free trade. Outraged at what she learned at the factory, Besant published her findings, to which Bryant & May reacted in a heavy-handed manner. This led to strike action from all 1,400 women workers.

The strike was censured by the *Times*, but supported by socialists such as George Bernard Shaw and Sydney Webb (an early member of the Fabian Society and co-founder of the LSE), and led to the unionisation of the women. It is considered to be the first strike by formerly unorganised workers to gain national publicity and led to the formation of many new labour unions across the country. Bryant & May eventually yielded to the strikers' demands, but such was public feeling that the Salvation Army was able to raise money to set up a rival match factory in the East End using the more expensive but much safer red phosphorous. It was soon producing six million boxes a year, at three times the price of Bryant & May's. All of this reflects very badly on the Quakers of course, and demands careful consideration. Does it undermine the general proposition of Quakernomics as an ethical capitalism, or is it an exception that proves the rule?

Let us start by considering the nature of the raw economic activity embodied in the sale of matches. To the average family the humble match was in fact one of life's essentials: no cooking could begin without it, and no heating of water for drinking or sanitary purposes was likewise possible (the tinder box had long been abandoned by 1888). So what price should a match be? If Bryant & May made a fortune from manufacturing them, did they not pay the workers too little, charge their customers too much, or flout safety regulations, or all three? Clearly the higher the price charged for the match the more they could pay the workers, and the more they could meet safety standards, including switching production to the safer red phosphorous – which is what they had set out to do. So why did they, for example, not charge three times as much for a match, like the Salvation Army? Or to put it another way, what is the *real* value of a match? This is a fundamental kind of question in economics, along with what is the *real* value of the labour contributed by the worker?

Classical economics answers both questions by saying that, with perfect competition, the price of the match and the price of labour reaches an equilibrium. Manufacturers compete to make matches, driving down the price, and workers compete for jobs, driving down wages. Classical economics asserts that at equilibrium, wages will settle at a rate sufficient to buy the products of industry, including all of life's necessities. In our ongoing discussion of subsistence, this is clearly a theory about wages with little supporting evidence. But for products it clearly means that there is no 'real' value or price that can be put on a match, for example. New production methods will drive its price down and down. Indeed, today, who could possibly say that matches are 'expensive'? And for the working families of Victorian Britain, when do we hear complaints about the price of matches? Clearly as an essential, most people could pay higher prices, and they did for a while volunteer to do so when buying matches from the Salvation Army. Those higher prices guaranteed better working conditions and freedom from phossy jaw. But so would have action by the British government, like that in America and Sweden, to ban the import of white phosphorous matches.

In the end sympathy for the cause ran out, and the general public abandoned their principles and started buying the cheaper matches from Bryant & May, which eventually bought up the Salvation Army factory when it went bust. Customers most likely *could* have gone on paying the higher price – but it would mean less for other essentials, and so market forces won over social conscience. The Salvation Army match boxes carried a message of social justice: 'Lights in Darkest England' they said on one side, and 'Our work is for God and humanity – Help the Darkest England Scheme – Bear one another's burdens' on the other. Are these not suitable slogans for the Quakers? Are not Quakers everywhere ashamed that it fell to another religious group, the Salvation Army, to fight for economic justice in such a way?

All I can do here is to present another side of the story. According to Patrick Beaver, author of a book on Bryant & May, no less than Charles Booth mentions the Bow match-works in his *Life and Labour in London*.[52] Booth points out that the low wages – which were the main issue in the strike – were in fact down to the irregularity of attendance of the matchgirls and seasonal variations in the work. Bryant & May, like most good employers, preferred to share work out rather than lay off staff in seasonal downturns, which included the summer months when demand for matches was lower. The *hourly rate* of pay at Bryant & May was in fact above average, but this was not noticed by the socialist reformers. Beaver also points out that after the dispute was settled the London Trades Council (a labour organisation) investigated and issued a report in which 'it was actually shown that most of the charges levelled against the company were without foundation' and that wages at the factory were in fact fifteen to twenty per cent higher than in comparable firms. Journalists who were inspired by the romantic image of the first major strike by women in Britain visited the factory and were generally surprised at the good working conditions, and landed up eulogising working practices at the factory.[53] A reporter for the *Record* visited the works, prompted by sensational accounts of dividends gained at the cost of starvation, exhaustion, and effectively slavery, only to find 'in all more than a thousand hands, and they were without doubt some of the most light-hearted workers I have ever come across [...] most of the girls seemed to be remarkably well nurtured and many of them had bright rosy cheeks which contrasted pleasantly with the pale and sickly countenances of many mill-hands in Lancashire.' A militant feminist of the era, Millicent Garrett Fawcett, also wrote in glowing terms of the conditions and the lengths gone to in order to eliminate phosphorous poisoning.

According to Beaver, the traditional white phosphorous was eventually replaced with a completely safe version developed by French chemists. In 1900 Bryant & May acquired the British patent rights to this substance, and struck a deal with the British government: if the government permanently banned white phosphorous, it would share the patent with all other match makers in the country free of charge. This was agreed and the 1910 act led to the elimination of white phosphorous and the dreaded phossy jaw from Britain.[54] The failure of the government to act earlier to ban the import of cheap matches, and its eventual action in 1910, demonstrates the issue of the 'level playing field' in free market capitalism. Left to itself the free market might throw up a Salvation Army match factory for the ethical production of a commodity, but it would not survive market forces for long: in contrast it was government action that eliminated the downward commercial pressures that had forced Bryant & May to use cheaper and more dangerous chemicals.

Perhaps Bryant & May redeemed themselves with their offer to the government in 1910, perhaps, in fact, the transgressions of the factory were grossly exaggerated, or perhaps by that time the owners were no longer Quakers anyway. What we do know is that there was no official Quaker condemnation of the firm. More research is really needed to gain a clear picture of the Matchgirls' Strike, but it serves well as an example of the forces of free market capitalism and how those forces are often tamed for the good by legislation.

Chapter 6

QUAKERS IN SCIENCE, CHEMICALS AND PHARMACEUTICALS

Britain led the world in the technologies at the centre of the Industrial Revolution, and also led the world in science. But it was the trial and error of technology that dominated industry for a long time, industrial production only later becoming an activity more driven by the discoveries in pure and applied science. Peter Mathias, the Cambridge historian of the Industrial Revolution, puts it like this:

> By and large innovations were not the result of the formal application of applied science, nor a product of the formal educational system of the country. Great determination, intense curiosity, quick wits, clever fingers, luck, capital or employment and a backer to survive the period of experimenting, testing, improving were more important in almost all fields than a scientific training.[1]

Hence the early achievements of the Industrial Revolution arose without much formal underpinning in science, but after about the middle of the nineteenth century this changed. My favourite example is that of the Atlantic telegraph cable project, floundering under the direction of an engineer, and rescued by the scientist William Thomson, later Lord Kelvin. The engineer represents the earlier archetype, one whose persistent trial and error led to success, though also very often to failure, while Kelvin represents the new approach to industrial innovation based on hard science. The successful cable was laid in 1866 after Kelvin had taken over and based the enterprise on better theories of mechanical stress and the science of electromagnetism. Chemicals, pharmaceuticals and such household products as soap and starch were all produced for centuries based on unsystematic discovery, and were changed by the emerging scientific discipline of chemistry, augmented by relevant branches of physics such as thermodynamics.

Our Quaker entrepreneurs fit the picture painted by Mathias very well, of great determination, intense curiosity, quick wits, and so on. The Darbys for example had no education in science, especially not at university level, and knew little about the physics or chemistry of their iron making.[2] Ransome, as we saw, discovered the chilled steel method of ploughshare casting after molten metal spilled on the foundry floor. Pure science of the form pursued by Newton or Kelvin for example was not the natural instinct of the Quaker entrepreneurs in general, though here we look at some exceptions.

Quaker Scientists and Botanists

Early Quaker or Quaker-born scientists include John Dalton, father of modern atomic theory and contributor to the fields of meteorology and colour blindness, and Thomas Young, known for 'Young's Modulus' and the famous 'Young's Double Slit Experiment' in optics which led to the theory of wave particle duality in physics and the later discoveries of quantum theory. Young was disowned by the Society of Friends for joining the Church of England, which he did in order to study at Cambridge. Luke Howard is best known for his nomenclature for clouds, which put the science of meteorology on a firm footing. The early work of Elizabeth Brown on sunspots led her travel widely to seek solar eclipses. She was appointed head of the solar section of the Liverpool Astronomical Association and later the director of the solar section of the British Astronomical Association.

Later Quaker scientists include Arthur Stanley Eddington who is as well-known in astrophysics as Dalton is in chemistry, and whose writings inspired the mathematician Alan Turing. Eddington is famous for the expedition to observe the solar eclipse of 1919 that provided one of the earliest confirmations of Einstein's theory of relativity. Sir Francis Galton, the founder of eugenics, was born into a Quaker family and was Charles Darwin's half-cousin, sharing the common grandparent Erasmus Darwin. Galton's work on eugenics is probably as much an embarrassment to the Quaker tradition as it is to real science. Kathleen Lonsdale was a chemist who confirmed the chemical structure of benzene originally proposed by Friedrich August Kekulé. Lonsdaleite, a rare form of diamond found in meteorites, was named in her honour, and has an interesting Quaker connection: it was two Quakers who had much earlier proved that diamond was a pure form of carbon. Jocelyn Bell Burnell – an astrophysicist like

Eddington – discovered radio pulsars. She went to a Quaker school and several times served as clerk to the sessions of the Britain Yearly Meeting. George Ellis is a professor of mathematics and theoretical physics and is an active Quaker who won the prestigious Templeton Prize for progress in religion. He has co-authored scientific works with Stephen Hawking.

Quakers in Britain hold an annual conference called Yearly Meeting in which a Quaker is invited to give what is known as the Swarthmore Lecture on the theme of the meeting. Perhaps the earliest given by a Quaker scientist was in 1915 by Silvanus P. Thompson (1851–1916), who was for many years the principal and professor of physics at Finsbury Technical College. In 1929 Eddington gave a talk called 'Science and the Unseen World', reprinted in 2007 with a new foreword by George Ellis, and in 1953 Kathleen Lonsdale gave the Swarthmore Lecture on the theme 'Removing the Causes of War'. The 1989 Swarthmore Lecture was given by Jocelyn Bell Burnell on the theme of suffering, and is a poignant call to remember and honour the things that are broken in life as well as the wholesome and successful.

The Quaker scientists are important, I would argue, because they complete the picture I have drawn so far of compatibility between religion and capitalism with a picture of compatibility between religion and science. As Burnell put it: 'In both Quakerism and science you must be completely ready to revise what you hold to be the truth; you always hold things provisionally, and you are always open to revising them.'[3] And, as I just pointed out, from about the middle of the nineteenth century capitalism and its enterprises were to increasingly rely on the sciences.

Botany and biology were disciplines prominent in the Victorian period and important for industrial capitalism partly because the trade in plants of all kinds is a wealth-creating industry in its own right, partly because advances in these sciences have led to vastly greater food production, and partly because these early studies led to developments in pharmacology and medicine. The Quaker transatlantic correspondence included the shipment of many seeds, roots, cuttings and pictures of newly discovered species, including a mountain magnolia.[4] Raistrick devotes a whole section to botanists in his chapter on Quaker scientists, and suggests that 'to them we do, indeed, owe a goodly proportion of our present garden and medical plants.'[5] Amongst these botanists were three fellows of the Royal Society (FRS), Peter Collinson, William Allen (mentioned earlier) and John Fothergill. And amongst the oddest-sounding contributions to modern ears perhaps is from Quaker botanist John Coakley Lettsom, who introduced the mangel-wurzel (a beet vegetable) to Britain as a food crop.[6]

John Fothergill was also a doctor, as were the Quakers Thomas Hodgkin, Joseph Lister and Alfred and Ada Salter.[7] Of these Joseph Lister is best known as the pioneer of antiseptic surgery, though he had ceased to be a Quaker in the years of his successful practice, and long before 'Listerine' mouthwash was named after him. His later honours included presidency of the Royal Society and a peerage, but he was recognised by the Quaker doctor, Alfred Salter, as 'a man of simple habits – extremely modest and forgetful of himself, with a devotion to truth, a passionate love for humanity, and a remarkable serenity of character.'[8]

Emden tells us that John Fothergill was one of the most popular doctors in London, and that Benjamin Franklin said of him: 'he could hardly conceive that a better man ever existed.'[9] Fothergill maintained extensive correspondence with America and a longstanding friendship with Franklin.[10] Fothergill's practice was one of the largest in London. His philanthropy was widespread, extending to a substantial contribution to the founding of the famous Quaker school at Ackworth; his botanical collection passed to public ownership in what is now West Ham Park (as mentioned in the Introduction); and a flowering shrub from south-eastern America bears his name. Fothergill's contribution to medicine lay in an instinct for the truly scientific – that is knowledge acquired through observation rather than received through tradition. Hence in 1747, during an outbreak of throat infections that was claiming the lives of many poor children, he spurned the usual treatment by bleeding, and recommended instead good diet, cleanliness and care, and medication with cinchona bark, its main active principle being quinine. Raistrick tells us: 'The number of his successes was very large, and the extent of consultations added to his unremitting care of the poor caused him about that time to be working normally some sixteen to seventeen hours a day.'[11] Fothergill subsequently published a paper identifying the throat infections as a form of scarlatina (scarlet fever), which brought him fame and opportunities for wealth, but he turned them down in favour of his work with the poor.

The Quaker scientists, botanists, chemists and doctors we have just examined all operated within early industrial capitalism, and form a necessary sector in a rounded economy. The state funded very little of their activities – unlike in twenty-first-century economies – and so they were nearly all involved in turning a profit somewhere in order to maintain their activities. Hence they form an important part of our Quaker 'total capitalism'.

Clock-Makers

While pure science is not perhaps an instinctive pursuit of the Quaker – though with notable exceptions as we have seen – a craft like watch-making certainly is. Mathias tells us: 'The engineering industry of the late eighteenth century thus saw a meeting between two widespread older sorts of skills: the skills of the blacksmith, carpenter, and millwright taken up to the standards of accuracy of the watch-maker.'[12] We see this trajectory in the Darbys: a yeoman ancestor who owned a blacksmithing forge led to a Darby who machined cast-iron cylinders for steam-engines. Benjamin Huntsman, we may recall, was a watch-maker who turned into one of the great innovators in steel, but there are two more Quaker watch-makers of note: George Graham, who invented the modern form of orrery, and Daniel Quare, who invented a repeating watch movement.

George Graham was a Cumberland Quaker who became a freeman of the Clock Makers Company in 1695 and Master of the Worshipful Company of Clockmakers in 1722 in honour of his services to the industry. He was elected FRS in 1721. Some of his achievements include the great mural quadrant at Greenwich Observatory, the discovery of the cyclical variation of the terrestrial magnetic field, and the discovery that auroras are related to magnetic field variations. Around 1730, George loaned approximately £200 to John Harrison so that he could start work on his marine chronometer known later as H1, the instrument that led to Harrison's conquest of longitude – and the maritime dominance of Britain. George was commonly known in the trade as 'Honest George Graham'.[13]

Daniel Quare was a West Country clock-maker whose Quaker beliefs led to him being fined for refusing to pay tithes and then fined again for refusing to pay for the militia who arrested him, this time losing two clocks and two watches to defray the costs. Further fines for observing Quaker practices followed, but he was eventually taken into William III's favour, and is said to have made a watch for him. Quare was one of the few watch- or clock-makers considered equal to George Graham.[14] He was in fact a watch-maker to several Royals, and won Charles II's favour over a rival whose claim for a patent for a repeating watch Quare opposed on the grounds that he had invented it first, a claim subsequently upheld in the history of watch-making. King George II so highly regarded Quare that he offered to appoint him as the king's watch-maker, but Quare declined as he would have had to swear an oath of loyalty.

Other Innovators

Windsor tells us that 'Famous Quaker names stand out when we turn to the porcelain and English china-clay industries. Three such names remain with us – those of Cookworthy, Champion and Wedgwood.'[15] The inclusion of Wedgewood here may well be mistaken, as he is widely considered to have been a Unitarian (though he may have attended Quaker schools when young). But Cookworthy and Champion were interesting Quaker innovators in this field. Raistrick says this: 'William Cookworthy is remembered among the many technical inventors who contributed to the establishment of the manufacture of this country, as the discoverer of the Cornish deposits of China clay, and the founder of the English porcelain industry based on their use.'[16] Cookworthy was another typical Quaker polymath: self-taught in Latin and French, a supplier of bulk chemicals and drugs, involved in the construction of lighthouses, a translator of Swedenborg, an experimenter with furnaces, and a devotee of astronomy. His Quaker family had been ruined by foolish speculation on the South Sea Bubble, and he was taken into the apothecary business of Silvanus Bevan.[17] It was in Cookworthy's fifties that lengthy investigations yielded the discovery of three deposits of china clay in the West Country, which to date have yielded some one hundred and twenty million tons for the making of porcelain. His was not a Quaker financial success story however, and neither did a second Quaker, Richard Champion, succeed in making a commercial go of it, perhaps because Wedgewood drained his resources by challenging the patent he held. Neither did the Quaker network come to the rescue in this case, although Joseph Fry, later of chocolate fame, invested £1,500 in the business. It closed not long after, apparently leaving him only a beautiful set of vases to show for it.[18]

Capitalism and Chemicals

As a short digression on capitalism I want to mention an incident at an academic conference where I was speaking about a German enterprise called Digital Art Museum, which is both a commercial gallery and a vehicle for research into the history of computer art. I had been challenged at question time about how 'prices' were set for the artworks, and wasn't this 'capitalist' and a 'commodification of the art object'? I later spoke to the young lady who asked the question, who was herself an artist. She didn't sell her works, because – it turned out – she had inherited a house from an aunt and lived off the rent. 'You little hypocrite!' I responded, as her story sunk in, and then had to apologise and back-pedal as I saw the offence I had caused. 'Hypocrite' was in fact the wrong word, as that implies dishonesty, and there was no doubt that the woman was sincere. What came home to me in this exchange however was how she had failed to think through the conflict between her Marxist principles and her 'bourgeois' existence. Quakers, it seems, never fell into this trap, which is why their example is so useful in contemplating the real nature of capitalism.

In my local Quaker Meeting books are laid out on the central table, including the Bible and the sourcebook of modern Quakerism, *Quaker Faith and Practice*. Along with these are some children's books. I was taken by the contradiction posed by two of them, a little like the contradiction facing the artist lady in my digression above. One of them tells the story of Luke Howard the meteorologist, making a big thing of how success comes with perseverance: a Quaker story for children. Another book conveys a typical environmental message for children: that nasty factories pollute the atmosphere and kill nature, but if we recycle and live more natural lives the planet will be a better place. The contradiction here lies in the fact that Quakers were at the forefront of building 'nasty factories', none more nasty than chemical works (though a match factory, as we saw, could be bad enough), and that Luke Howard was in fact a genius in the mass production of chemicals.

All of us in Western-style economies, beneficiaries of modernity, have lifestyles of comfort and opportunity not dreamed of at the dawn of the Industrial Revolution. But our schoolbooks and later education do little to uncover the harsh realities of factory production that provide us our homes, goods, transport, entertainment, medicines and food – all the 'upstream' processes as it were – or the harsh realities of what happens to our sewerage, household and industrial waste – all the 'downstream' processes. Industrial chemicals are central to all of this, but our gaze only extends a fraction of the journey that our goods make towards and away from us, and never takes in how chemicals are involved in those journeys. Hence, by now focussing on the Quaker chemical industries, we begin to get a little deeper into the true workings of industrial capitalism. The furnaces at Coalbrookdale may have struck us as 'dark satanic mills', but the romance of the family firm, the entrepreneurial spirit, and the sheer beauty of the Iron Bridge in the picturesque surroundings of the Severn Valley, along with the homely nature of the cooking pots turned out there by the million – all this may have made up for the initial negative assessment of factories blackening and ravaging the pristine forests of the region. But chemical works with their poisonous substances, vats and miles of piping are much harder to fall in love with. This is by way of introduction to an outstanding Quaker firm, Crosfield's, makers of soap products and related chemicals.

Crosfield

The Crosfield's soap factory in Warrington was a typical Quaker enterprise, set up in 1814 by Joseph Crosfield. In the late 1830s it was producing about nine hundred tons of soap a year. By the 1860s it was the fifth largest soap producer in the country, later shifting more to chemical production and finally being absorbed into Lever Brothers and then into the Unilever empire. Joseph lost every penny of his £1,500 capital in the first year, and a group of Friends had to be appointed to advise him through these financial difficulties. However his later success brought him profits that he invested far and wide, and also led him to spread his wealth through philanthropy. He was remembered on his death as one of the most able men of Warrington, despite his being anti-Establishment and having campaigned for many radical causes, including on behalf of the Anti–Corn Law League. Walvin tells us that he established schools, a mechanics institute, libraries and a bible society in Warrington,[19] the latter being typical, as we have seen, of the Quakers in that it was funded by them but served other denominations.[20]

   A. E. Musson, author of *Enterprise in Soap and Chemicals*, says: 'From a few scrappy extraneous pieces of evidence, however, in local newspapers, etc., it appears that the firm's employees were more happily situated than workers generally.'[21] The managers knew most of their staff by name and provided pensions for long serving employees, according to Windsor.[22] Alongside other familiar aspects of industrial paternalism, such as a sick fund and works outings, Crosfield was even supportive of trade unions, speaking out in their favour as a necessary counterpart to the power of employers. Joseph's son George continued the business, leading its diversification into chemicals, and taking interest in a local bank and the Warrington & Stockport Railway, of which he became auditor.[23] This is another illustration of the generalised economic activity, typical of the age, but also of what I am calling the 'total capitalism' of Quakernomics.

The development of the soap factory took, as all such businesses do, periodic injections of capital to take advantage of new industrial processes. The advent of steam was also quickly adopted, for heating, melting and power, as was a major advance in soap making: the use of sodium silicate. A licence for this and other patents were bought in along with scientific expertise – in the shape of Dr Karl Markel, a German chemist – marking the early transition from an industry with its roots in antiquity and its discoveries slow and unsystematic, to the science-led paradigm of modern manufacture. In this case the Quaker industrialists made few significant innovations in their field, though Crosfield's took out some patents, but were quick to adopt the patents of other, often German, firms, and also bought the rights to 'Persil' from the German company Henkel – a household brand name that has survived far longer than Crosfield's 'Perfection' soap.[24]

Three generations of Crosfields ran the company up to the point when it was incorporated in 1896, an inevitable move as their great rivals, including Lever, had already done so. Interestingly in 1907 the reliance on German scientific expertise ended with the then unusual move of taking scientists from the research departments of British universities.[25] This development can be taken as emblematic of the central role that science henceforth played in such industries, and how state-funded education and research supported them.

Soap is a typical household product that we use daily and give no thought to. Yet in its manufacture lies many of the nastiest chemicals, both acids and alkalis, and in the early days of the Crosfield's works, they and other Merseyside soaperies were often taken to court by local residents and farmers complaining of nuisance and damage to animals and crops.[26] Although alkalis are the key ingredient in soap that makes them both cleansing and anti-bacterial, sulphuric acid was then used in the making of alkaline soda, which in turn generates hydrogen chloride gas. This gas is quickly absorbed by moisture, for example in the lungs, to create a strong corrosive acid. Contrast this picture with that of the Liverpool International Exhibition of 1866 where Crosfield's won a gold medal for its 'Perfection' soap, prompting the *Warrington Guardian* to wax lyrical on its virtues, as 'incapable of injuring the most delicate fabric or the tenderest of skins […] made from the purest of materials [...]' The *Illustrated London News* followed with: 'it combines the most extraordinary lathering powers with absolute PURITY and NEUTRALITY.'[27]

This contradiction – I would suggest – is typical of the contradiction at the heart of industrial capitalism, whether run privately or by the state. The Crosfield company produced chemicals such as caustic soda, silicate of soda and glycerine as much as soap, and even in the manufacture of soap itself we find a considerable range of industrial chemicals and processes involved. Steam power was used, as mentioned, and also steam for heating – a very nasty combination of high temperatures and caustic materials, while high-temperature furnaces were required to melt silicates, all of which are a continual threat to the health and safety of workers, even today. Our morning bath, shower, or face-and-hands wash all rely on soap or similar products: we feel clean and protected from germs. Yet how many schoolchildren have been taken to a soap or chemical factory or been in some way enthused about such a thing? The well-meaning environmentalism taught to children will create in them the same contradiction as my artist faced: they are the daily beneficiaries of something they have been taught to vaguely mistrust. Quakernomics on the other hand teaches a clear-eyed picture of the bigger process, from the unromantic chemical factory upstream of the supply of our goods – our 'Perfection' soaps – to the unromantic disposal downstream of our waste.

I don't mean any of this as a justification for industrial pollution or the abandonment of environmental concerns. But we should teach our children what is at stake here, and give them some idea of what has to be really overcome if we want to rein in the impact of our lifestyles on the planet.

Allen & Hanburys

We turn now from chemicals to pharmaceuticals, and no Quaker company stands out more in this field than Allen & Hanburys. From the East Coast line into Liverpool Street station, as I mentioned, one can still spot their sign on their old factory at Bethnal Green. This Quaker enterprise was founded in 1715 and, in a parallel with Crosfield's, now finds itself part of a well-known twenty-first-century giant, in this case GlaxoSmithKlein. It has been remarked that 'its history is synonymous with the development of the British pharmaceutical industry.'[28]

The Quaker history of the company involves, as happens so often, a network of relations. The Quaker emphasis on honesty gave rise to their innumerable banking operations, but second to that field in the necessity for an honest reputation must lie pharmaceuticals. Silvanus Bevan, the Welsh Quaker who founded the company, along with his partners and successors, maintained that reputation over generations as the company expanded and built factories in London, Ware and Hertfordshire. Bevan set up his initial business in Plough Court, off Lombard Street, the famous financial centre. His Quaker connections were many, including taking William Cookworthy as apprentice (as mentioned earlier) and his marriage to the daughter of Daniel Quare, the clock-maker to royalty discussed above. He was elected FRS in 1725 on the proposal of Sir Isaac Newton. [29] Silvanus was joined in the business by his brother Timothy, who married twice: first time to Elisabeth, daughter of David Barclay of Lombard Street, and second time to Hannah, daughter of Joseph Gurney of the Norwich Gurneys.

In 1792 Bevan offered the Quaker William Allen a clerkship, and before long Allen took control of the firm. In 1797 he in turn took Luke Howard into partnership.[30] Howard had already set up a pharmacy in Fleet Street and had a gift with chemicals, as we observed, and he left Allen's business in 1807 to concentrate on their manufacture. In 1806 Allen married Charlotte Hanbury, thus cementing links with another prodigiously business-minded Quaker clan. Allen himself was committed to the abolition of slavery, and knew both Thomas Clarkson and William Wilberforce.[31] Plough Court became one of the centres of the anti-slavery movement.[32]

Allen was linked to other leading radicals of his day, including James Mill, Jeremy Bentham and Robert Owen, and was involved in the takeover of Owen's experiment in New Lanark Mills. Like the Quaker clock-maker, Quare, Allen's reputation brought him into frequent contact with royalty, and he struck up a friendship with Alexander I of Russia, visiting him in Moscow and Vienna, the latter trip undertaken to secure the Emperor's help in ending the slave trade.[33] Apparently in his trip to Moscow in 1819 he conversed with the tsar for over two hours, touching on the New Lanark experiment and the work of Elizabeth Fry, and on the tsar's suggestion they concluded their meeting with a short period of silent prayer.[34] Allen had given up sugar in protest against the role of slavery in its production, and is said to have refused a sweetened tea offered to him on another occasion by the tsar in Verona.

The frequent meetings of Quakers with rulers and princes drew criticism at times, but had precedent in the extraordinary meeting between George Fox and Oliver Cromwell in 1655. Fox had been arrested, but prior to his interview had written a letter that must have moved Cromwell deeply. In their meeting Fox spoke to Cromwell as he did everywhere about peace and truth, and in his journal records this on parting company with Cromwell that day: 'As I was turning, he caught me by the hand, and with tears in his eyes said, "Come again to my house; for if thou and I were but an hour of a day together, we should be nearer one to the other"; adding that he wished me no more ill than he did to his own soul.'[35] Fox was freed after this, and met Cromwell a number of times before his death. For the Marxist revolutionary all this is difficult: communists want to sweep away power structures represented by people like Cromwell and foreign princes, but here is Fox, in one sense a social revolutionary, yet completely at home with and welcomed to the seat of power. Quakers clearly took their cue from Fox in this respect, and their ability to mingle with rulers was invaluable in the pursuit of both their businesses and their activism. William Allen exemplifies this characteristic in Quakers, a tradition which could be summed up in the phrase 'speak truth to power', the title of a polemical booklet published by Quakers in 1955.[36]

Allen conducted scientific research, as well as being a member of various scientific societies, including the Linnaean Society, and was elected FRS in 1807, having refused it earlier. Along with another Quaker scientist he delivered a paper to the Royal Society proving that diamond was pure carbon, a nice forerunner of the work of the Quaker scientist Kathleen Lonsdale, mentioned earlier. Plough Court 'had by that time become one of the centres of scientific research in London', according to one historian.[37]

As the pharmaceutical business expanded it leased buildings in Bethnal Green, in the East End of London, and most of its manufacturing was transferred there, though in time factories were also set up in other parts of the UK and abroad. Its cod liver oil, for example, was manufactured in the Lofoten Islands and other locations in Norway. The firm's great period of expansion followed its adoption of limited liability status in 1893, growing to produce a huge range of products related to medicine, including baby foods, surgery equipment, hospital furniture, ambulances, even 'milk-cocoa' and 'horse balls' (a veterinary product), constructing a business empire that was world-wide. It was only the advent of retailers like Boots Chemists that eventually reduced the firm's presence in the high street, and led to its takeover by Glaxo.

John Bell & Co. and Corbyn, Stacey & Co.

Two more important Quaker pharmaceutical firms need to be mentioned: John Bell & Co. and Corbyn, Stacey & Co.[38] In 1798, aged only 23, John Bell opened his business as a chemist and druggist at 338, Oxford Street. Bell took only two years to pay off the capital he had borrowed from his family. He was typical of the move away from the tradition of the apothecaries – who largely moved into medicine – towards the new industry of pharmaceuticals, in the transition from herbalism to modern medicine, and in which Quakers played a prominent role. In another typical pattern John's son, Jacob, being born into the wealth created by his father's business, rather abandoned Quaker principles and was disowned by the Kingston Monthly Meeting in 1855.

The Wellcome Institute, established by pharmaceutical philanthropist Sir Henry Wellcome, records the Quaker Thomas Corbyn (1711–1791) as a 'wholesale and manufacturing chemist and druggist', mentioning too that his nickname was 'Pope Corbyn' on account of his strict adherence to Quaker doctrine.[39] Corbyn was both a principal member of the Society of Friends in London and traded widely on the other side of the Atlantic, his drugs produced to a very high standard. His enterprise includes all the elements of Quaker success so far described, with one additional feature: trading through the Quaker network across the Atlantic. Walvin comments: 'From Nova Scotia to Barbados, he dispatched pharmaceutical goods to Friends for sampling and distribution, knowing that they would transact his business fairly and honestly.'[40] One could almost say that this gave him an unfair advantage over non-Quaker rivals.

Reckitt & Sons

We conclude this brief survey of chemicals and related products by looking at a Quaker starch manufacturer, whose name still lingers in household brands: Reckitt & Sons. Chemicals in various forms are essential to industrial capitalism, are mass produced in factories, can be a blessing in the form of soap, safety matches or medicines, or can blight lives and whole landscapes: think of Bhopal in India where victims of perhaps the worst accident ever in industrial chemical production has left a legacy of sickness and litigation to this day. The techniques of mass production in chemicals have also been applied to *food*. Again, cheap food – like cheap soap, matches and medicines – help billions of people on lower wage scales make ends meet, but is also responsible in various ways for new health epidemics like obesity and diabetes. Industrial capitalism, it seems, is everywhere a mixed blessing, and therefore requires highly developed regulatory frameworks, food being a particularly good example. The Quaker producers of medicines and foodstuffs gained their reputation – and wealth – by being scrupulous over purity, in a time of rampant and criminal adulteration.

Walvin tells us that 'The Reckitt chemical company in Hull, which began life as a small starch business, had almost 5,000 workers by the early twentieth century.'[41] It was founded in the 1840s by Isaac Reckitt who acquired a recipe for the manufacture of starch. (Dickens has David Copperfield tell us that the proctors he worked with wore starch 'to as great an extent as it is in the nature of man to bear', indicating its importance in Victorian times.) At the time of the Irish potato famine, potatoes for the basis of starch manufacture were understandably scarce, but sago was not, and Reckitt patented a method based on it. His son James was 23 years old at this point, and it was he who built up the business and diversified its range to include blue and black lead and biscuits – the latter product line later finding its way to the Quaker firm of Huntley & Palmers. (One *ought* to be nervous that food is a 'product line' of the chemical industry, but thus is the history of food production under industrialisation.) Emden tells us that James Reckitt wanted working conditions for his employees as ideal as possible. This included security of employment, insurance against accident and illness, pensions, and sharing in the firm's prosperity 'in proportion to the annual dividend on the ordinary shares'.[42]

We saw earlier that the Quaker Lead Company, amongst other Quaker concerns, also made sure to mitigate the vagaries of the business cycle – especially in the ravages of unemployment it visits on the workers – by careful stockpiling and other measures. This is part of a business plan that has little to do with profits, or the direct concerns of the employers, but everything to do with the position of care that an employer is placed in with respect to a workforce. Like other Quakers James Reckitt also set up worker housing, in this case a Garden Village of six hundred homes. He was a pacifist and committed to the anti-slavery movement. Emden tells us that on his death 'the city of Hull, for which he had done more than any other individual, mourned him as though he had been a Royal personage.'[43]

Chapter 7

QUAKERS IN FOODSTUFFS AND LUXURIES

In this chapter we turn to look at the production of foodstuffs and the strange habit of Quakers in manufacturing luxuries. First we turn to Joseph Sturge (1793–1859), famous for his work to end slavery, and commemorated in Birmingham with a statue for his contribution to civic life. The statue was renovated in 2007 to commemorate the 200th anniversary of the abolition of the British slave trade, and is inscribed with the words: 'Charity, Temperance and Peace'. In Jamaica Sturge worked with Baptists to create villages for freed slaves, and helped purchase the land for a village of a hundred families: it is still called Sturge Town. We briefly look at Sturge here because he was originally a farmer and then a corn merchant; he also contributed to the railways and went on a peace mission to Tsar Nicholas I.

When we start to consider the fundamentals of economic justice the question always returns to food. If the income of a poor family is more than sufficient to buy adequate food then all else is possible: health, education, enterprise. If not, a family struggles at or below subsistence and every moment of the day is consumed in hunger and the anxiety of hunger. 'Corn' is the old-fashioned word for all grain in England, including wheat, rye, barley and oats, of which wheat is the most important. A yeoman farmer who produced enough grain for his family and some left over for sale had made the daily bread possible, even though the diet would be greatly enhanced by seasonal vegetables and some meat and dairy produce in small quantities.

Joseph Sturge bought and sold grain, though he refused to supply grain to the distilleries. With grain one encounters an early set of issues in capitalism: the power that corn merchants had to set prices, and the forerunners of so-called financial 'derivatives': options and futures. We also discover the role of the Corn Exchange, a feature of many rural towns that played a vital role in the economy of earlier times. In Japan rice was so important as a grain that it formed an effective currency (you can see this in the film *The Seven Samurai*), and the rice brokers of Japan were the forerunners of that country's modern banking system. Sturge as a corn merchant or factor was part of a vital body of British merchants who enabled farmers to sell their grain and to hedge to some degree against the vagaries of weather – from which principle we now have financial hedge funds. The historical hedging of corn meant that price fluctuations were to some extent smoothed out, and that could make all the difference for a family on subsistence wages and prevent the desperate but understandable recourse to rioting when prices rose out of reach. At the same time corn traders like Sturge were blamed when prices did go high, and the anger of hungry people could lead to attacks on them: indeed, a Quaker corn merchant was assaulted in Chelmsford in 1799. It is no wonder then that Adam Smith wrote:

> The unlimited, unrestrained freedom of the corn trade, as it is the only effectual preventative of the miseries of a famine, so it is the best palliative of the inconveniences of a dearth [...] No trade deserves more the full protection of the law, and no trade requires it so much, because no trade is so much exposed to popular odium.[1]

Whether we agree with Smith or not, it is clear that the price of basic food items is what mostly determined whether wages were at subsistence or above. But the Quakers became famous, not for basic foodstuffs, but for luxury items.

The Issue of Luxuries

We come shortly to the Quaker industries that include perhaps the best-known Quaker brand: Cadbury's. These industries also present a conundrum: why, when the Quakers were so diffident about luxury in their own lives, if not in outright condemnation, did they run industries that produced chocolate, sweets, biscuits, tea and beer? After all, William Allen gave up sugar in tea because of the slave trade. Is it not a contradiction that Quakers were at the forefront of the temperance movement, yet ran for a while the largest brewery in the world? It is at the very least a contrast to the picture painted above of serious Quaker scientists, and doctors like Fothergill ministering to the urban poor. Yet the theme returns us to the central pursuit of the Quaker entrepreneurs through the Industrial Revolution and beyond: manufacturing. It is here that Quakers employed the greatest number of working people and in which their practice of industrial welfare is most pertinent to the history of industrial capitalism and its ethics. The Quaker confectionary industries also turn out to embody some of the most advanced Quaker attempts at welfare and philanthropy, built on the profits generated through highly rationalised and innovative production methods.

But first, the issue of luxuries in the lives of the urban working poor. The Quakers were deeply concerned, not just about the working conditions of their employees, but also about the quality of their lives beyond the factory gate. We saw of course that they were not unique in this, and that Engels and Disraeli represent such concerns from the left and right of the political spectrum respectively. While all were agreed that the issue of drink could not be avoided, those on the right usually declared its abuse an inherent moral failing of the uneducated, while those on the left usually protested that working people were driven to drink out of desperation at low wages and appalling working and living conditions. The Quakers sided with the left here, and their promotion of drinking chocolate was a direct attempt to provide a harmless substitute for alcohol. Leaving aside the paternalism of this – an issue everywhere present in Quakernomics – what justification is there in this approach? I would argue that in the relevant literature, both fiction and non-fiction, we find many accounts of working people where all kinds of ready pleasures are turned to as a relief from the drudgery of the working day. Novelists including Dickens, Disraeli, Zola, Tressell, Steinbeck and Sinclair were keen observers of the working classes, and record their reliance on alcohol, coffee, sex, confectionary and gambling as regular distractions. The surveys from Engels, Booth and Rowntree confirm the same. It is in this context that the temperance movement was significant, and led Quakers to promote it vigorously and to promote drinking chocolate just as much, hoping to provide in the temperance bar as attractive an atmosphere as that of the public house.

Fry

The story of Quaker chocolate begins with Joseph Fry (1728–1787), another typical early Quaker polymath. The name 'Fry' is considered to have its origins in an Old English word meaning 'free born', indicative perhaps of yeoman ancestry again. Joseph Fry was apprenticed to an eminent doctor in Basingstoke, and then moved to Bristol where his medical practice flourished. He left this to set up a soap factory based on his skills as a chemist, the firm much later merging with Lever Brothers.[2] Leaving the soap business, Fry then became a highly respected letter founder, his son Edmund later continuing that business, and in 1758 the University of Oxford commissioned the company to create a fount of Greek types. Joseph Fry was also involved in publishing books including editions of authors such as Virgil and Milton. As mentioned earlier, he also assisted Richard Champion by taking a share in the Bristol China Factory, as porcelain also demanded his skills as a chemist. But most of these activities were incidental to his main business of merchandising, including the sale of chocolate, cocoa 'nibs' (pieces of cocoa bean formed by roasting, cracking and shelling the bean) and cocoa. Emden comments: 'Dr Joseph Fry is practically the originator of the British cocoa and chocolate industry.'[3]

In fact Fry's interest in chocolate began when he started to prescribe cocoa to patients as a nutritional supplement – as many apothecaries did – and so when he started to manufacture it he had a steady stream of customers in his patients.[4] To begin manufacture he had to purchase a patent from an established Bristol maker of cocoa, and so set up his first factory. In 1795 the family business purchased a Watts' steam-engine for grinding cocoa beans. A newspaper article of the time declared: 'It is astonishing to what variety of manufactures this useful machine has been applied!'[5] These details on the powering of factories are important, I suggest, because so much of Quaker wealth, indeed nearly all wealth derived in the Industrial Revolution and continuing today, has its origins in processes using non-human energies: coal provides a huge impetus over water, wind and animal power, as discussed earlier. At the same time the mass production of luxuries like cocoa and chocolate brought down costs and so placed them within range of working people, and that meant in turn that massive new markets opened up, over and above the wealthy families of Bristol and Bath who were Fry's early customers.

As Quakers, the Frys were as Puritan as any. Their factory on the river Frome was notable for the piety of morning Meeting, attended by the entire workforce between 9:00 and 9:20, which included sung hymns.[6] The Fry family collectively engaged in many of the usual Quaker enterprises of the time, including railways, participating in the civic life of the town, and yet finding time to write religious works and practice philanthropy. They dominated the chocolate industry for a long period, favourably placed in the trading port of Bristol, and taking up contracts with the British Navy. In 1847 the Fry brothers had succeeded in producing the first solid chocolate bar in Britain, meaning that the product could now be eaten as a solid rather than taken as a drink.[7] The first experiments produced something not that palatable, but they persisted with many innovations, in the teeth of competition from continental chocolatiers, now also experimenting with mass production.

Fry's was the chocolate act to follow, and the Cadburys, starting in the trade much later on, had a lot of catching up to do. However, by 1919, it was Cadbury's who bought out Fry's, not the other way round, as we shall see.

Cadbury

We now come to the quintessential Quaker brand, Cadbury's, the name most likely to be recognised as Quaker, and 'Bournville' as a wrapper label that may be recognised as the name of a model worker village. But I have a confession to make: I have never liked Cadbury's chocolates. My excuse is a childhood often spent in Vienna and hence a preference for continental confectionary. I only make the point because it might dispel the suspicion that the account given here is in some way tinged with the romance of British chocolate products. For me, that is not the romance. Instead, in reading a biography of George Cadbury, I discovered both the archetypal Quaker businessman-philanthropist, and someone rather appealing to me: a man whose religion took a deeply modern and private form. I should also admit that I cannot be indifferent to one specific instance of his countless acts of philanthropy, perhaps something of an irony for me: the boarding at Bournville of 18 impoverished Viennese children after the war in 1918, their return with money and gifts, and the supply of three tons of chocolate for children in Vienna, leading to his being fondly remembered there as the 'Chocolate Uncle'.[8]

But whatever one's taste in confectionary, or feelings about the personalities, the Cadbury story cannot fail to be an account of an astonishing achievement. It has of course been told in great detail by many authors, one of the most recent accounts being found in *Chocolate Wars* by Deborah Cadbury. What makes her book so pertinent is that it traces not just the history of Cadbury's but draws our attention to a feature of capitalism with considerable ethical implications: the hostile takeover bid. In this case it was by Kraft over Cadbury's, which effectively put an end to one of the greatest social experiments ever carried out by an industrialist family.

But first, a little of the Cadbury industrial history. The Quaker domination in confectionary in the nineteenth century, through Cadbury's, Rowntree's and Fry's, is a good parallel with the Quaker domination of iron making in the eighteenth century. The sheer scale of these confectionary enterprises derived again from the unique Quaker combination of innovation, capitalisation, networking and industrial welfare, the latter providing above-average and highly motivated workforces. These factors are all present in the Cadbury story, beginning in 1794 with the move by Richard Tapper Cadbury, from a farming background into Birmingham, to set up shop.[9] By 1824 his son John had set up a tea and coffee outlet in the same street, and then branched out into the new craze: cocoa, 'a most nutritious drink for breakfast'. In 1831 his experiments in grinding cocoa were so successful that he installed a steam-engine for the purpose – though we saw that this was first undertaken by their Quaker rival, Joseph Storrs Fry, much earlier, in 1795. As with Fry, the early customers were the wealthy, and in 1854 Cadbury's received the Royal Warrant as manufacturers of chocolate and cocoa to Queen Victoria. Much of their success was due to an obsession with purity, and their determination to beat Dutch rivals.

It is one of John Cadbury's sons, George, who becomes perhaps the key Quaker in this family to shape their chocolate business, and, indeed, the industry. Like almost all the Quaker entrepreneurs, George Cadbury was apprenticed within the Quaker network, in his case to Joseph Rowntree in York. It was in this period that the Rowntree family themselves entered confectionary, in 1862, with Henry Rowntree taking over the cocoa factory and shop of another Quaker, Samuel Tuke.[10] Although on good terms with the Fry dynasty, business rivalry was perfectly legitimate in the Quaker world, and George Cadbury, in pressing the government for new adulteration laws, forced Fry and other chocolate makers to reduce the cheapening additives to their cocoa. Acts of Parliament in 1872 and 1875 required manufacturers to list all their cocoa ingredients, a beneficial move for the public mostly driven by Cadbury.

In 1878 Richard and George Cadbury found a rural site outside Birmingham with good rail and canal links at Bournbrook, renamed it Bournville, and opened their new factory there. In 1893 they bought an additional 120 acres of adjoining land and built a model village on it, not, it should be added, confined to Cadbury workers.[11] It was perhaps to be the pinnacle of all such Quaker experiments, of which there were many examples stretching back to the 1820s in Britain, Ireland

and the colonies. Indeed the Cadbury brothers were embarking on what was both a business expansion and a deliberate large-scale social experiment, and both had plenty of sceptical onlookers. We will return to George Cadbury later as a typical Quaker social reformer, but here we simply trace a brief history of the company after his death in 1922. It had been incorporated in 1899 but some of its best-known product lines, such as Cadbury's Milk Tray, were developed in the early part of the twentieth century, and in 1919 the company was merged with J. S. Fry & Sons, leaving Cadbury's and Rowntree's as the remaining Quaker confectionary giants – not always on good terms with each other. Other factories were built but by 1938 Bournville alone had ten thousand staff, a huge operation. In 1969 Cadbury's merged with Schweppes, and followed on by buying up other food brand names. It even licensed the Hershey Company to manufacture some of its lines in America. In 2010 Kraft Foods made a takeover bid for Cadbury's, at a time when Hershey was also interested, but was beaten off by Kraft. To the widespread disapproval of the British public, Cadbury's was taken over by Kraft in February 2010. Sir Adrian and Sir Dominic Cadbury, former chairmen of the company, warned shareholders in a letter in the *Daily Telegraph* that Kraft might not live up to its claims, but market forces prevailed: shareholders put their financial interests before loyalty to the particular brand of responsible capitalism represented by Cadbury's.[12]

Rowntree

Joseph Rowntree was to become a renowned chocolate magnate and social reformer, leaving behind three trusts at his death in 1926 which not only survived into the twenty-first century but have become four, devoted respectively to social change, political reform, peace, and social justice – all deeply Quaker concerns. By the end of the nineteenth century Rowntree's employed over four thousand workers. The company provided them with a library, free education, a works magazine, a social welfare officer, a doctor, a dentist and a pension fund, and built a model village called New Earswick in Yorkshire, comparable with Bournville, Saltaire and Port Sunlight (the latter two being the subject of a later discussion). Rowntree apparently said of it: 'I do not want to establish communities bearing the stamp of charity but rather of rightly ordered and self governing communities.' His son Seebohm Rowntree carried out an extensive study of poverty in York (as mentioned earlier), inspired by the philanthropy of his father.

Cocoa essence had been the key to the success of Fry's and Cadbury's, but Rowntree for some reason was not so enthusiastic about it, and hence his business lagged. In 1879 he took an interest in the fruit pastilles developed by a French confectioner called Gaget, and began to sell his own version in 1881, which turned around the fortunes of the company.[13] (Although this sweet is now universally associated with Rowntree's, Allen & Hanburys also made a version in their day.) By avoiding head-on competition with cocoa essence, and creating a market for a new product, Rowntree shows again something subtle about competition: it is never really successful when emulating exactly what another company does, but succeeds at a tangent. Even so, this new success had to be consolidated by yielding to the spell of cocoa essence.

The twentieth-century history of Rowntree's is a little like Cadbury's: it merged with another major confectioner, Mackintosh's, in 1969, and finally succumbed to a hostile takeover from its great continental rival Nestlé in 1988. Though smaller than Cadbury's or Fry's, Rowntree's had still been one of the nation's biggest employers, and this led to industrial action at one stage in its history, to the bewilderment of its Quaker owners.[14] An event in the 1930s showed another stage in the transition from Quaker tradition: a legal dispute between Rowntree's and Cadbury's over the Aero chocolate bar. Rowntree's had promoted the new product as more easily digested than Cadbury's 'old-fashioned' milk chocolate, and took out some dubious patents on its manufacture. Deborah Cadbury tells us that the 'possibility that the dispute could be settled by the Society of Friends was considered. This was, after all, how Quaker firms resolved their differences in the past.'[15] It was not to be, however, and the companies resorted to lawyers in the end, leading to a settlement in 1937. This was perhaps another milestone in the fading of the Meeting as overseer of Quaker business activity.

Biscuits: Huntley & Palmers, Carr's and Jacob's

We now take a quick look at some other familiar high street brand names that all had Quaker origins: Huntley & Palmers, Carr's and Jacob's, all in the biscuit business.

Huntley & Palmers, founded in 1822 by the Quaker families of the Palmers – related to the Clarks of Street – and the Huntleys from Gloucester, was at one time the world's largest biscuit producer.

I mentioned earlier that some biscuit lines were taken over from the Quaker firm of Reckitt & Son; this was in 1866. Huntley & Palmers became one of Reading's largest employers, and its factory had its own railway system and steam locomotives. At the heart of their success lay the biscuit tin, embossed and decorated, and destined to become both a collector's item and a symbol of the British Empire. The Quaker connections faded in a few generations, however, and Emden, writing in the 1930s, reported all links broken.[16] Nevertheless, the philanthropy of the founders was equal to that of other major Quaker employers, and the company made several notable gifts to the town, including to the university and the Royal College of Music.

The brand name of Jacob's persists on the contemporary packaging of their famous cream crackers. The company was originally founded by Quakers in Dublin around 1885, which takes us back to Ireland where a number of businesses flourished within a Quaker network at least as active as that in England. Eventually both Jacob's and Huntley & Palmers were absorbed into Associated Biscuits. Carr's (famous for their water biscuits) was another Quaker enterprise, this time founded in Carlisle. It was also absorbed by Associated Biscuits in the end.

Tea

When we come to tea, only one Quaker name still echoes faintly in the high street: Horniman's. This may in fact be more due to the museum of the same name in South London, but in the early days Quaker merchants were often involved in tea selling, including William Tuke, Samuel Fothergill and John Horniman, the latter's business eventually being taken over by the Lyons chain. Horniman's son was a typical Victorian naturalist and built a museum to house his collection, presenting it to Dulwich in 1901.[17] The building was of note because the architect, Charles Harrison Townsend, had also designed the Bishopsgate Institute and the Whitechapel Gallery. Emden tells us that for early Quakers it was almost an impossibility to enter the tea market because it was controlled and monopolised by the East India Company, resulting in half of English tea being contraband in efforts to evade this monopoly. William Tuke was amongst the first Quakers in 1835, after the monopoly was finally rescinded, to announce 'Free Trade tea', while his real social contribution lay in his humane treatment of the insane.[18] Samuel Fothergill was a Quaker activist working, for example, to reconcile colonists and Native Americans, all funded by his tea business (in which the young George Crosfield was apprenticed).[19] It seems that the profits from Quaker tea found philanthropic outlets, but probably on a much smaller scale than from Quaker cocoa.

Brewing

Emden tells us of a Quaker brewer called William Lucas who struggled with his conscience over his trade, deciding in the end that total abstinence was certainly 'irrational, unchristian, and inexpedient', while temperance was quite acceptable.[20] And so the brewery at Hitchin stayed in the Lucas family for some generations. It is also true that until clean drinking water became available to the masses in the great cities weak beer was a better alternative (David Copperfield drinks it from childhood on in Dickens' novel) – though not so good of course as tea or cocoa. Many other Quakers were brewers, and so it is not surprising that, given their industry, energy and financial clout, one of their enterprises should land up as the biggest brewery in the world in its time: Barclay, Perkins & Co. In 1789 it was known as Thrale's and had one Quaker in management, John Perkins, but was up for auction – overseen by Samuel Johnson. In response to one rather tepid inquiry he famously said: 'Sir, we are not here to sell a parcel of boilers and vats, but the potentiality of growing rich beyond the dreams of avarice.'[21] In the end the American Quaker, Robert Barclay, bid for it, backed by Quaker bankers David Barclay and Silvanus Bevan II, and so this particular 'potentiality' fell completely into Quaker hands and business acumen.

The growth of the business – by 1810 production was over two hundred thousand barrels a year – and the installation of a Boulton & Watt steam-engine (which was to last for a hundred years) turned the Anchor Brewery, occupying over thirteen acres, into something of a tourist attraction. Visitors included the Prince of Wales, Napoleon III, Ibrahim Pasha of Egypt and the Italian nationalist Giuseppe Garibaldi. It also included the German statesman Otto von Bismarck, who was central to the introduction of state welfare programmes in that country. The brewery's Russian Imperial Stout was widely sold on the continent and its products were so well known that there were references to the brewery in the novels of Charles Dickens: apparently Dick Swiveller claimed of their beer in the *Old Curiosity Shop* that there was 'a spell in every drop against the ills of mortality.' Also, it was a job at 'Barclay and Perkins' that Mrs Micawber recommends to her husband in *David Copperfield*. Although Dr Johnson himself was disappointed at his pecuniary rewards from the original auction, his face was eventually to appear on the labels of Barclay's bottles, as the 'Barclay's Doctor' brand gained fame at home and abroad. An upright figure of a jovial Dr Johnson clutching a pint pot became the brewery's emblem.

Dickens mentions not just Barclay's in connection with Mr Micawber's hopeless ambitions but also another brewery with Quaker ownership: Truman, Hanbury & Buxton. Sampson Hanbury was a Quaker with family connections to the Gurneys, while Thomas Buxton married Hannah Gurney, sister of Elizabeth Fry. Buxton was an abolitionist, social reformer and an MP later made a baronet, having turned from his Quaker roots to the Church of England, though not without first making that classic Quaker move: the introduction of a steam-engine to the works. He appears on the British £5 note in the background to Elizabeth Fry, as mentioned in the Introduction.

I used to know the Truman brewery, as it was located in Brick Lane where I often strolled after work. Part of the old factory was then used as an art supplies shop and its wares were set out on tables perched on the old tiled malting floors. It was never the largest brewery in the world, merely for a long time the largest in London. Its site today, including shops, fashion markets and cafes, would make a perfectly good last stop on a possible 'Quaker tour' from West Ham, via the Gurney obelisk, Bryant & May, Allen & Hanburys and the commemorative Kindertransport sculptures at Liverpool Street station, being only a few minutes' walk from there.

Chapter 8

QUAKERS IN TRADING, BANKING AND FINANCE

We have now pretty much surveyed the manufacturing side of Quakernomics, looking along the way at Quaker scientists and doctors, all part of the 'total capitalism' that they pursued. One of the reasons for going into the history at such length is to show, in addition to the Quaker microcosm, what is true for the economy at large: it relies on an extensive interdependence of entrepreneurial activity, bolstered by the increasing role of science, and the necessary background of medicine and education for the health and productivity of the workforce. This interdependence is an organic, unplanned phenomenon, which, as it developed, required regulatory frameworks and policing to keep pace with it in order to mitigate its worst side-effects on the population and environment. Socialists often deplore the competitive nature of capitalism as its worst feature, but within the interdependence that is another of capitalism's key features there exists in fact much cooperation, and a great deal of that embodies an unsung and important trust and friendliness, even between rivals or between entrepreneur and bank manager. On this note we now look at the major remaining activity of the Quakers in rounding off their 'total capitalism': finance.

An early indication that Quakers were not only wealthy but involved in banking comes from the fact that the Bank of England in 1694 made provisions in its founding charter for Quaker owners of a minimum £500 of bank stock to be excused the usual oath.[1] This entitled them not only to participate financially but also to vote in elections for the board and governor. Although we now regard the Bank of England as a picture of Establishment, it was then regarded as an outsider's bank founded by dissenting and immigrant financiers in the City.[2] We find it hard to imagine today, but in the eighteenth and early nineteenth centuries almost anybody could set up a bank. At its most basic a bank takes in savings at one rate of interest and lends the money out at a higher rate, thus making a profit. (It is worth noting perhaps that some renowned economists, including John Maynard Keynes, have suggested that the level of bank lending is not in fact constrained by the level of bank deposits.[3] However in the extensive literature on this subject no data to support this idea has ever been put forward.) The person approaching a bank for a loan is only interested in obtaining the loan at the lowest possible rate of interest, but the saver or depositor has much more on their mind: is the banker trustworthy? Is my money *safe*? It is the question of trust that led so many Quaker businessmen to enter banking: whatever legacy of suspicion might attach to the Quaker religious brand, as it were, it was easily outweighed by its reputation for trading honesty.

In economics textbooks much is made of the origins of banking in the activities of goldsmiths – and we look at a famous Quaker example – but in reality far more banking evolved out of the activities of merchants. Lending was one important function, of course, but the other key operation of a bank is the payment system: shifting money as a movement parallel to that of goods and services. Provincial banks in port cities and trading towns sprang up everywhere to serve such financial needs of the Industrial Revolution, and before long Lombard Street in London became the national banking hub, the equivalent then to the City today. Quaker bankers formed a significant part of this activity, and by the twentieth century their legacy was behind two of the so-called 'big five' high street banks: Lloyds and Barclays, both formed by the merger of many smaller Quaker banks.

The early banks effectively created the commercial currency of the day, quite apart from the issue of notes and coins legalised by government through the Bank of England and the Royal Mint. The private banks issued their own banknotes and, more importantly, dealt with what was called 'commercial paper' – effectively IOUs written out by merchants whose local reputation was sufficient to guarantee the paper as a form of money. In 1844 the Bank Charter Act restricted the private printing of banknotes, passing that power exclusively to the Bank of England. It was a Quaker bank, Fox, Fowler & Co., which was to be the last English bank to issue its own banknotes, up to the time that it was bought out by Lloyds in 1921 (its quota of £6,256,000 notes passing to the Bank of England).[4] No new banks since 1844 have been permitted to issue currency in the UK, and under the terms of the 1844 act the merger with Lloyds ended the older issuing custom.

With the Credit Crunch of 2008 many well-educated people realised that their knowledge of banking was rather limited as they struggled to understand journalists' reports into the crisis. In its twenty-first-century form it certainly has evolved from the time of the early Quaker banks, but the issue of trust is easily grasped. We trusted the bankers and they failed us. How? By taking stupid risks with our money. The history of Quaker banking is therefore highly instructive of the nature of banking in general and the central role that risk takes in it. Banking is also central to industrial capitalism because it provides the capital for new enterprises, and for existing ones to adapt and expand. Without banks, or some form of lending at interest, there would have been no Industrial Revolution.

Lawyers, Stockbrokers and Accountants

There is more to finance than banking, however, so before concentrating on the Quaker bankers it is worth mentioning that Quakers also became notable lawyers, stockbrokers and accountants. We know this from Emden in his account of three Quaker families: the Seebohms (originating in Germany and with interests in steel, law and banking), the Braithwaites (law, banking and stockbroking) and the Waterhouses (accountancy, law and architecture). Edwin Waterhouse co-founded the accountancy practice of Price Waterhouse that is now part of PricewaterhouseCoopers, while his brother Alfred was a famous architect of the Victorian Gothic Revival, best known for designing the Natural History Museum in London.[5] A life insurance company with a clear reference to Quakers still in its name is Friends Provident, founded as a mutual friendly society for Quakers by Samuel Tuke and Joseph Rowntree. Up to 1915 only Quakers were eligible for policies and membership while up to 1983 a minimum of five Quakers had to sit on the board of directors of this firm.

One thing is clear in Quaker history: that George Fox himself was 'good with money'. When he left his family on a journey of self-discovery at the age of nineteen he had a substantial legacy from his father which he not only lived on but managed to increase over a lifetime with wise investments, and in turn left a respectable inheritance.[6] If you add to this meticulous record keeping, fear of debt and Meeting oversight of monetary matters, it is not surprising that Quakers were successful in stockbroking, accountancy and banking. Law is a little different of course, but here too, the experience of the early persecutions and the

extensive legal research carried out by Friends, including Fox, in order
to defend themselves in the courts, became a powerful tradition within
the society. For any businessman a knowledge of the law is essential, and
forms part of the framework for rounded capitalist activity.

Usury

One more digression is needed before looking at Quaker bankers
and the relationship between trading and banking: a look at the issue
of usury. The term 'usury' strikes us perhaps as vaguely Biblical,
and there is a good reason for that: historically, most religions have
forbidden the lending of money at interest as immoral. A writer and
activist on world debt, Ann Pettifor, has been a leader of the Jubilee
2000 movement for the forgiving of third-world debt. She believes
that much contemporary lending, in particular to developing nations,
is tantamount to usury and that Christian leaders should renew their
arguments against it.[7] But what is usury exactly? Is there a moral
lending at interest, and above a certain rate a lending that is usurious,
and therefore immoral? Pettifor points to the argument between
Martin Luther and John Calvin as a turning point in the Christian
history of lending: Luther railed against usury, where Calvin argued
that interest is lawful, provided it did not exceed a certain rate.[8] In the
Jewish tradition the issue was settled like this:

> Thou shalt not lend upon interest to thy brother: interest of money,
> interest of victuals, interest of any thing that is lent upon interest.
> Unto a foreigner thou mayest lend upon interest; but unto thy
> brother thou shalt not lend upon interest; that the LORD thy God
> may bless thee in all that thou puttest thy hand unto, in the land
> whither thou goest in to possess it. (Deuteronomy 23:19–20)

The First Council of Nicaea in 325 CE forbade clergy from engaging in
usury, but as Jews were not bound by usury laws in respect of non-Jews,
they became merchant bankers to the Christian world. Then, as Calvin's
Protestantism set Christians free from the usury laws, the beginnings of
industrial capitalism were made possible.

So where does legitimate lending end and usury begin? This is a
difficult question, but at the extremes it is an easy distinction. The
economic historian Niall Ferguson paints a vivid picture of usury in
the Glasgow estates where he grew up in his book *The Ascent of Money*.

He even includes a photo of an infamous loan shark, Gerard Law, being arrested by Glasgow's Illegal Money-Lending Unit. Such a police unit is needed in every desperately poor working district where loan sharks operate at astronomical interest (in fact most British cities run something like an Illegal Money Lending Team to this day). Ferguson tells us that Law would lend money at 25 per cent a week, which comes to over eleven million per cent compound interest a year.[9] Such usury was found everywhere in the lawless slums such as those that George Cadbury visited in the Victorian period. But in respectable twenty-first-century high streets in the wake of the Credit Crunch so-called 'pay-day loan' facilities proliferated. They are mostly quite legal, but their compound interest per annum is in the thousands – and rarely made explicit. Quakers attempted to eradicate such practices amongst their workforces as we have seen, and worked instead to build up legitimate banking institutions.

Goldsmith Bankers and John Freame

Because the use of gold as money has a long history, the goldsmith bankers are a good place to start to consider the nature of banking. The story of goldsmith banking involves these two innovations: the use of gold receipts or promissory notes as paper money, and what is known as the 'fractional reserve system' of lending out a large proportion of what was deposited. (In fact fractional reserve banking is the basis of all modern banking.) The goldsmith's written receipt, or title of ownership, circulated as a form of currency, passing from hand to hand. It is better to call it a 'bill' or 'bill of exchange' because the bill was in fact regulated in its structure: it would be countersigned by each recipient, and returned once there was no more space for signatures. But the bill illustrates the key idea in the birth of banking: whatever the uses of gold and silver bullion or coins as ultimate currency, paper was much more convenient and could be issued by anyone who was trusted. Coins were usually minted under the authority of the Crown, while paper 'money' had a far greater usage by volume of transaction, particularly as the Industrial Revolution got underway. However, the obvious problem with paper money lies in the possibility of fraud.

We saw that the Quaker John Freame is credited with the founding of Barclays Bank in 1690, though his shop in Lombard Street which he set up after his apprenticeship was then called Freame & Gould.

His partner Thomas Gould was also from a prosperous Quaker family, and in time Freame and Gould married each other's sisters – a typical in-house Quaker arrangement, as it were. Freame was apprenticed to a London Quaker goldsmith and was entering a business open only to the rich: his own partnership would have needed between £500 and £3,000 start-up capital then, something like £300,000 to £2 million in today's money.[10] Apparently apprentices in the London goldsmith banks were central to their informal 'clearing' arrangements, a system now done on a massive scale electronically.[11] In 1695 London Yearly Meeting placed a large deposit with Freame & Gould: £1,100 or around £660,000 in today's money. The size of this deposit shows two things: that Quaker 'central' had command of substantial sums, and that it trusted Freame's bank, then of only five years' standing. In 1711 Freame became clerk to Yearly Meeting, the most responsible of posts within the Society of Friends in Britain.

Like most ventures in those days, a goldsmith's bank was interested in wider commercial activity, and we saw that Freame's bank became stockholders in the Quaker Lead Company as it also did with its precursor, the Quaker-dominated Welsh Copper Company.[12] This is historically interesting and relevant to today's world of banking: Freame was both a banker for and partner of the mining company. For a banker to have an involvement with a company they are bankers for is now frowned on in America and Britain, but in Germany it is still practised, and allows for bankers to make proper risk evaluations of a company, and a company to have secure streams of funding. Freame financed the experiments of Dr Wright in lead and silver refining, discussed earlier, and received delivery of silver 'cake' from the company on its way to the Royal Mint. In 1736 John Freame's son, Joseph, took James Barclay, his sister's husband and also a Quaker, as a partner. The enterprise was operating as a typical city bank of the period, laying the foundations for the global banking enterprise that would take the Barclays name, and which in its early days as a joint-stock enterprise was often called the 'Quaker Bank'.

Although many textbooks on economics and banking suggest that modern banking arose to a significant degree from the goldsmith bankers, a Victorian authority on the subject suggests in fact that goldsmith banking operated on a 'trifling scale'.[13] It may sound glamorous, but it was a different kind of bank that handled the bulk of early transactions: one that grew out of the activities of merchants.

Merchants and Banking: Pease, Backhouse and Gurney

The Quaker Lloyds of Birmingham and the Quaker Gurneys of Norwich illustrate this second major route whereby banks came into being: through financial services by and for domestic industries. Manufacturers in the early Industrial Revolution needed markets that provided a steady demand, and would often make loans to their clients out of their profits in order to keep business going. They also took in deposits from small tradesmen, paying no interest and issuing deposit notes that again were a form of money or currency. Regional banks began to flourish in the eighteenth century. The first bank outside London was established in Bristol in 1716, a natural development in a city made wealthy by overseas trade. By 1810 there were 650 regional banks, all based on whatever the local merchants traded in, and it is no surprise therefore to find successful Quaker merchants taking this obvious step into financial services.[14] We saw earlier that Edward Pease, the 'Father of the Railways', came from a family made wealthy in the wool trade. His father Joseph had set up the Pease Partners Bank which had something like one hundred and ninety accounts in the last half of the eighteenth century, and Edward continued to be active in the bank. It eventually ran into trouble in 1902, when it was taken over by Barclays.

The local rival to the Pease Partners Bank was J. J. Backhouse, founded by a Quaker family whose wealth came from flax and linen, and who also made the natural transitions from manufacturing to merchandising to banking. When Jonathan Backhouse and Anne Pease married the two banks formed an alliance, and we saw that they became the principle financiers for the Stockton & Darlington Railway. We also saw that the Earl of Darlington had objected to the railway on the grounds that it would interfere with his fox hunting, but in fact the earl took his animosity to the project to much greater lengths. The vulnerability of any bank operating the fractional reserve system is that customers can turn up on any one day and demand more of their cash than is held in reserve. Any hint that the bank cannot pay, and word gets round. Hence more customers turn up, precipitating the dreaded bank 'run' – as so well dramatised in Frank Capra's film, *A Wonderful Life* (1946). The earl plotted to ruin Backhouse by buying up his banknotes and then presenting them all at once for redemption in gold, thus triggering a run. The story goes that Backhouse heard of the plot and raced to London to obtain sufficient gold to cover the paper money.

On his return to Darlington his carriage lost one of its four wheels, but by redistributing the gold he managed to balance the carriage and arrive in time to exchange it for the banknotes presented by the earl's agent. Apparently the quiet Quaker completed his triumph by telling the agent that should the earl wish to sell his castle he would pay for it in the same metal.

This is no doubt a story that satisfies the Quaker dislike of the landed establishment, but it also illustrates why fractional reserve banking is vulnerable and requires very careful management. The fact that Backhouse had his reserves held in London is typical of the pyramiding of banking services through the country at the time, but that he had enough gold and quick access to it was down to his skill and integrity as a banker. For the Peases, either their judgement or luck ran out in 1902.

The Pease banking venture arose from the wool trade, while the Backhouse venture arose from flax and linen; the Gurneys in Norfolk established their banking empire again on the basis of wool. In fact their banking history went back to the seventeenth century, but developed later as they became middle-men providing loans for the worsted spinners to pay wages. These arrangements were eventually formalised in the establishment of the Gurney Bank in Norwich in 1770. Banks evolved out of many industries and trades, and shops which provided loans or deposit services were common and often later became banks. In Yarmouth a Quaker bank had its origins in the import of Swedish iron, and was absorbed like many other local Quaker banks into the Gurney bank in Norwich.[15] The Gurneys were a large family and their wealth was so well known that a character in a Gilbert and Sullivan opera even sings his desire to be as 'rich as the Gurneys'. At one point the control of the bank passed to John Gurney whose sons and daughters included notable reformers – Elizabeth Fry being the most famous – and the banker Samuel Gurney. The latter is known for his partnership in the ill-fated company of Overend & Gurney, and was singled out by Karl Marx for sarcastic comment in the third volume of *Capital*.

Many families made rich in the Industrial Revolution made the journey from manufacturer to trader to banker. Further down the line small regional banks would merge with larger ones or disappear. The Pease bank, the Backhouse bank and the Gurney bank in Norwich were all eventually subsumed within Barclays, the great Quaker bank into which flowed so many similar Quaker tributaries.

Barclays Bank

Robert Barclay (1648–1690) was a Scottish Quaker and the author of *An Apology for the True Christian Divinity*, a defence of the Quaker religion published in Latin in Amsterdam in 1676. Barclay experienced persecution, but his work made him second only to George Fox in promoting Quakerism, and he eventually found favour in court and was appointed the governor of the East Jersey colony in America. It was his grandson David Barclay II who was the Barclay partner of Freame & Barclay, and also a proprietor of Barclay, Perkins & Co., when he and Silvanus Bevan took over the Anchor Brewery in Southwark. Robert Barclay was effectively the theologian of the Quaker movement, while David Barclay II gave the name to a banking empire that survived the 2008 Credit Crunch without government assistance, though later became mired in scandal.

In the 1980s a campaign was launched to boycott Barclays for its operations in apartheid South Africa, which it eventually capitulated to. In 2008 it picked up the remains of Lehman Brothers for peanuts, and in 2012 found itself at the centre of the Libor-fixing scandal which forced out three of its top executives. What, people were asking in 2012, had happened to its original Quaker ethos? Part of the answer surely must be that in the making of things it is hard to have many conceits, but in the movement from manufacturing, to trading, to banking, and finally to the anonymity of a modern joint-stock or PLC finance house the fundamental truths of economic activity are long left behind.

Lloyds Bank

We return now to the history of Lloyds bank, with its origins in that favourite Quaker metal: iron. It also takes us back to Birmingham, a city in which the Quakers flourished and made many contributions to civic life. Commerce had grown steadily in the city for a long time, all without the benefit of a formal bank, until the Quaker, Sampson Lloyd II, along with John Taylor, the Birmingham 'button king', set up Taylors & Lloyds in 1756. This move was to see profits for the Lloyds from banking exceed that of iron manufacturing within a space of only six years.[16] The fact that it is easier to make money out of money than out of iron is not just a Quaker experience, but perhaps an experience inherent to capitalism, and no doubt a big factor in the 2008 Credit Crunch. Before long the Lloyds business in Birmingham set up a new partnership in Lombard

Street, where, as we have already seen, Quakers took a prominent place, and from there the business continued into its twenty-first-century form. In the 1750s however there were barely a dozen banks in the country outside of London.

In the early years Birmingham, an unincorporated town of thirty thousand inhabitants, had no formal banking services so most gold deposits were made with goldsmiths in London. Loans were conducted outside of the banking system using what was known as an inland trade bill or bill of exchange. The *form* of the bill was regulated by Parliament but it was entirely issued by private traders, including of course the goldsmiths we looked at above. Each bill was in effect an IOU specifying who had to pay whom how much. Such bills would generally have to be paid within sixty days, and in that time could circulate much like a bank note. Clearly it would only circulate amongst those who knew the reliability of the payee. For example the bills of exchange of the Quaker Lead Company circulated as currency in North Wales and were 'discounted' in Lombard Street, a sign that the venture had become established and successful.

In this early period of banking the private issue of notes and coins was common, and Taylors & Lloyds issued notes of £5.5 and £1 denominations: sums of money that were then worth perhaps sixty or more times their modern value. A shortage of official coinage – that is coins minted by the Crown – could seriously hamper trade in those days, and for a while Taylors & Lloyds issued seven shilling notes which were apparently very popular.[17] I rather love this fact as I am old enough to remember the 10 shilling note, and also remember the popular expression 'bent as a nine bob note' ('bob' being slang for shilling). I doubt if whoever originated the phrase would have realised that the British banking system had two centuries previous come close to issuing such a thing – a seven bob note. The shortage of 'official' money, that is coins of the realm, is in fact an important part of the commercial and monetary history of the Industrial Revolution, as we begin to understand that most of the money in circulation had entirely unofficial origins as bills of exchange along with privately issued notes and coins.

The black horse as the symbol of Lloyds bank came from the sign of premises they took over later, originally set up by a goldsmith in 1677. It converted into a joint-stock company in 1865, becoming Lloyds Bank Limited in 1889. It suffered ignominy in the 2008 Credit Crunch, when it had to be bailed out by the British government: the taxpayer subsequently holding a 38 per cent stake in it (though this was not as catastrophic as the case of RBS/NatWest which required an 83 per cent government stake). Lloyds was subsequently forced to offer many of its branches for sale.

Overend & Gurney

Lombard Street has historically been the London home for bankers, a number of which, as we have seen, had Quaker origins. Richardson, Overend & Co. (Overend & Gurney for short) was formed in 1800 at 65, Lombard Street, joining the Quaker Lloyds at 14 and the Quaker Barclays at 54. Another Lloyds, not Quakers this time, also set up a coffee-shop in Lombard Street, which eventually became the world's leading insurance market: Lloyds of London. To top this Allen & Hanburys, the Quaker pharmaceuticals company, was located at Plough Court, just around the corner. Overend & Gurney was founded as a business for the novel purpose of dedicated bill-broking, which proved a success. It soon became the greatest discounting-house in the world. Bills of exchange were circulating with massive total sums at stake, and formed a basic kind of credit which could be loaned to companies needing cash for start-up or expansion – or for speculation. During a financial crisis in 1825, Overend & Gurney was able to make loans to many other banks. The house became known as 'the bankers' banker' and took many previous clients from the Bank of England.

In 1809 the Quaker Samuel Gurney of the Norwich bank took over and led the company to its early successes. He died in 1856 but his successors, in an astonishingly small period of time, made a series of catastrophic financial deals that took it to ruin. They managed to take a world-famous bank, second only to the Bank of England, and make such disastrous errors of risk assessment that it collapsed in 1866, on a day so bleak for the whole British economy that it was called Black Friday. The collapse of Overend & Gurney was the single greatest Quaker commercial disaster. The fall led Marx to write to Engels: 'DEAR FRED, The Gurney affair AMUSES me immensely. I have studied this damned CASE in all the DETAILS [...]'. It led Walter Bagehot, the editor in chief of the *Economist* at the time, to write an important book on banking, in which he urged a clarification of the purpose of the Bank of England and proposed reforms largely taken up in the aftermath of the crash. Above all it should be emphasised however that this crash was neither just a part of Quaker history nor a remote part of early capitalism. It played an important role in strengthening the Bank of

England which may well have prevented a similar run on a British bank taking place again for an astonishing length of time: almost a hundred and fifty years. It was the run on Northern Rock in 2007, heralding the Credit Crunch in Britain, that was to be the next British experience of such a thing.

One could say that the differences in financial practice in the intervening century and a half – including astounding new technologies and financial instruments – are in fact negligible compared to the similarities: hidden away in an atmosphere of secrecy and commercial confidentiality, bankers make bad judgements on loans and then follow the initial errors with worse ones as do so many gamblers when under pressure. In effect we get here to the heart of capitalism, the wider understanding of which is perhaps the *only* safeguard against further repetitions.

Why did the Quakers behind Overend & Gurney fall from Quaker standards? The writer Geoffrey Elliott devotes a whole book to the fate of the company, *The Mystery of Overend and Gurney*, in which he points out that most of the errant bankers had been to Grove School, a leading Quaker school attended by Sir Joseph Lister, Alfred Waterhouse and Thomas Hodgkin (a Quaker doctor whose name is lent to Hodgkin's disease), and whose ethos should have ensured its pupils' long-standing honesty and sobriety.[18] More precisely, how was it that the wisdom of Samuel Gurney was lost in a single generation? He epitomised Quaker tradition and values. He once permitted a clerk he found to have committed fraud to escape to the Continent rather than be prosecuted and hanged, and was often called to parliamentary committees attempting then, as now, to 'fathom the inscrutable workings of the financial markets'.[19] As an example of Gurney's philanthropy it was suggested by the president of Liberia, the state founded for freed slaves, that the area between the capital Monrovia and neighbouring Sierra Leone, if purchased, would help enormously to stifle the existing slave trade. The following day the president turned up to collect a personal draft for £1,000 from Samuel, the other half of the necessary funds promised by Samuel if the British government would not come up with the balance.[20] When Samuel Gurney died in 1856 his estate was worth over £50 million in today's money, despite his prodigious philanthropy, much of it to London's East End, for example the Poplar Hospital for Accidents, the first casualty hospital for dockworkers, and the Royal London Hospital (another landmark I walked past for many years on my way to work).[21] It is for this reason that the obelisk was erected to his memory in Stratford, East

London, by grateful parishioners. How could a son of such a man, even if amongst non-Quaker directors of the company, go so badly wrong?

By the 1850s the company was discounting £70 million of bills a year – around £3.5 billion in today's money. But, only four years after the death of Samuel Gurney, the firm tried to pull off a terrible stunt, striking at the Bank of England after it tightened its rules on supporting discounters. It attempted to orchestrate a 'run' on the Bank of England! It backfired, leaving the firm's reputation lessened; it was surely a sign that the new management had lost the sober vigilance of Samuel Gurney. Gladstone himself umpired the truce between the banks.[22] It might seem incredible to us now that a private bank should attempt to orchestrate a run on the Bank of England, all the more considering that the Quaker banker Backhouse resisted such an attack by the Earl of Darlington in such a dignified way, as we saw earlier.

It was John Henry Gurney who attempted to steer the company out of trouble from 1861, and whose further mistakes largely led to its spectacular crash. He had been an active partner in the Norwich bank, and joined Overend & Gurney rather late in the day. He was also personally liable for the company's debts to date. His arrival and painful realisation of the firm's liabilities meant that he was required to undo the excesses of the other directors, who were living high on what were by then illusory profits. Proper auditing had been abandoned – an absolute betrayal of Quaker principles. By 1865 Overend & Gurney was a company of two halves: a profitable core business of bill discounting, and a junk portfolio mostly based on shipping lines where ships were re-mortgaged and where bills in the name of respectable 'front' men hid the truth of financial disaster.[23] The solution they hit on was to make a limited liability company out of the firm, to 'float' it on the Stock Exchange. It could have worked. It didn't. The firm was reorganised as a joint-stock company in August 1865, and failed less than a year later, on 10 May 1866. The financial crisis it set off was comparable to any major financial crisis since then, including the Credit Crunch of 2008. The bank rate rose to 10 per cent for three months, and more than two hundred companies, including other banks, failed as a result. On the brink of disaster the firm did what all banks do: they ask for help from the central bank of their nation, in this case the Bank of England. It was true that the Bank of England might have had a grudge against the firm for mounting a run on it earlier, but the fact was that the books of Overend & Gurney told a simple truth: their liabilities so far exceeded their assets that nothing could be done. It went under owing nearly

£1 billion in today's money. As the largest bill-broker in the country, and with a huge investment portfolio, its end impacted on millions of people in Britain. The polite notice pinned to its door that announced the suspension of payments at 3:30 p.m. on 10 May 1866 gradually drew a larger and larger crowd of panic-stricken investors – and no doubt the ghoulish. This was financial death on a large scale. It was also a 'credit crunch', halting the flow of credit throughout a commercial system that was intimately dependent on it.

Six directors of the new Overend & Gurney company were sent to trial at the old High Court on charges of fraud, including the Quakers Henry and John Gurney. Unlike the public mood following the banking crises in 2008, the Victorians following the high-profile trial were generally sympathetic (apart from Marx it seems) and supported the final not-guilty verdict. Yet despite the huge publicity I cannot find any response from the Society of Friends. We saw that the Quakers made no public response to the matchgirls' strike at Bryant & May, despite national headlines over it. I am just as unsure why there was no response from the society to the crash of Overend & Gurney. Certainly I have found no mention of it or the subsequent trial in the Quaker publication *The Friend*. But I have suggested that Meeting oversight of business was anyway waning in this period, perhaps partly because of the laxer rules as to who exactly was a Quaker, or perhaps because of the complexities of business, particularly after the Limited Liability Act of 1855.

Bagehot's Verdict

I mentioned Walter Bagehot above: he was an English businessman, essayist and journalist who became the editor in chief of the *Economist* in 1860, which had been founded by his father-in-law. The *Economist* today still has a column and blog named in honour of Bagehot. In 1873 he wrote *Lombard Street: A Description of the Money Market*, partly as a reaction to the financial collapse of Overend & Gurney. But more than this Bagehot presents one of the best-respected histories of banking and the role of credit in commerce to date, widely quoted again in the aftermath of the 2008 Credit Crunch. He says of his day for example: 'We have entirely lost the idea that any undertaking likely to pay, and seen to be likely, can perish for want of money' (where 'money' means 'loan' of course). He goes on to suggest that a citizen of the Elizabethan period, even if they had been able to invent the railways, would not have been able to collect the capital to build them.[24] As he says: 'English trade is carried on upon borrowed capital to an extent of which few foreigners have an idea, and none of our ancestors could have conceived.' [25] Bagehot describes how the savings of a county 'with good land but no manufactures and trade' greatly exceeds what could be lent out in such a rural setting, and how these savings were firstly deposited in local banks, then sent to the London banks, mostly in Lombard Street.[26] In turn this surplus was lent to the industrial districts through the mechanism of bill-broking. In their turn, the Lombard Street banks deposited their surpluses with the Bank of England, which therefore became the apex of the national banking pyramid. As Bagehot sums it up: 'Thus English capital runs as surely and instantly where it is most wanted, and where there is most to be made of it, as water runs to find its level.' One could say that the present eminence of the City of London as a financial centre is based entirely on this historical development. Bagehot's verdict on Overend & Gurney is interesting:

> In the first place, an hereditary business of great magnitude is dangerous. The management of such a business needs more than common industry and more than common ability. But there is no security at all that these will be regularly continued in each generation. The case of Overend, Gurney and Co., the model instance of all evil in business, is a most alarming example of this evil. No cleverer men of business probably (cleverer I mean for the purposes of their particular calling) could well be found than the founders and first managers of that house. But in a very few years the rule in it passed to a generation whose folly surpassed the usual limit of imaginable incapacity. In a short time they substituted ruin for prosperity and changed opulence into insolvency. Such great folly is happily rare; and the business of a bank is not nearly as difficult as the business of a discount company.[27]

We saw earlier that Edward Pease advised his sons that a 'business is not an estate'. He meant that inheriting a business meant the continuity of exactly the same hard work and ethical standards across the generations as in the founders of it, rather than the relaxation into inherited wealth. Overend & Gurney is the exception to the normal Quaker ability to run businesses successfully down the generations. Bagehot may have been right to say that in general there is no security in a business kept in a family and handed down, but the Quaker tradition usually shows otherwise. Bagehot's simplest summary of the crash is painful to hear however: 'And these losses,' he says, 'were made in a manner so reckless and foolish, that one would think a child who had lent money in the City of London would have lent it better.'[28] Ouch.

There is no doubt that the collapse of Overend & Gurney is the single worst failing of Quakernomics. On the other hand it was only one out of 74 Quaker banks, the vast majority of which were highly trusted. But I would suggest that banking is a special kind of business: you could say that banks are the engines of collective economic risk taking. The entrepreneur, in the memorable phrase of Keynes, needs 'animal spirits' – sheer daring – to be who he or she is. Society at some level seems to recognise this when forgiving bankers, either literally as the Victorians seemed to have done with the Gurneys, or financially, as when we collectively bail them out (even if we now direct fury at their bonuses). All countries in the world have turned to their central banks, and nationally run deposit insurance schemes of various kinds, to protect this industry. When an iron-maker goes bust it affects just that firm and perhaps a few local suppliers. When a bank goes bust it can take two hundred firms down with it.

Chapter 9

QUAKERS IN CULTURE

When it comes to a chapter on Quakers and the arts, media and culture, well, it is rather bound to be a short one. Almost no individual or group rises above their time in all respects. If the Puritan tradition was instrumental in giving the Quakers their essential mixture of religion and capitalism, it also shaped them in another significant way: it made art and aesthetics foreign to them. There are notable exceptions of course, but on the whole the Quakers are a typical Puritan group whose soul simply does not resonate with the arts, and who were shaped by a historical anti-Catholic movement insisting on the total removal of imagery and iconography from places of worship. I have commented already that the Quakers were disinclined to Romanticism of either the English Wordsworthian type, or the German idealist type, and that this was a great strength. However, what this means is that Quakers contributed very little to the culture of their day, having little presence in the visual arts, music, theatre, opera, novels or journalism. In turn the Quakers were barely represented by artists or writers in their work, and this is one reason perhaps why their record of philanthropic entrepreneurship is so little known. It also means that the Quaker 'total capitalism' that I am presenting does have something of a gap in it – beyond arms and spirits. A fully rounded economy needs the arts as much as anything else, and it is often works of the imagination that shape the attitudes of a population to every aspect of life, including the economic. But let us look at some exceptions, which show once again that if Quakers put their mind to something, they make a commercial success of it – even if not always a critical success.

We saw that Francis Darby developed the art casting department at Coalbrookdale. Raistrick points out: 'The world at large was just realizing the flexibility of cast iron – it was the first real "plastic" medium which could produce or reproduce carved and sculptured ornament in infinite number. Architects were awakening to the possible beauty of cast iron in rails, balconies, gates and in finer ornament.'[1] Darby's products on show at the Great Exhibition were an expression of just this new aesthetic, though the *Illustrated London News* thought the centrepiece of the Coalbrookdale stand, the ornate dome, to be 'one of the most pretentious works' in the exhibition. Other critics were no kinder, commenting that the technical proficiency of the ironfounder was remarkable, but the profusion of styles mere confusion.[2]

More encouraging perhaps was the response to the typefaces of Joseph Fry and his son Edmund, discussed earlier. In addition to the Quaker firm of type-founders Pine & Fry in Bristol, a Quaker in Gloucester, John Bellows, set up a printing business, which also led him to linguistics. Not only was he the first in the county to use a steam-engine to operate his presses, he wrote the most important French–English dictionary of his day and made important archaeological discoveries still remembered in his home town. In later life he travelled much, visiting Tolstoy and a Russian religious group with beliefs rather like the Quakers, the Dukhobortsy or 'Spirit Wrestlers', who were much persecuted for their pacifism. Emden gives us an unusual glimpse into the world of Victorian business regulation in an account of the outcome of the Factory Act for Bellows. In 1868 his printing works were inspected under the new regulations and found to be exemplary in respect of working conditions – something we would expect of a Quaker firm – but in addition a friendship grew out of this meeting resulting in Bellows marrying the inspector's sister a year later.[3] The inspector is not always to be feared, therefore, as the 'dead hand' of government interference. And Bellows could not have succeeded as a printer without some aesthetic sense.

But perhaps most endearing of the Quakers in the visual arts of the Victorian era is Francis Frith, a photographer whose records of Victorian Britain are still highly prized and sold via the Internet. I say endearing, because Frith clearly spanned the Protestant theology of his tradition and the Romantic impulse writ large. He hated his Quaker boarding school in Birmingham, being 'the most insipid and mechanical portion of existence', loved mathematics, metaphysics and poetry, and succumbed to the obligatory nervous breakdown as a young man.[4] He was later successful in business with a printing company, reaching an astonishing turnover of around £8 million a year in today's money, and retired aged 34 as a man of independent means. Like many Victorian gentlemen he then embarked on fabulous voyages up the Nile, being repeatedly robbed and captured by brigands, and partaking of crocodile chops.[5] But he was already making a name as a photographer, taking with him crates of heavy and fragile glass plates. This time the mainstream was impressed by the emerging technological art. The *Times* commented that his works 'carry us far beyond anything that is in the power of the most accomplished artist to transfer to his canvas.'[6] He subsequently applied the usual Quaker obsession for industry to capture just about every city, town and village in the British Isles on photographic plate (and in true Quaker style established a firm that was one of the largest photographic studios in the world). The photographic archive that he left behind is a real national treasure,[7] but so is he, I would suggest, for a photographic portrait in which he appears in Egyptian clothes, suggesting the archetypal English romantic.

One can find other odd instances of Quakers in the arts: for example, a little later on two Quakers would have a significant impact on the design of the London Underground, both in its corporate identity – including logos, poster design and marketing – and also in the architecture of its stations. Frank Pick was the chief executive of London Transport for many years, and was born into a devout Lincolnshire Quaker family. He commissioned many striking posters for the Underground and appointed Charles Holden, an architect who attended Meeting and regarded himself as a Quaker, though he did not formally join. Holden's many Underground stations include Arnos Grove and Southgate, and his best known building is perhaps Senate House for the University of London.

The Quaker architect Alfred Waterhouse designed the Natural History Museum, as mentioned earlier, and also many other civic buildings such as Manchester Town Hall. He also designed mansions for wealthy Quakers and the Lake District home where Beatrix Potter spent her summers. Emden records that Sir Reginald Theodore Blomfield, another notable Victorian architect, said of Waterhouse that he had 'a great affection for that horrible red terra-cotta combined with red brick.'[8] Is there no escape from aesthetic censure of Quaker efforts in the arts? (Personally, I like the style.) Another Quaker architect, Hubert Lidbetter designed Friends House in Euston, the main Quaker meeting house in Britain. I have to confess that while I have enjoyed many visits there, including working as a sound engineer for a spirituality conference, I have never quite fallen in love with the building ... preferring red terracotta and brick.

Two American Quakers stand out in their artistic fields: James Turrell in fine art, and Joan Baez as a singer-songwriter. The parents of Baez became Quakers in her early childhood, and she retained their interest, particularly in relation to pacifism and social issues. While the latter emanate clearly from the Quaker tradition, engagement in the arts does not, and so there is no particular artistic movement that Quaker artists have in common.

Finally, I want to mention two novels with Quaker themes. I have already introduced David Morse's novel, *The Iron Bridge*, and need to just add that he is a practising Quaker himself. The other novel, *Dazzle of the Day*, is by Molly Gloss, who is not a Quaker as far as I understand. Both novels have an environmental science-fiction flavour (Gloss is a close friend with fellow science-fiction writer Ursula K. Le Guin). In *Dazzle of the Day* a group of Quakers decide to leave a blasted Earth on a spaceship, and, hundreds of years later, have to make the difficult decision whether to make their home on a rather low-grade planet or continue wandering in space. This provides for a marvellous exposition of the Quaker Business Method – the way that Quakers make big decisions.

The early Gurneys were supporters of the arts, including theatre and painting, but this was rare amongst Quakers. I would have to conclude by saying that a Puritan religion, with a founder as adamantly anti-art and anti-music as George Fox, is bound, even as it makes astonishing adjustments to each turn in modernity, to be a little tone deaf to the aesthetic.

Chapter 10

THE QUAKER SYSTEM

I have coined the term 'total capitalism' to mean the pursuit of the complete spectrum of activities necessary for an economy including: science, technology, chemicals, manufacturing of heavy goods, essentials and luxuries, transport, marketing, publishing, the arts, banking, investment services, law, stockbroking and accounting. I think I have demonstrated that the Quakers as a group were able to pursue this, though with some small gaps here and there, particularly in cultural activities. George Fox exhorted his followers to follow trades that he considered legitimate – 'innocent trades' – so this excluded the manufacture of spirits or arms, as we have seen. There are of course other trades obviously repugnant to the Quakers such as those involving recreational drugs, gambling or prostitution, whether legalised or not. Despite these gaps, the record of Quaker total capitalism is, I believe, remarkable, going far beyond that of any other non-conformist Christian group of the period, and quite possibly beyond what the Jews, the Jains and the Parsees achieved in commerce. What anyway marks Quakernomics as unique amongst such religious groups is that it was central to the very emergence of the Industrial Revolution, as we have seen.

This total capitalism of the Quakers means we can examine their enterprises as a microcosm of the wider economy, and hence examine questions as to what an ethical capitalism looks like in the round. If Quakers had been restricted to just one or two areas of economic activity, one might form an inconclusive opinion as to ethical capitalism. For example, if the Quakers had confined themselves to the production of luxuries, then perhaps the social experiment of Bournville would not be applicable to the bulk of working people. But we have seen that Quakers were big employers in most fields so their industrial relations have a universal promise. When we add Quaker banking as a *largely* ethical banking practice the picture is completed. If, as I believe I have demonstrated, Quakernomics was at the heart of, or indeed shaped, the new working life of people leaving the land for the factories of the Industrial Revolution, then it also has a message of hope about how the worst aspects of that experience can be avoided. More perhaps: accounts of working life in Quaker factories often suggest an advance on the uncertainty and limited horizons of life as subsistence farmers on the land. I don't agree with Marx that industrial capitalism rescued millions from 'rural idiocy', as he put it, because that is to denigrate the yeoman smallholder, and is the sentiment that led to the destruction of the *kulaks*. But we cannot doubt that the city offers new opportunities.

The Scale and Causes of Quaker Business Achievement

It is worth recapitulating the *scale* of Quaker business activity. Deborah Cadbury, in her book on the Quaker confectioners and their rivals, points out that some four thousand Quaker families ran nearly three hundred businesses.[1] And as Danny Boyle so effectively visualised, Abraham Darby kick-started the Industrial Revolution with his breakthroughs in iron making. We can add too that Coalbrookdale went on to become the largest iron foundry in the world and cast the Iron Bridge, and that Benjamin Huntsman made a parallel breakthrough in the casting of steel, to have a profound impact on the Sheffield cutlers. Ambrose Crowley's business was the largest ironmongers in Europe, while the Bristol firm of Reynolds, Getley & Co. were the largest tinplate works of their kind in the world, and Lloyds & Lloyds were amongst the largest manufacturers of steel tubes in their field. Robert Ransome pioneered chilled iron ploughs and interchangeable plough parts as his contribution to agriculture, and his company became the largest manufacturer of plough and agricultural equipment in Britain and influenced agriculture around the world. Quakers ran the largest lead and silver mines in the country and developed the reverberatory furnace for the smelting of those metals. We saw that Joseph Fry founded the British chocolate industry and was the first to use a steam-engine in grinding cocoa. Between them, Fry's, Rowntree's and Cadbury's dominated the confectionary market, while Huntley & Palmers were biscuit and biscuit tin makers for the Empire, and the largest producers of biscuits in their day. Joseph Pease became 'Father of the Railways', while *Bradshaw's Railway Times*, Thomas Edmonson's ticketing machines and Charles May's sleeper fasteners all shaped the emerging rail industry. Quakers at one time produced a fifth of all soap in the country. Quakers ran 74 banks, and the initially successful Overend & Gurney pioneered bill-broking, was the largest such broker in the world, and was second only to the Bank of England before it crashed. Quakers ran one of the largest match factories in the world, and at different times ran the largest brewery in the world and the largest brewery in London. Francis Frith set up one of the largest photographic studios in the world, while Quakers took a leading role in the design of the London Underground, and a Quaker was the architect of the Natural History Museum. Quakers developed one of the world's largest pharmaceutical companies in the world, were watch-makers to kings, and invented the modern orrery. Not mentioned earlier is the Victorian cement producer founded by Quaker Edmund Wright Brooks that became the largest employer in Essex.

They also introduced the mangel-wurzel to Britain ... perhaps one of their lesser triumphs.

These are just the British successes. America also had its share of Quaker entrepreneurs, not least those who established the world's largest whaling industry on Nantucket Island, and amongst which families were the Starbucks (as mentioned in the Introduction). Quakers founded Sandy Spring Bank, the largest bank in the state of Maryland. A Quaker family soap and candle business started in Philadelphia by Joseph Elkinton eventually became PQ Corporation, a leading world-wide producer of inorganic chemicals. America's second largest steel producer and largest shipbuilder, the Bethlehem Steel Corporation, was founded by the Quaker Joseph Wharton. The Quaker merchant Johns Hopkins, an American entrepreneur, abolitionist and philanthropist, lent his name to famous institutions. On the other hand the American Quaker Oats company, still in business today, was not in fact founded by a Quaker. Instead the term was used in branding to suggest that the product and its manufacture met Quaker values. Although the US picture of Quaker success is a little more patchy than in Britain, there is no doubt that it further represents their reach. Finally it is worth mentioning that the founding board president of Tokyo Telecommunication Engineering was a Japanese Quaker called Tamon Maeda. His company later became Sony.

How did they do it? What was the secret of Quaker business success? How could a mere one per cent of the population or less create businesses that could claim anything up to 60 per cent of national productivity in their various enterprises? In the first instance the answer is honesty. This honesty was born of religious belief and religious persecution, the latter being a severe test of a person's integrity. As Quaker leaders put it: 'trade and other occupations show forth truth to the world', which indicates how this honesty was understood in the commercial setting. Unlike perhaps other Protestant groups whose success was understood as indicating an 'elect' destined for salvation, success for Quakers merely tested all the time their determination to 'live in truth'. As Raistrick puts it: 'In a world that was unstable, where speculation was rife and where business morals were generally lax, the stability, honesty and independence of the Quaker attracted business to him.'[2] Emden tells us that Quakers were the first to discard bargaining as shopkeepers and set fixed prices for goods.[3] This apparently aroused suspicion and perplexity to start with and lost customers, but not for long: fixed prices told a story of honesty and reliability.

But many manufacturers, traders and bankers are honest people, and quietly demonstrate truthful living without any religious belief or affiliation. The Quakers had more than honesty, though their 'brand' as it were relied heavily on it, in particular in banking. As we saw with Quaker Oats, even non-Quakers attempted to exploit it. The real secret weapon of the Quakers lay in their extensive networking, as developed through Meeting, their schools, the tradition of apprenticeship to Quaker businesses, and in marriage and travel, as we have seen. Walvin comments thus on Quaker material flourishing: 'It was, however, a prosperity which followed a pattern of mutual self-help, meticulous bookkeeping and financial scrutiny, and all under the watchful eye of the local Quaker community.'[4] The Meeting was at the centre of Quaker life, and it developed various structures despite having no priesthood or hierarchy, including the Meeting for Business – in which both religious and other collective decisions were made – and the appointment of Elders and Overseers. We have seen a number of times that Meeting would act as moral guardian of the ethics of enterprises run by their members. Bristol Quarterly Meeting considered the sale of sheepskin coats to the British Army by Clarks of Street wrong because the coats kept British soldiers alive to kill Russian soldiers. Joseph Fry, the banker, not the chocolatier, was disowned for going bankrupt. As a result his wife, Elizabeth Fry, was disowned by Ratcliff and Barking Monthly Meeting in May 1829 and she found herself unwelcome back home amongst local Friends in East Anglia and even found it hard to get her son into a Quaker school; the ethical horror in which bankruptcy was held, and the collective response to it, was incredibly strong amongst Quakers in that period.[5] Pacifism and the avoidance of debt were taken very seriously indeed.

The fear of debt was so much part of the fabric of Quaker thought that Emden suggests that 'children were educated as if existence had only two dangers: "debt and eternal punishment".'[6] He adds in a footnote that eternal punishment is a doctrine not typical of Quakers, which rather leaves debt as life's principal danger. Walvin points out that 'Monthly Meetings were asked "to be properly watchful one over another, and early to caution all against running beyond their depth, and entangling themselves in a greater multiplicity of trade and business than they can extricate themselves with honour and reputation."'[7] Taking Norwich as an example, the local Meeting investigated 60 insolvencies between 1701 and 1773, and in 26 of them Gurney family members were involved in the investigation.[8] They were also involved, naturally enough, in the investigation of Joseph Fry's insolvency, and it fell to one of Elizabeth Fry's brothers to urge that 'painful justice' be applied – painful for the ties of family too. The response of Meeting would vary: in genuine cases where insolvency was caused by factors beyond control, financial support might be available; where misjudgement was a cause there might be a reprimand; and where any kind of irresponsibility or deceit was involved there would be disownment. Meeting would also be stern with any Quakers found to be avoiding the due payment of taxes, or in general 'endeavouring to diminish any of the customs, excise or any other public dues.'[9] The perception of them as law-abiding citizens was essential and all Quakers were urged 'to render unto the king what is his due, in taxes and customs payable to him according to the law.'

The Quaker schools contributed to bringing young people up with the Quaker ethos, and also to the essential networking between families. Apprenticeships of a family member into the business of another Quaker family meant that further contacts were established and business skills passed on, while marrying between Quaker families often cemented business links. The history of 'sufferings' as we saw, and the endless record keeping of distrainments, led to meticulous record keeping in financial matters too. 'Few groups kept records like the Quakers', Walvin tells us, 'family records; genealogies; birth, marriage and death statistics; private letters and diaries; minutes of local, regional and national meetings.'[10] He adds that they invented and perfected a form of census predating the official census system used in Britain by a century.

And businesses need businesses. Commercial activity requires a host of coordinated materials or services, and the essential interconnectedness of commercial activity became ever more obvious with increasing specialisation. Quakers were able to draw on each other in this way, but above all, Quakers *travelled*. Wherever they went, they would of course be guests of other Quakers and attend their Meetings, and so their network spread across Britain and into the heart of commerce in London, and also spread through America and the colonies. Walvin tells us that the Quaker home was where business deals took place, the counterpart to the gentleman's club perhaps, which was much relied on by other businessman for general commercial networking.[11]

Finally, businesses need finance. In commenting on Richard Reynold's involvement in Coalbrookdale Walvin writes: 'It was an evolving pattern: acquisitive Friends financed their own and other industrial and commercial ventures by lending at below the market rate, confident that their investments were safeguarded by the ethical standards and rigorous scrutiny of the local Quaker community.'[12]

The Fading of the Quaker Ethic

What caused the historic Quakernomics to fade away? The Quakers today are an active religious group whose core values have not changed, yet clearly they are no longer pre-eminent in business. There are of course a number of factors, but the chief amongst them is probably the emergence of the joint-stock or limited company as the new powerhouse of business, displacing the family-controlled firm. We already considered the takeover of Cadbury's by Kraft as symbolic of this process, a gradual shift that eroded Quaker control of their companies throughout the twentieth century. Windsor says: 'As with the Lloyds, the story of Joseph Crosfield and Sons [...] draws to an end with the advent of limited liability status.'[13] As with the Lloyds and the Crosfields, so it was with countless other Quaker businesses: they were incorporated in order to secure the greater investment needed to compete with their rivals, and as a result Quaker control of boardrooms declined.

But other forces were also at work. We have seen many times that businessmen and scientists born into Quaker families would drift out of the Society of Friends, drawn to the wider social status offered within the Church of England, or simply to be able to go to university, as with the scientist Thomas Young. Geoffrey Elliott wrote of the Quakers that 'The Trollopian subtleties of social standing were not for them'.[14]

This captures well the Quaker independence from fashionable society, but with wealth came the temptation to move in such circles, and some fell prey to the glamour of exactly that social standing. The great ironmaster Ambrose Crowley III, born to Quakers, became an Anglican, a Tory MP and was knighted: such moves drew many successful entrepreneurs out of the ranks of the society, for example the Crosfield sons also left for Anglicanism.[15] A book on business and religion in Britain includes a table of Quaker businessmen with separate columns for those who stayed 'plain', those who became 'worldly' and those who resigned.[16] There are many famous Quaker business names in the latter two categories. Indeed it was not always clear whether individuals held the status of Quaker when they ceased to attend Meeting, because this lapse was not always followed up and ended in disownment.

'A carriage and pair does not long continue to drive to a Meeting House' is an old saying in Quaker circles.[17] Sons and grandsons of wealthy Quakers rarely stayed 'plain' and often left or were disowned by the society. We have of course seen many exceptions: the Darbys continued for generations, and George Cadbury only gave up riding his horse to Meeting in Birmingham when he exchanged it for a bicycle; he could have afforded a 'carriage and pair' many times over. Many of his descendents remained Quakers.

However, it is also true that as many joined as left the Quakers, drawn by their simple ethos, and often attracted by their pacifism, and so for the two centuries from the first Darby in 1700 to the last of the Crosfields around 1900, Quakernomics persisted despite wealth. It was the shareholders who really displaced the Quaker ethos, though perhaps also it was down to increasingly unforgiving commercial rivalry. We can take the Aero dispute between Cadbury's and Rowntree's to symbolise both this and the end of Meeting involvement in Quaker businesses.

We can imagine the total economic output of the Quakers, the 'Gross Quaker Product' or 'GQP', on a graph in the centuries of their operations. I picture it as a lopsided bell curve with its peak in the late Victorian period, a steep rise in the early eighteenth century, and a long tail reaching eventually into the twenty-first. Different curves could be drawn for different parts of the world, though I have been focussing mostly on England and Ireland. It would take some considerable research and number crunching to put figures to this curve, and to then compare it with national GDP through the period. Even at its peak, I have no way of guessing what proportion GQP would be of GDP. It is clear however that the area under the GQP graph represents a huge gross production of goods and services by successful enterprises which at the same time embodied a serious attempt to link business with social improvement. It is not a question of one-off voluntary philanthropy here but a *systematic* application of a business philosophy that touched nearly all sectors of the economy. I hope that I have shown that Quakernomics is a big enough phenomenon for that philosophy to be taken as a serious challenge to the view that capitalism is intrinsically evil – as Michael Moore insists upon – or the view that attempts to moderate capitalism for social ends would destroy entrepreneurial energy and profit, as free market extremists insist upon.

As the Quaker presence in business faded, something else took over however: the transfer of its ethos from the private sphere to the state, combined with the growth of the unions. The elective ethics of Quakernomics with its paternalist basis became the sphere of a minority of family-owned businesses, while the new battles would be fought between corporations and unions, with legislation progressively granting by right to the worker what was previously a matter of enlightened management. Following a photographic record of Quaker traces in London we look at how Quakers, through their participation in public life, contributed to the broader movement towards economic justice and the slow and at times uncertain progress towards the eradication of subsistence wages.

QUAKER TRACES IN LONDON

Figure 1. West Ham Park in East London

Dr John Fothergill was a Quaker physician and botanist remembered in West Ham Park simply as a philanthropist. He purchased Upton House estate in 1762, where he established greenhouses and a unique botanical collection. Honoured by Benjamin Franklin and recognised for his pioneering medical work, his name lives on in this part of the park, known as the 'Fothergill Bed'. After his death the estate passed to the Quaker Gurneys, and for a while Elizabeth Fry lived there, and was at one point visited by the King of Prussia. The Park was purchased for the public in the 1870s, with a large proportion of the funds raised by the Gurney family.

Inset: The park notice board records some of this Quaker history.

Figure 2. The Gurney Obelisk in Stratford

The Gurney memorial drinking fountain in Stratford, East London, was erected in honour of the Quaker banker and philanthropist Samuel Gurney, brother of prison reformer Elizabeth Fry. Its location just by a branch of Starbucks lends itself to reflecting on another part of Quaker history: the Quaker whaling town of Nantucket in which the Starbuck family were prominent. Herman Melville named the first mate in *Moby-Dick* after this family, and the founders of the coffee chain chose the name for their brand, apparently being greatly fond of the novel.

Inset: The inscription on the memorial.

Figure 3. The Bryant & May Match Factory

Entrance to the Bryant & May match factory in Bow, East London, now
apartments. The huge scale of the Victorian brick-built factory is best
appreciated from the rail line that runs along its southern perimeter.
The factory was built by Quakers but its reputation for introducing the
life-saving safety match into Britain is overshadowed by the Matchgirls'
Strike of 1888. Some sources praise the exceptional working conditions
and efforts gone to by the management in preventing the terrible
industrial disease of 'phossy jaw' – a cancer caused by working with white
phosphorous – while others condemn the owners for exploitation of the
workforce. It was in its time one of the largest producers of matches in
the world, and in 1910 its management persuaded the government to
ban white phosphorous in match production.

Inset: A blue plaque placed on the factory gatehouse commemorates the role of Annie
Besant in leading the Matchgirls' Strike.

Figure 4. Allen & Hanburys in Bethnal Green, East End

The Allen & Hanburys factory in Bethnal Green, now renovated as light industrial units and hemmed in by new apartment blocks. This Quaker company was in its time the largest pharmaceutical company in the world, with a huge range of products and a presence on every high street. Its headquarters was originally in Plough Court, off Lombard Street. 'Allenburys' blackcurrant pastilles were a rival to Rowntree's Pastilles in their day, and the tins remain collectable items.

Inset: The Allen & Hanburys name is still visible from a distance, and from the Bethnal Green train station.

**Figure 5. The Kindertransport commemorative
sculptures at Liverpool Street station**

The Kindertransport commemorative sculpture at the main entrance
to Liverpool Street station. It marks the escape from Nazi Germany
and Austria of thousands of children, brought to Britain via Harwich.
Quakers played a key role in this. The girl standing with the suitcase
could have been my mother, in traditional Austrian dress and pigtails,
who also brought with her a violin (as shown in the sculpture).

Inset: A second commemorative sculpture on the lower concourse has an inscription on
the rear which reads: 'Dedicated to The Religious Society of Friends – The Quakers. For
instigating the Kindertransports and their unique role in getting the British Parliament to
change legislation in order to accept the children into Great Britain.'

Figure 6. The Truman Brewery, Brick Lane

One of the Truman brewery buildings in Brick Lane, East End. Though only the Truman name survives at present, the Quaker partners in this firm, Sir Thomas Fowell Buxton and Sampson Hanbury, helped make this the largest brewery in London in its day. It is mentioned in Dickens' *David Copperfield* as a possible employer for the hapless Mr Micawber. Buxton was famous for his abolitionist role and appears in the background to Elizabeth Fry on the British five pound note; in a typical Quaker arrangement he married Fry's sister, both part of the Norwich Gurney Quaker banking dynasty. Visitors to Brick Lane today know the buildings under the name 'Truman', but adjoining streets record the real history: Buxton Street, Hanbury Street and Quaker Street, so named because of a Quaker Meeting House built there.

Insets: A blue plaque commemorates Buxton's role in the anti-slavery campaign, while the defunct company office at 91 Brick Lane still records the name of the company as 'Truman Hanbury Buxton & Co Ltd'.

Figure 7. Lombard Street, City of London

View along Lombard Street towards the unfinished 'Walkie Talkie' building. Lombard Street was London's early financial centre, a name synonymous with banking and the title of Walter Bagehot's famous book on the subject. It was also a key Quaker location in that both the modern Barclays and Lloyds banks were founded there by Quakers. Several traditional signs still hang in Lombard Street; visible here is that of the Trustee Savings Bank, now merged with Lloyds. Birmingham Quakers founded Lloyds Bank and adopted the sign of the black horse in their London branch. Further along on the left is a modern block that has displaced the old headquarters of Barclays, which was founded by Quakers under the sign of the black spread eagle. On the right, opposite a church building, is Plough Court.

Insets: Street signs. Plough Court is important in Quaker history because Allen & Hanburys was founded there as a pharmaceutical company (and retained its company offices in Lombard Street well into the twentieth century). It became not only a centre for scientific work in medicine but also a centre for the anti-slavery movement.

Figure 8. Blackfriars Bridge

A view of Blackfriars Bridge on the river Thames. The ironworks for the bridge were manufactured by the Quaker firm Lloyds, Fosters & Company, a move which unfortunately bankrupted it. This did not prevent the bridge being opened by Queen Victoria in 1869. The firm was one of the first in the country to adopt the Bessemer process for steel production.

Inset: On the northern approach to the bridge an ornate drinking fountain can be found bearing an inscription mentioning Samuel Gurney, MP, as the chairman of the Metropolitan Free Drinking Fountains Association.

Figure 9. Plaque commemorating the Anchor Brewery
This plaque commemorating the Anchor Brewery stands in Park Street, Southwark, close to the site of the original Globe Theatre. The plaque records the ownership of the brewery between 1781 to 1955 by the Quaker firm Barclay, Perkins & Co. The Quakers bought it at an auction overseen by Samuel Johnson, installed a steam engine that lasted a hundred years, and expanded its operations to make it the largest brewery in the world. Mentioned by Dickens in several of his novels, it was visited in its heyday by dignitaries such as the Prince of Wales, Napoleon III, Ibrahim Pasha of Egypt, Giuseppe Garibaldi and Otto von Bismarck. Dr Johnson failed to make much money from his role in the sale, but was rewarded in another way: an upright figure of a jovial Dr Johnson clutching a pint pot became the brewery's emblem.

Figure 10. The Coalbrookdale Gates, Kensington

The Coalbrookdale Gates are located by Kensington Gardens in Hyde Park. As one of many small cast plaques at the base records, it was 'Designed and Cast by the Coalbrookdale Company for the Great Exhibition of 1851'. After the exhibition the gates were moved to their current location. The Coalbrookdale Company was founded in 1700 by the Bristol Quaker Abraham Darby I. Five generations of this Quaker family ran the ironworks, at one time the largest of its kind in the world. More than that, Darby invented the smelting of iron with coal and coke, and the sand casting of iron, two innovations which kick-started the Industrial Revolution. It was his grandson Abraham Darby III who designed and built the Iron Bridge, considered iconic of the Industrial Revolution, the first iron bridge in the world.

Inset: One of the small plaques near the ground, recording the origins and subsequent renovations of the gates.

Figure 11. Natural History Museum, Kensington

The Natural History Museum was designed by the Quaker architect Alfred Waterhouse. He was famous for neo-Gothic, Renaissance, and Romanesque revival styles and was perhaps one of the most financially successful of Victorian architects. He also designed Manchester's town hall and a country home that was the summer residence of the young Beatrix Potter.

One of his brothers, Edwin, co-founded the accountancy practice Price Waterhouse, now part of PricewaterhouseCoopers, and another brother, Theodore, founded the law firm Waterhouse & Co., which is now part of Field Fisher Waterhouse LLP.

Figure 12. Friends House, Euston

The Friends Meeting House on Euston Road is a familiar landmark to Londoners. It was built in 1927 to designs by Irish architect Hubert Lidbetter, who was a Quaker. It is the headquarters of the Quakers in Britain.

Inset: A cornerstone on the building records the name of the architect, close to a sign bearing the official name of the building: 'Friends House'.

Part III

QUAKERS, SOCIETY AND SOCIAL JUSTICE

Chapter 11

QUAKERS IN PUBLIC LIFE

In the first publication to draw together Quaker business achievements, Paul Emden's *Quakers in Commerce* of 1939, the Quaker legacy is summed up like this:

> Quakerism, indeed, made its chief impression, not as one might perhaps expect, upon theology or philosophy, but upon social history; and in almost every department of social and moral progress – Amelioration of Housing Conditions; Social Organisation of Factories; Relief of the Poor and Sick, Care for the Insane, Protection of the Aborigines; Prison Reform; Revision of the Criminal Code; Suppression of the Opium Trade; International Arbitration – Quakers were amongst the pioneers and very often they stood at first alone.[1]

Emden adds a few further items: abolition of slavery, promotion of the temperance movement (at times Quakers were in the lead on this), and education of children and adults. Quakers also sat on all kinds of public bodies, roles that might be unpaid, attract only expenses, or be remunerated at levels significantly lower than comparable executive roles in commerce. Put broadly, we can call this a participation in public or civic life. And wherever that participation flowed from principles which Quakers held ahead of their time, we can give it the contemporary name of 'activism'. As we have seen Quakers were not divided between those who entered public life on the one hand and those who engaged in commerce on the other: they were mostly one and the same individual, and this is what gives Quakernomics its character. At the same time the history of Quaker persecution tinged this participation in public life with the continuous consciousness of the outsider, one who not so easily forgets those still in poverty or despised by the mainstream.

Of course some Quakers devoted more of their life to activism than
to commerce, but they were generally only able to do this because of
the profits from family enterprises. At times it is also true that Quakers
were active in public life in order to further their ventures, such as
when Pease and Backhouse pursued the necessary Railway Act through
Parliament. But the picture I want to paint here – pulling together many
references already made – is one of a continuum between commerce
and public life, between capitalism and civic virtue. In other words
I want to show that Quakernomics was enmeshed in public life far
beyond the occasional narrow lobbying that commerce demands. It
pursued a civic good from beyond the factory gate into all spheres of
governance and civic life.

Fellows of Societies

How though do outsiders, with vivid memories of their persecutions,
become insiders? Warily, perhaps, but interested in new forms of
association. The Royal Society is an interesting example of an
institution founded with virtually no historical precedent. Its full name
was the Royal Society of London for Improving Natural Knowledge,
and was granted a Royal Charter by Charles II in 1660, around the
time of the birth of Quakerism. Sir Isaac Newton was its president from
1703 to 1727, on whose recommendation the Quaker Silvanus Bevan
was appointed a fellow in 1725. Apart from Bevan, we have seen that a
number of Quakers became fellows (or 'FRS' for short). These include
John Bellers in 1719, Peter Collinson in 1728, John Fothergill in 1763,
John Coakley Lettsom in 1773 (no doubt for contributions to science
beyond the mangel-wurzel), William Allen in 1807, Luke Howard in
1821, John Dalton in 1822, Charles May in 1855, Daniel Hanbury in
1869 and John Eliot Howard in 1874. Kathleen Lonsdale was one of
the first two women ever appointed FRS in 1945, while perhaps the
most recent Quaker appointee was George Ellis in 2007. As pointed
out earlier it took a long time before the pure science of the type
pursued by the Royal Society became central to industrial capitalism,
perhaps two centuries from its founding. But no modern economy
can operate without its equivalent now – its function dissipated right
across the research establishments of the publicly funded university
sector – and it was perhaps the philosopher Leibniz who did most to
establish similar organisations in such countries as Russia, Germany
and France.

Quakers have a natural gift for organisation, and the Royal Society benefited from this, as the following passage from a book on science and religion shows:

It is important to stress the centrality of this small group of Quakers and ex-Quakers in maintaining the organisational structure of the Royal Society. Not only was Birch one of the Secretaries for a thirteen-year period, but he served on Council for a total of eighteen years, while John Bellers, Silvanus Bevan, John Collinson and the ex-Quaker instrument maker George Graham also served on Council, the last two on a number of occasions. The three practising Quakers in this group must have looked conspicuous in their plain, black dress and broad hats.[2]

In fact the Royal Society represents exactly the type of new institution open to non-conformists that allowed Quakers, whatever their reservations, to participate in new spheres of public life. We saw that William Allen was elected to a similar organisation, the Linnaean Society of London, devoted to the biological sciences. John Coakley Lettsom founded the Medical Society of London in 1773, now one of the oldest surviving medical societies in the United Kingdom, possibly the world. He was also a founder-member of the Royal Humane Society in 1774.

Another unique institution – the Fabian Society – was co-founded, as we saw, by the Quaker Edward Reynolds Pease in 1884. In 1895 Pease, along with Sidney and Beatrice Webb, became trustees of the fund used to found the London School of Economics. Pease had inherited a sizeable Quaker fortune (he had Peases on one side and Frys on the other), and attempted at one stage to convert the working classes of Newcastle to socialism – a venture in which he had no success.

Honours Accepted and Refused

But Quakers were just as likely to turn down honours and recognition, not so much as a result of their persecutions, but from the certainty that all people are equal in the eyes of God. They were certainly wary of an establishment that had persecuted them, but they were more wary still of their own consciences. We saw that Benjamin Huntsman refused to accept fellowship of the Royal Society, for example, despite the tenor of the organisation as purely scientific, and we saw that the Irish Quaker, John Grubb Richardson, turned down a baronetcy from David Lloyd George.

Arthur Raistrick, the author of three books of industrial history I have
extensively drawn on in this volume, refused an OBE from Harold
Wilson, declining the honour in a letter that began 'Dear Harold, I am
deeply disappointed in you'.

Many Quakers did accept honours, however. The Quaker Joseph
W. Pease was made a baronet by Gladstone, and his son, also called
Joseph, became the first Quaker peer, under the title Lord Gainford.[3]
Things did not go so smoothly for James Reckitt, however, who initially
accepted a baronetcy, also from Gladstone. Reckitt's wife was displeased
at this affront to Quaker principles, and Reckitt had to 'withdraw by
telegram the acceptance he had sent by letter'. When the offer was later
repeated Mrs Reckitt relented.[4] We also saw that Abraham Darby II and
Benjamin Huntsman refused to take out patents on their innovations,
though other patents were taken up by Quakers, including by the first
Abraham Darby. We return shortly to a more detailed consideration
of George Cadbury's social activism, but it is worth listing here some
honours that he refused over a lifetime. These include requests to stand
as an MP for the Liberal Party from Gladstone in 1892 and from Lord
Rosebery in 1895. He refused appointment to the Privy Council, an
advisory position to the sovereign, and he also turned down an honorary
degree from the University of Birmingham.[5]

The Quakers and Moravians Act of 1833 paved the way for Quakers
to join Parliament by allowing them to substitute an affirmation in place
of the traditional oath. Joseph Pease, son of the Quaker called the
'Father of the Railways', was the first Quaker elected to Parliament,
just prior to the act, in 1832, but not without some complications. The
Peases, like most Quakers in Parliament, were Liberals. Others elected
to Parliament amongst the Quakers we have already looked at include
Edmund Backhouse and John Bright, while not mentioned so far include
Charles Gilpin (a Liberal who supported the repeal of the Corn Laws,
the Poor Law, prison reform, the anti-slavery movement and abolition of
the death penalty), John Ellis (a railway director with similar interests),
and more recently Philip Noel-Baker (more on him shortly).

Windsor notes: 'The Crosfields, like many Friends, were active in
the Liberal cause. Since 1832 they had turned to the working classes
for a coalition of capital and labour, a union of the useful and the
industrious against the non-producing, rent-charging, royalty-exacting
landowners.'[6] This implies that Quakers were generally unsympathetic
to Conservative interests, but in fact a number of Quakers later became
Conservative MPs. Parliament has many attractions, and cynics like

Charles Dickens saw nothing beyond the many corruptions possible to those holding high office. But Quakers acted in Parliament, as elsewhere, in good faith. They believed that matters of social justice were to be pursued and resolved there and so were active in all the key debates of their day on wages, working conditions, slavery, war, and so on. But of course Quaker activism was not confined to this particular route.

Some Outstanding Quaker Activists

One of the earliest Quaker activists was John Bellers (1654–1725), an influence on Robert Owen. Bellers holds that rare historical distinction of basking in the admiration of Karl Marx, who said he was 'a veritable phenomenon in the history of political economy'.[7] Bellers was apprenticed as a cloth merchant and was a close friend of William Penn, founder of Pennsylvania. Bellers wrote tracts – an ubiquitous method for the activist of the day – on social issues such as education, health provision, care for the poor, support for refugees, a plan for a European State, and an argument for the abolition of capital punishment. He was elected FRS in 1719, as we saw. His most famous work is *Proposals for Raising a College of Industry of All Useful Trades and Husbandry* (1695). Bellers' *Proposals* is interesting because it shows a typical Quaker trait: the linking of social activism with profit. It begins by declaring 'the ill provision for the poor in England one of the greatest reproaches to our Christian profession.' ('Profession' at that time meant the declaration of religious belief, hence 'professors' were in modern terms preachers. There was no concept in Bellers' time of religion belonging to the private sphere.) His idea was to bring the poor together in one place and train them so as 'they may be made of equal value to money (by their raising a plentiful supply of all conveniences of life.)' Essentially he was appealing to the self-interest of those who might fund such an adventure, and, as this was a document addressed to Parliament, expressed the desire that it may 'make England the mart and treasury of Europe', and appealed hence to the self-interest of the government. Given the patronising tone towards the poor and the mention of profit it is all the more surprising that Marx praised it. But we need to understand the setting of its time: it was advocating things we have long taken for granted but then considered radical. Educate the poor? That was highly radical in his day, so we should forgive the strange language of Bellers's tract: 'There is three things I aim at: First, Profit for the rich, (which will be life to the rest.) Secondly, A plentiful living for the poor, without difficulty.

Thirdly, A good education for youth, that may tend to prepare their souls into the nature of the good ground.' The proposals never attracted sufficient sponsors, but he was instrumental in setting up the Quaker Workhouse at Clerkenwell, another institution we are now horrified at, but which was also a radical attempt to help the poor. Dickens, in setting up a home for 'fallen' women, was acting on the same impulse.

Neither Bellers' 'Colleges' for the poor nor the Clerkenwell Workhouse were successful, indicating that idealism of this sort soon founders on the many practical difficulties of uniting the long-term poor and the infirm with profitable labour. The same is true in prison reform: centuries of effort to provide inmates with dignified and properly remunerated work have often failed, leaving the 'chain gang' at one extreme and enforced idleness at the other. This is a good place to point out that the 'Protestant work ethic' and 'the spirit of capitalism' are not universal impulses and aspirations, and that all those who do not share them – and who are not idle or criminal – have little alternative beyond jail or the monastery in a civilisation built on these values. The hippy and 'slacker' movements attempted to live between the cracks of capitalist modernity, as did the Bohemians before them (I come from such a background), but the legacy of the Protestant work ethic makes such alternatives ever harder to pursue. There is nothing in Quakernomics that can resolve that particular question. Bellers epitomised the work ethic – as do most Quakers – and his vision did not include alternatives to 'profitable' work. At the same time we need to understand the circumstances that informed his vision: the continuation whilst in prison of useful trades by the Quakers, made possible by the Meetings for Sufferings which ensured they had the materials to do so. In York Castle, for example, Quakers imprisoned under the usual persecutory laws of the period produced linen, stockings and lace.[8]

John Bright, the son of Jacob Bright, a self-made and successful cotton manufacturer, was born in Rochdale in 1811. Jacob was deeply religious and sent John to Quaker schools in Lancashire and Yorkshire. This Quaker education helped to develop in Bright a passionate commitment to political and religious equality. In 1843 he was elected to Parliament where he campaigned for the repeal of the Corn Laws and supported universal suffrage and the secret ballot. Being an ally of the controversial Richard Cobden, who was at the centre of the Corn Law reform and also a pacifist, Bright was regarded with suspicion on his entry to the House of Commons, but soon made his reputation for oratory. The Corn Laws are of interest to Quaker history because they were seen to be part of the 'Old Corruption' including the Church, the landed gentry and the Establishment (senior politicians, industrialists, civil servants, judges, barristers and so on). As Walvin points out the campaign against the Corn Laws 'could promote economic self-interest in alliance with the social good.'[9] Bright has been mentioned before in connection with the trade that brought him wealth – cotton – and all we need to add here is that he was a great influence on the steel magnate, Andrew Carnegie, as we shall see.

Having experienced prison many times in the early days, it is not surprising that Quakers retained interest in its reform for a long time. Elizabeth Fry (1780–1845) is perhaps the most famous of the early Quaker prison reformers, mentioned earlier as a member of the Gurney family and wife of Joseph Fry, the failed banker disowned by the Society of Friends. Elizabeth Fry's philanthropic work extended to establishing a night shelter for the homeless in London after seeing the dead body of a young boy one winter. She also opened a training school for nurses, which inspired Florence Nightingale, and had several audiences with Queen Victoria, who contributed financially to Fry's causes. Robert Peel passed several acts of Parliament to further the cause of prison reform, and since 2001 Elizabeth Fry and her work have been commemorated on the British £5 note.

Fry herself had no source of income beyond that of her family and Quaker network (she had eleven children), but it is part of the bigger picture to understand that Quaker business wealth – in this case largely from banking – was always at the ready for the kind of philanthropic work that she pursued. Apparently she had an immensely calming personality, being also a gifted preacher, and had some success in that difficult venture of providing useful employment to prisoners.[10] Despite the trauma of her husband's business failure and disownment, and a personal nervous breakdown at one point, her persistence led her to be one of the most famous reformers of her time. We saw, for example, that William Allen found himself discussing her work with Tsar Alexander I of Russia in 1819.

Turning now to George Cadbury, I want to show that he can be taken as the archetypal example out of all the Quaker philanthropists – many of whom were no lesser individuals – and so is an essential figure in contemplating the ethical capitalism of Quakernomics. We find in him a saintliness of the kind that may have prompted Tawney to assume that the Quaker enterprises were 'peaks' which did not alter the general commercial climate (as we will see later on), and also find in him the human limitations of a businessman at one point facing a terribly difficult strategic decision with enormous financial and ethical implications.

I have to admit that I am focussing on George Cadbury partly because of an excellent and detailed biography of him by the journalist A. G. Gardiner. There was a link between subject and biographer because Gardiner became the editor of the *Daily News*, a paper bought by George Cadbury as a way to oppose the Boer war. But Gardiner resigned over a disagreement with Cadbury in 1919, and so his publication of the biography in 1923 should not be seen as the outcome of too close a coincidence of views; neither was he a Quaker. Gardiner's portrait of Cadbury shows a man growing up in a deeply religious household, yet gifted with the traits of the successful entrepreneur, one with the adventurer's instinct. George's brother Richard was equally talented and hardworking, but Gardiner says of George: 'the channel of his mind was narrower and the current swifter. He had no aesthetic tastes, and of personal ambition in the ordinary sense he had no trace.'[11] He epitomised the Protestant work ethic of making money solely for philanthropic ends. The Cadbury business teetered on a knife edge of profitability for many years, and the brothers were on the verge of giving up at one point. But as the company became successful they were able to raise wages for the workforce and engage in wider social action. In fact, Gardiner points out: 'They felt keenly the insufficiency of the standard of payment that existed, and while still losing heavily, gradually raised the scale above the normal wretched payment then current in Birmingham.'[12] Their empathy for the working poor of Birmingham was honed by their commitment to the Adult School Movement, introduced to that city by the Quaker Joseph Sturge. Earlier, George had witnessed the creeping industrialism that brought a number of evils in its wake: the first and defining factor being low or subsistence wages, as a result of which workers were particularly vulnerable to the 'jerry builders', the publicans and the loan sharks. George had personally seen the wretched conditions described so well in social research surveys and in fiction of the time, when he had accompanied his parents on visits to the poor in Birmingham slums.

Hence George's first response, apart from raising wages, was to financially support and teach in the Birmingham Adult School. At the age of 20 George taught each Sunday morning from 7:00 to 7:30, initially under the supervision of a Quaker alderman, William White. At first it was a small group of boys, and then an entire class, named

Class XIV, with which he subsequently held an unbroken connection for half a century, and which numbered some three hundred. The men could be ex-thieves or drunkards, and would be sent to fetch errant members from the 'unimagined wildernesses of courts and alleys, pausing here at the door of an unspeakable hovel and passing there into a cavernous interior...'[13] Gardiner paints a Dickensian picture for us of the working poor of Birmingham amongst whom George Cadbury became a familiar figure. Towards the end of his life the 'members' of the Adult School known to George numbered in the thousands, and he never failed to send a special gift to the class on Sunday: a great box of flowers. Gardiner tells us this: '"Mr. Cadbury's flower" became a sort of emblem in hundreds of homes in Birmingham.'[14] Each man would take one home, and apparently it became a regular sight to see a child run out to find out which flower father had brought home that Sunday. George regarded it as a message of hope intended more for them than their parents.

The Adult School, though dear to George's heart, was only a small part of the greater social activism that he pursued. His father had been central in shaping Birmingham's civic development and George continued at the heart of the struggle against the forces of indifferent and exploitative capitalism that lobbied powerfully against regulatory 'interference'. Indeed, here lay a great difference between the approach of John Bright and the Cadburys; as Gardiner says of George: 'He was a social reformer always in advance of the thought of his co-religionist John Bright'.[15] Bright even opposed a Parliamentary act to prevent adulteration, so strong was his opposition to state interference in private business. We can understand his position perhaps as a throwback to the stout yeoman independence at the heart of the Quaker demographic, but this adamant free market position was at odds with most Quakers who, like the Cadburys, began to see that their principles of social responsibility required significant state regulation to promulgate. We saw that the Conservative MP Bill Cash was enamoured enough of Bright's political philosophy to write a biography of him. But the general tenor of Quaker thinking, as Liberals, was to lobby the state to intervene more, not less, in the cause of social and economic justice.

George declined an honorary degree from the University of Birmingham, as mentioned earlier. He had been amongst its first subscribers, with a gift of £5,000 (perhaps £250,000 in today's money), and the establishment of a lectureship in civic design and town planning. The first lecturer so appointed acknowledged George in this way: 'To his example we largely owe the fact that town-planning is now an accepted phase of municipal activity'.[16] He further attributed the existence of the Town Planning Act to George's influence, along with powers given to public bodies in England 'to control the development of their growing towns.' The key aspect of this control, as far as George was concerned, was the suppression of slum landlords and predatory traders, including publicans and usurers. But why should George Cadbury refuse this simple honour? It was certainly part of his natural reluctance for such things, but there was another motive, it turns out: he thought that his name was too controversial, and would arouse much hostility, and therefore would hinder the work of the university. In fact the brothers faced considerable opposition, and regular slander, over their experiments in social justice. The accusations made against them – such as reserving jobs and houses just for Quakers – had no foundation in reality, except for one.

The most difficult accusation flung at the Cadburys by their detractors was that they had for a period bought cocoa from São Tomé where working conditions were no better than slavery. George gave flowers to working men for their children, a sensitive gesture, but if he had to he was tough enough to sue in the courts. The accusation over cocoa slavery was printed in the *Evening Standard*, which pursued rival policies to that promoted in Cadbury's *Daily News*, and became the subject of a libel action brought by George. As with the Bryant & May situation, the events appear complicated, but the trial judge made it impossible for a hostile jury to clear the *Evening Standard* of the charge. Libel it was and the Cadburys were cleared of the accusations against them as unfounded in fact. However, although all costs were awarded against the *Evening Standard*, the jury gave contemptuous damages to the Cadburys of one farthing.[17] Gardiner is convinced that the Cadburys had done everything in their power to investigate the conditions of the cocoa workers, and shifted suppliers once reliable information was available. Deborah Cadbury fills out the story with the picture of a rather frail 70-year-old George giving evidence at the trial, and greatly relieved that the 'slanders hurled against us had been cleared'.[18] His nephew William Cadbury had been the key figure in this episode: more on him shortly. It was of course a political and much publicised trial, fought by the leading barristers of the day. Edward Carson, the counsel defending the *Evening Standard*, had previously defended the Marquess of Queensberry against Oscar Wilde's libel action and won. The Cadbury trial essentially represented a clash between the philosophies of Unionist conservatism which opposed free trade – arguing that exploitation of this sort was an inevitable outcome – and the Liberals who supported it. The ethics of it, however blameless the Cadburys may have been, stood at the heart of modern globalisation right into the twenty-first century – and there are no easy answers now, as then. Wages at or near starvation and slavery level may have been on the way out in the developed world, and in particular in its vanguard, Bournville, but has this scourge merely been pushed out of sight in a far-away developing country?

George Cadbury's whole life was devoted to turning industrial capitalism from a potential exploitation of ordinary working people to a system that served them. The question of sourcing raw materials in countries with nothing to mitigate that exploitation stands over his entire legacy: we return to it shortly.

Slavery, Pacifism, the League of Nations and the United Nations

We have already seen that many prominent Quakers were active in the anti-slavery movement. Although early Quakers owned slaves in America it was typical that they should be ahead of their time in abandoning this practice and then seeking its universal end. Hence why the accusations of the *Evening Standard* were so hurtful to the Cadburys. Quakers were involved in the movement to end the opium trade, and of course in the temperance movement, rather to the discomfort of some Quaker brewers.

We have seen that pacifism is a central Quaker belief, though this was not dogmatically held, and in the American Civil War some Quakers did take up arms, and not all were disowned for it. Pacifism is often misunderstood as an entirely passive stance, but for the Quakers, work towards peace and preventing war is as important as refusing to serve. Quakers met with Tolstoy, and, whether it was through such direct contact or through reading their literature, or both, Tolstoy was greatly influenced by them in his pacifism.[19] In turn Ghandi, a self-professed disciple of Tolstoy, must have indirectly also owed some of his pacifist thinking to the Quakers. Tolstoy suffered much vilification for his pacifism, and the Quakers too have been subject to prejudice on that count. When John Bright made an impassioned speech against the Crimean War it lost him his seat in Parliament.

Here I want to briefly focus on a more recent Quaker, Philip Noel-Baker (1889–1982) who was heavily involved in the formation of the

League of Nations. As a young man he was an athlete and ran for Britain at the Stockholm Olympic Games in 1912. During World War I he organised and led the Friends' Ambulance Unit attached to British troops in France, and afterwards became the first Sir Ernest Cassel Professor of International Relations at the University of London. We saw already that he was later elected as a Labour MP to Parliament, but he was also a renowned campaigner for disarmament who received the Nobel Peace Prize in 1959. In 1944 Noel-Baker was placed in charge of British preparatory work for the United Nations and the following year helped to draft the charter of the UN at San Francisco.

The connection between the UN and the Quakers does not stop there however: the Quaker United Nations Office (QUNO), set up in 1948, has operations both in New York and Geneva. Its parent body, the Friends World Committee for Consultation, has consultative status at the UN, alongside other religious organisations such as the Brahma Kumaris. Along with contemporary institutions like the various Rowntree Trusts, the QUNO is part of the Quaker legacy for peace and social justice in the twenty-first century. In 1947, the Quakers, represented by their two great relief organisations, the Friends Service Council and the American Friends Service Committee (which published *Speak Truth to Power*), were given the Nobel Peace Prize for their work. Another Quaker, Emily Greene Balch, the leader of the Women's International League for Peace and Freedom, shared the Nobel Peace Prize in the previous year with John Mott of the YMCA. This is a good place to also mention the work of the Quaker Eric Baker, a founding partner of the human rights organization Amnesty International, and who also served for a while as head of Quaker Peace and Social Witness.

The link is clear between Quaker activism at all levels, including such international forums as the UN and Amnesty International, and Quaker economics. Although activism draws in funds from all kinds of external sources – we saw for example that Queen Victoria gave financial assistance to the projects of Elizabeth Fry – Quaker wealth was a huge part of the story in early Quaker activism. So much fundraising is of a matched nature where initial backing is followed by further funding streams. Having their own industrial wealth as a base meant that Quaker activism could operate at much higher levels than charitable bodies starting from scratch. Quakernomics, then, is a philosophy of wealth creation which sought from the outset to put its wealth to social ends. We shall compare this philosophy later on with its opposite: one that declares that wealth creation has no business in civic life other than the generation of profit.

Chapter 12

INDUSTRIAL WELFARE AND QUAKER LAPSES

As Walvin says: 'While Quakers fought to distance themselves from the taint of commercial failure or wrong-doing, they were also not entirely happy with the rewards of success.'[1] This unease ran through their history and the evolution over time of their identity and manner of doing things in the world. The answer, again and again, was philanthropy. Walvin tells us that in 1768 Quakers were enjoined thus: 'let us impress it especially upon Friends in affluent circumstances, to submit to a becoming frugality in their manner of living, in order to relieve the wants of the needy of all denominations with a liberal hand.' Philanthropy is not random, however, and the 'needy' exist in a hierarchy of circumstances, from the absolutely desperate to the fraudulent. Hence a proper understanding both of poverty, and of its causes, was of great interest to the Quakers.

We saw earlier that Seebohm Rowntree published his *Poverty: A Study of Town Life* in 1901, rather late in the history of Quaker philanthropy. Its most important message was that a third of the population of York lived below the poverty line, even when in work, a figure almost identical to that in London. In other words wages at or below subsistence were still a reality at the start of the twentieth century, two hundred years after Alfred Darby I initiated the Age of Iron. Rowntree explains in his introduction that he did not want to draw on existing government reports (of the type most likely used by Engels, Marx and Disraeli); rather, he wanted to use an 'intensive' method, focussing on a single area, rather as Booth had done (with whom Rowntree corresponded).[2] Hence he decided to investigate every wage-earning family in York, all 11,560 of them. His breakdown of the causes of family poverty is revealing. The most significant factors were death of the principal wage earner (15 per cent), largeness of families (22 per cent), and low wages while in regular work (52 per cent).[3] For low wages to be far and above the most significant factor in poverty was an indictment of industrial capitalism in its first two hundred years. Whatever the prophets of the free market might say about wages finding a natural level, it is clear that the level for half of the workers in York was inadequate for raising a family, and this despite the above average wages provided by one of the city's leading employers, Rowntree's. At the same time Rowntree wanted to distinguish between 'primary' and 'secondary' poverty, the former being due to the kind of factors listed above, and the second made worse by wasteful spending, such as on drink.[4]

In a chapter on the pubs in York Rowntree comments on his visits to them: 'In a round of the public-houses which the writer made on Saturday evening in May 1901, the fact of their social attractiveness struck him very forcibly. It points to the need for the establishment on temperance lines of something equally attractive in this respect.'[5] I must admit I warmed to Rowntree on reading these lines. I can imagine him genuinely struck by the sociability of the working man's bar, even though he was himself a chocolate heir and a member of a religious group of the utmost sobriety. Indeed, unless one can enter such a place and find it genuinely attractive, it is hard to tackle any question of social justice with a clear eye. A literary contrast to the scene we can imagine of Rowntree in a bar might be early in Goethe's novel, *Faust*, in 'Auerbach's Cellar in Leipzig'. The protagonist, at a similar social remove from the working man, enters the bar, but the fantastical outcome is far from congenial and leads to violence. I would suggest that Goethe represents the romantic vision which rarely engages with the realities of life, preferring to endorse the superiority of the poet and the honour of duelling, while Quakers in contrast represent a deeply practical engagement with people of every social standing. While on a literary theme, Melville's protagonist in *Moby-Dick* – a man of astonishing erudition and culture – is deeply at home in the cut-price bar in Quaker Nantucket in the novel's opening. Melville chose the setting well for his purpose, which was to convey a radical equality.

Walvin tells us that Winston Churchill was urged to read Rowntree's *Poverty* at a dinner with Liberal politicians and was moved by the work. Apparently he wrote of it: 'Although the British Empire is so large, the poor cannot find room to live in it [...] they would have had a better chance of happiness, if they had been born cannibal islanders of the Southern seas [...] this festering life at home makes world-wide power a mockery, and defaces the image of God upon earth.'[6] It is easy to write this kind of thing; much harder to do anything about it of course.

Given the key role that poor wages played in poverty, Quaker employers, as we have seen, did their best to provide above average levels of pay. But beyond that, if they could create housing and facilities that were not 'Rachmanised', i.e., run by racketeers, and if they could provide sociability through temperance rather than drink, and if they could eradicate the usurers, then they would have made enormous strides to mitigate the worst impact of industrial capitalism on the working poor. Hence the model village, model town and garden city.

We have seen that Quaker model villages, epitomised in Cadbury's Bournville, were built out of company profits. Perhaps the first Quaker model village was in fact Portlaw in Ireland, built by the Malcomson family, who started a cotton mill in Co. Waterford in 1825. By 1844 the model village had 1,800 workers, and may well have been a pattern for later Quaker model villages, including Bessbrook in 1845 and Bournville in 1893. If Bournville became the quintessential Quaker model village, it also became a pattern for the world, inspiring many business and political leaders to visit and return – often to foreign countries – with plans to build something similar. These even included the American chocolate manufacturer Milton S. Hershey, of Hershey Bar fame.

Some Quaker Lapses

But despite all these efforts we have seen that Quakers as a group could fall from their high standards and make the same errors of judgement as other capitalists preoccupied with profit, or perhaps just the survival of their company. These include the collapse of Overend & Gurney, possibly the matchgirls' strike at Bryant & May, and events leading to the accusations in the *Evening Standard* that Cadbury's cocoa derived from modern-day slavery.

Other Quaker lapses include the odd behaviour of Joseph Rowntree in poaching employees and expertise from other companies, a kind of industrial espionage, early in his career. Walvin comments: 'Here was a prominent Quaker, upon whom praise has been lavished in high-toned abundance, who spent part of the formative years as head of his company actively poaching from other businesses'.[7] We also saw that Edward Wright, who developed the reverberatory furnace for smelting lead and effectively ran the Quaker Lead Company in the 1720s, had, along with other Quakers, fraudulently invested company funds in the South Sea Bubble. We saw that Samuel Galton, a Quaker with interests in science whose descendent founded the 'science' of eugenics, was disowned for manufacturing arms, though, strangely, was not prevented from worshipping at the Bull Street Meeting House in Birmingham. Coalbrookdale at one point cast some two thousand cannon and ancillary equipment for war, despite their pacifist principles. Marx accused Quaker mill owners of exploiting children, though I have not been able to trace the history of this.

What the Quaker lapses do show is that business is ever-evolving, and that all necessary attempts to regulate it are sometimes just playing catch-up, or clean-up, after the event. But the Quaker ethos itself is all the clearer for acknowledgement of these dangers: it is a determination backed by energy and money to make business socially responsible.

Cocoa Slavery

We return now to perhaps the greatest challenge that the outside world ever posed to the ethical capitalism of Quakernomics: the production of cocoa for Cadbury's, Fry's and Rowntree's by virtual slave labour on the island of São Tomé for a number of years. I want to present a few more details about this as a way of exploring how any attempt at an ethical capitalism by a group, even as large, determined and well-organised as the Quakers, is located within a sea of *unethical* capitalism. In the almost complete vertical integration of the Coalbrookdale operation Quakers had control over most aspects of the business, and we saw that once horse teams were brought under company control, abuses of workers in this incidental trade could be eliminated (and no doubt horses better treated). But abuses beyond Quaker control remained vast. The cynic will have already noted with glee the Quaker lapses within their control, and has an infinitely greater dataset to draw on to declare that capitalism beyond their best efforts shows itself as intrinsically a force for evil in the world. I can't answer the determined cynic, but I can moderate what might look so far like a naive and over-optimistic vision of Quakernomics, using the example of the cocoa slavery issue.

While the works by A. G. Gardiner and Deborah Cadbury exonerate the Cadburys from *any* blame over slavery in São Tomé, the author Lowell J. Satre, in a book-length treatment of the issue, is more measured. Apparently warning bells sounded in 1901, but it was 1909 before Cadbury's – and with them Fry's and Rowntree's – ended cocoa imports from the island. Eight long years of virtual slavery. As Satre's book chapter titled

'Careful Steps and Concern – or Dragging Feet and Hypocrisy?'
so eloquently puts it, doubt remains and the jury at the libel trial were
not entirely convinced by the Cadbury case. And here is why: the
cross-examination of William Cadbury by Carson at one point took
this turn:

CARSON: The cocoa you were buying was procured by atrocious
            methods of slavery?
CADBURY: Yes.
CARSON: Men, women and children taken forcibly away from
            their homes against their will?
CADBURY: Yes.
CARSON: Were they marched on the road like cattle?
CADBURY: I cannot answer that question. They were marched in
            forced marches down the coast.
CARSON: Were they labelled when they went on board ship?
CADBURY: Yes.
CARSON: How far had they to march?
CADBURY: Various distances. Some came from more than a
            thousand miles, some from quite near the coast.
CARSON: Never to return again?
CADBURY: Never to return.
CARSON: From the information which you procured, did they go
            down in shackles?
CADBURY: It is the usual custom, I believe, to shackle them at
            night on the march.
CARSON: Those who could not keep up with the march were
            murdered?
CADBURY: I have seen statements to that effect
CARSON: You do not doubt it?
CADBURY: I do not doubt that it has been so in some cases.[8]

Do not William Cadbury's admissions here cast a pall over the entire
ethical claims of the Cadbury business? If not over all of Quakernomics?
I have to admit that in all the material I examined in relation to the
Quaker enterprises, this created the most difficulty for me. A major
cause within Quaker activism had been the abolition of slavery, yet
here was William Cadbury in 1909 – long after the Slavery Act of 1833
abolished slavery within the British Empire – admitting that cocoa
used in the model factory of Bournville was produced by slave labour.

Does one not choke on one's morning cocoa, 'a most nutritious drink for breakfast', according to their advertising? Doesn't the slogan 'Absolutely Pure, Therefore the Best' now ring hollow?

On reflection, however, I think that this doubt should hang over capitalism in general, not Quakernomics. Under cross-examination one is only permitted to answer the question. But the missing qualification, which no doubt William Cadbury would have wanted to make, and which was extensively established in the trial, was that he was only sure of the facts once he had made his own much-publicised trip to São Tomé. In reality the Cadburys had invested a great deal of time and money, and also diplomatic effort with the Foreign Office, to establish facts, and to give the Portuguese authorities time to prove what they kept asserting: that they had abolished slavery in their colonies. This was the assurance given to Cadbury's time and time again. What Cadbury's was up against was a diplomatic jungle in which the *government* dragged its feet, not wishing to offend its trading partner. The answers that William Cadbury gave to Carson were about facts that, once he was sure of them, caused the immediate cessation of cocoa purchasing from the island.

However this doubt should remain, I think: perhaps Cadbury's pursued the wrong strategy. From the outset William Cadbury, with George's backing, was determined to improve conditions on the island, should the rumours they heard in 1901 prove to be true. Their rationale was this: that if they just walked away from the problem, by ceasing purchase of the crop, bad conditions would continue or get worse. Indeed, when they finally pulled out, despite their lobbying in America, other firms bought up the cocoa. But I think that the Quaker ethos over-extended itself here. The sea of unethical business practices in which Quakernomics stands as a largely ethical island was simply too big for any hope of success in this particular case. The diplomatic stalling by the Portuguese and British authorities – a veritable art-form of course – was part of a machine too large for even the combined forces of Cadbury's, Fry's and Rowntree's to fight. We saw that Bryant & May did persuade the government in 1910 to create a level playing field for phosphorous in Britain, though even that was too late for many victims of phossy jaw. But the chances of establishing a level playing field for black labour in colonial Africa at that time were infinitely smaller, and Cadbury's lost the gamble and also lost their moral high ground in the attempt. Racism was then too entrenched in the European philosophy of government and empire. Indeed Satre points out that public opinion at that time, influenced by the theories of Social Darwinism, was growing *less* sympathetic to the black African, not more.[9]

What this means for Quakernomics – and for any ethical capitalism – is that defeats from time to time are not just likely but inevitable. It is simply not possible to create an ethical capitalism that is unassailable, because of the interconnected nature of economic activity. The complete vertical integration of a business is rarely possible and efforts to insist on ethical practices in distant places are fraught with difficulty – still in the twenty-first century. There are accusations even today that some cocoa in the Ivory Coast is picked by child labour, effectively a form of slavery. The chief executive of the electronics giant Apple faced the same problems as George and William Cadbury did in 1909 in ascertaining the truth of labour practices in Apple's Chinese factories in 2012 – accusations of child labour were subsequently confirmed despite assurances by the authorities to the contrary. Hence the picture of Quakernomics presented so far has to be moderated with this insight: it is a struggle that is never-ending, and will bring failures from time to time. But, where the cynic just gives up on capitalism, Quakernomics keeps *trying*. If everybody gave up – and we will see arguments put forward for such a strategy in later chapters – the world would be a far worse place.

Chapter 13

QUAKERS AND OTHER ETHICAL CAPITALISTS

Walvin tells us: 'Few images of Victorian life remain more durable and popular than the bleak caricatures of the Industrial Revolution. Whatever historians have done to refine and modify them, these views persist. Yet even from the very early days of industrial change, certain employers sought to run their businesses without generating the worst forms of contemporary hardship and exploitation.'[1] The reader might be forgiven for imagining by now that Quakers were the only industrial capitalists of the age who practiced such philanthropy, but in fact there were many others, as Walvin implies. He qualifies his insight, however:

> There was a difference between these Quakers and other millionaire benefactors. Most others were above all else individualists: men who were edged towards such activities by personal factors – some religious, some secular. Quakers, however, came from a culture in which public service and good works were part of the warp and weft of their beliefs.[2]

Emden reminds us, as we saw earlier, that Methodism contained within it similar beliefs, and he goes on to include the Huguenots of France, the Calvinists of Geneva, the Covenanters of Scotland and the Puritans of England amongst those groups involved in commerce with philanthropic principles. While I have argued here that no religious group outside the Quakers ever achieved such a coherent presence in industrial capitalism on such a scale, the fact remains that the industrial philanthropy of these other groups, taken as a whole, was also highly significant, and it is worth examining some key, though perhaps solitary, examples.

In the autumn of 2011 the BBC screened a series called 'When Bankers Were Good', introduced by Ian Hislop, which looked at philanthropic

Victorian bankers including Samuel Gurney, George Peabody, Angela Burdett-Coutts and Natty Rothschild.[3] This series complemented Hislop's 'Age of the Do-Gooders'. Both of them were in effect a response to the challenge laid down by the British Conservative leader David Cameron with his idea of the 'Big Society', an idea presented as an alternative to what free marketeers castigate as 'big government'. Clearly, then, Quakernomics as a philanthropic capitalism could be taken as an argument for the 'Big Society', and against 'big government'. If millionaire and billionaire industrialists collectively placed significant portions of their wealth at the service of the poor, then why should the government raise taxes to do so? The history of Quakernomics is not exactly an argument against big government, however, an issue we return to. For now we look at philanthropy outside the Quaker tradition, in the legacies of Robert Owen, Milton S. Hershey, Titus Salt, William Lever and Andrew Carnegie, so as to gain a broader picture of it.

Robert Owen

Robert Owen (1771–1858) was a Welsh mill owner, social reformer and one of the founders of utopian socialism and the cooperative movement. We saw that the Quaker William Allen was involved in a group that included Owen, along with James Mill and Jeremy Bentham. Despite sharp differences with him, Allen had a financial interest in New Lanark, Owen's great experiment in industrial welfare. However Owen not only regarded all religions as 'based on the same ridiculous imagination', and criticised Allen for his Quaker beliefs, but also criticised him for his contacts with royalty in Europe and Russia.[4] But what is religiously ridiculous to one person is not to another, and in later life Owen turned to spiritualism. He is best known for his experiment with the model factory and village he set up in New Lanark, which was visited by social reformers, statesmen and royal personages, including Nicholas, later emperor of Russia. Owen eventually withdrew his interest in New Lanark, leaving Allen and the others still involved. One source suggest that 'in ruling the lives of his employees Owen was "as dictatorial as any hard-fisted mill boss [...] creating a closed society under benevolent despotism."'[5]

Owen was disgusted with the corrupt practice of the 'truck shop' – the company store – and, like the Quaker Lead Company managers, he opened an honest version with good quality products at little more than wholesale prices. He went further however because he based the shop on cooperative principles which became the foundation of the cooperative wholesale movement in Britain. 'Owenism' became an identifiable strand in socialist thinking, and has some common ground with the Quakers, but Owen seemed to want to place himself at the head of socialist movements, and lacked perhaps that deeply consensual nature that Quaker tradition inculcates in its members. His own writings show him at two removes from our concerns in this book. Firstly his utopian socialism is based on an imagined comprehensive overhaul of human nature, proposing for example: 'That the whole man must be re-formed on fundamental principles the very reverse of those in which he had been trained; in short, that the minds of all men must be born again, and their knowledge and practice commence on a new foundation.'[6] This, I would suggest, belongs more to evangelical religion than the sober Christianity or economics of the Quakers. Secondly, while cooperative ownership of businesses no doubt fosters a more ethical capitalism in those enterprises, it is a phenomenon too small to inform the real target of our enquiry here: how to make big capitalism ethical.

Milton S. Hershey and Chocolatetown

Milton S. Hershey (1857–1945) was an American confectioner from a Mennonite family who attended a Quaker school, and who modelled 'Chocolatetown' directly on Bourneville. (It is worth noting that in America there may be literally thousands of distinct Christian church organisations, out of which only three are known as the 'Peace Churches': the Amish, the Mennonites and the Quakers.) Hershey's philanthropy arose partly out of his childless marriage and the early death of his wife, resulting in his transferring the majority of his assets to an educational trust. Or, in a more romantic vein of speculation: did the fact that his wife's illness, which prevented the couple sailing on the Titanic and thus probably spared his life, incline him that way? In any case it is said of him: 'He was part of a forward-looking group of entrepreneurs in this country and abroad who believed that providing better living conditions for their workers resulted in better workers [...] Milton Hershey conceived of building a community that would support and nurture his workers. Developing the community became a lifelong passion for him.'[7]

As with Fry's and Cadbury's, Hershey's secured large contracts with the military for chocolate bars, and to this day the Hershey bar is an enduringly American product. The town named after Hershey where his factory was built is also a lasting legacy of philanthropic commitment to the civic sphere. At the age of 61 he anonymously gave away his entire fortune, an estimated value of $60 million in 1918, to endow a school for poor and orphaned boys.

Titus Salt and Saltaire

The life and work of businessman and philanthropist Titus Salt (1803–1876) is another example that closely resembles the Quaker pattern of industrialists. He entered Parliament, was honoured with a baronetcy, and created a model workers' village, in this case Saltaire in Bradford, West Yorkshire. We are not sure if he was Congregationalist by faith he but certainly endowed the village with a Congregational church, and also donated land for a Wesleyan Chapel, echoing the non-denominational pattern of Quaker tradition. He even forbade 'beershops' in Saltaire. He became one of the largest employers in Bradford and was its Liberal MP for many years. He was apparently a very private man and seemed to have no broader network for his philanthropy, outside the general connections required for a successful businessman.

William Lever and Port Sunlight

With William Lever (1851–1925) we can be surer of the Congregationalist origins of his philanthropy, though a later interest in Freemasonry led to the adoption of its principles in his company hierarchy. He was a soap manufacturer, and with his best-known product, 'Sunlight' soap, created fierce competition for Crossfield's 'Perfection' soap, as we saw (though a bigger rival was Pears). Lever built the model village of Port Sunlight near Liverpool, embodying similar philanthropic principles to Bournville.

Lever was a Liberal in politics and an MP for the Wirral constituency between 1906 and 1909. He used his maiden speech to the House of Commons to urge the government to introduce a national old age pension, such as the one he provided for his workers. His business relied on the import of palm oil and Lever has been criticised for the use of forced labour in the Congo in the horrific Belgian regime of the period, a practice decried by Belgian liberals but which continued up until independence in 1960. He was up against the same problems as Cadbury's, and their stories are a little intertwined because an anti-slavery activist working in the Congo thought the problems there far more significant than on São Tomé and didn't want the distraction of William Cadbury's efforts to deal with it.[8]

Andrew Carnegie

Andrew Carnegie (1835–1919) was the Abraham Darby of America, leading the enormous expansion of its steel industry in the latter half of the nineteenth century. Like another famous Scot, John Muir – who founded the American National Park System and the very tradition of ecology – Carnegie came from humble origins. His parents were weavers living in a single room cottage, who emigrated, like the Muirs, to America, where the young Andrew started as a telegraph messenger boy. In another parallel with Muir, Carnegie found his religion more in nature than in organised faith, though later in life he joined the Presbyterian Church. Hence his philanthropy did not arise, as with the Quakers, from the 'warp and weft' of received beliefs, but sprang from an inner impulse, perhaps inspired by the poverty of his childhood. We known much about his thinking from a tract he wrote called *The Gospel of Wealth*, which starts with this assertion: 'The problem of our age is the proper administration of wealth, so that the ties of brotherhood may still bind together the rich and poor in harmonious relationship.' Carnegie had become one of the richest men in America, but was determined that his family should inherit only in moderation. William K. Vanderbilt, son of the richest man in the world at his death, once said: 'Inherited wealth is as certain death to ambition as cocaine is to morality.' It is a common theme but Carnegie was absolutely serious about it. He, unlike so many rich people, was in favour of ever-higher death duties: 'The growing disposition to tax more and more heavily large estates left at death is a cheering indication of the growth of a salutary change in public opinion.' Not many of the super-rich seem to be cheered by any kind of tax, but Carnegie thought that this was the wisest form of taxation. He was happy to say that: 'By taxing estates heavily at death the state marks its condemnation of the selfish millionaire's unworthy life.'

Here he speaks just as a Quaker would:

This, then, is held to be the duty of the man of Wealth: First, to set an example of modest, unostentatious living, shunning display or extravagance; to provide moderately for the legitimate wants of those dependent upon him; and after doing so to consider all

surplus revenues which come to him simply as trust funds, which
he is called upon to administer, and strictly bound as a matter of
duty to administer in the manner which, in his judgment, is best
calculated to produce the most beneficial results for the community
[…] the man of wealth thus becoming the mere agent and trustee
for his poorer brethren, bringing to their service his superior
wisdom, experience and ability to administer, doing for them better
than they would or could do for themselves.[9]

There are several things to note in this remarkable passage. First that
he advocated an unostentatious living, as the Quakers did. Secondly
we cannot avoid the stark paternalism in the assumption that he would
do better for the poor than they could do for themselves (the Quakers,
I would suggest, evolved beyond this position in their thinking). But his
originality lies in this: that the surplus revenues of his business should
be considered as a *trust fund*. This is remarkable: it suggests an ethical
position in which surplus wealth is not owned by the entrepreneur, but
arrives in his or her hands as funds to be administered in trust for the poor.
At the same time Carnegie was not interested in conventional charity
which would distribute those funds as hand-outs, indeed he thought
such 'unearned' largesse to make things worse, not better. Hence his
legacy of educational trusts and establishments. His personal legacy was
mixed on at least one count however: the infamous Homestead Strike of
1892 at his main steel plant in Pennsylvania lasted 143 days and resulted
in 10 deaths and defeat of the unions.

As mentioned earlier, the Quaker John Bright was a great influence
on Carnegie, a 'favourite living hero in public life' for him, and Bright's
pacifism was part of the impetus behind Carnegie's interest in world
peace that led him to found the Carnegie Endowment for International
Peace in 1910. He later founded the Church Peace Union in 1914 on
the eve of World War I, and his vision was later incorporated into the
foundations of the League of Nations. All of this is well known, but I
have not found much acknowledgement of what should be an ethical
thunderclap to a selfish capitalism deaf to anything but profit: his idea
that surplus profit should be regarded as wealth held in trust for the poor.

Quakernomics and Ethics

In Chapter 10 I summarised the history of the Quaker enterprises as
a form of total capitalism. Having now brought together the various

enlightened practices and philanthropic ventures of the Quaker capitalists, and also considered the broader tradition of philanthropy beyond the Quakers, we can now summarise the claim I am making for Quakernomics as an ethical capitalism.

I introduced the idea of the 'Gross Quaker Product', or GQP, and a graph of this output for the two to three centuries of Quaker enterprise, and the idea that the area under the graph represents a substantial attempt at social responsibility, beyond which there lies the more fragmentary but substantial ethical capitalism of other philanthropists. We have now seen that profits generated by Quakernomics supported not just re-investment for growth and innovation of the enterprises themselves but the entry of Quakers into all aspects of public life, excepting of course the military. The profits of Quakernomics allowed Quakers to participate fully in the civic development of the new towns of the Industrial Revolution, shaping such things as town planning, labour laws, and the provision of education, health and pension rights. Beyond their immediate communities Quakers acted in Parliament and elsewhere to pursue the goals of peace, the end of slavery, and to mitigate the effects of alcohol abuse within the impoverished working classes. They were highly active in scientific societies, such as the Royal Society, and put their knowledge to good use in their industries, in pharmacy and in medicine.

The economists of the left and right are united in their interest in human flourishing but have different visions of exactly what this means. Since World War II they have also been united in seeking growth as the key to solving problems of social justice, as we will see. The Quaker vision of human flourishing contains within it an element that makes it left of centre: its emphasis on equality. This is couched in religious terms: 'to see that of God in everyone'. Rowntree went into the public houses of York and was moved by the palpable sociability of them; the Darbys worshipped with their workers – as did Fry and Cadbury – and in general the Quakers applied their principles of equality as far as they could while maintaining hierarchical management structures necessary for the running of businesses. They very often avoided honours, or accepted them only on the basis that it would further their philanthropic reach. But this reach was ultimately limited in a harsh world, and at times broke down. The various Quaker lapses that we have looked at should sober us as to the challenge that industrial capitalism ever poses, and in ever-changing guises. In arms, in bill-broking, in phosphorous, and above all in the disaster of cocoa slavery, the Quakers perhaps stumbled.

These exceptions should show that Quakernomics or any ethical capitalism is always a question of an endeavour that can fail, either through a momentary lapse of ethics, a lapse of judgement, or because the external forces of unethical capitalism become insurmountable.

We are now in a position to list the major evils of unregulated industrial capitalism, in advance of the second part of this book where we take a critical look at conventional economic thinking. It is important to stress that I reject many of the critiques of the left, including that of Marx, which declares capitalism an intrinsic evil. I have been arguing all along that Quakernomics, along with all forms of industrial capitalism, delivers the good things of life, 'the goods'. But I also use phrases like 'road-kill along the way' to economic flourishing, or the 'collateral damage' of industrial capitalism. I don't intend these terms cynically. Even when the ethics of the entrepreneur are impeccable the capitalism that flows from their efforts can have unintended negative consequences. And when the entrepreneur is careless or downright dishonest, the sheer scale of their enterprises and the nature of industrial production mean that the consequences can be terrible.

We have seen in the thinking of writers like Paine or Engels that unemployment is the first evil visited by capitalism on those disenfranchised from the earth. Once the means of production that nature bestows on the human animal are lost, the worker is at risk of being 'repudiated' by the employing class, as Engels puts it.

The second evil of industrial capitalism is perhaps subsistence wages. The spectre of unemployment is so awful in pre-welfare industrial societies that workers will accept wages so low as to only just prevent starvation. In post-industrial welfare societies we find that low wages can persist or return to the point where the state has to make up the shortfall, a form of taxpayer subsidy to private industry. The latter evil is not as harsh as the former, but it is still an indictment of industrial capitalism.

If employed, and even if wages are adequate, workers may face dangerous machinery, caustic or poisonous chemicals, or injuries from repetitive actions. The modern bugbear of 'health and safety' gone mad in popular thinking sometimes hides the realities of such dangers.

Finally, there are hazards to the environment that we are only just beginning to understand. Apparently 97 per cent of scientists who work in the field of climate change believe that global warming is due to human industrial activity. The accusation levelled against Quakernomics by Maggie Foster in *The Iron Bridge* has to be answered.

Part IV

INDUSTRIAL ETHICS AND ECONOMIC THOUGHT

Chapter 14

FROM MERCANTILISM
TO MARSHALL

I have constructed a detailed picture of the Quaker enterprises, the industrial welfare bound up in them, and the broader activism and contributions made to public life by the Quakers, greatly assisted by the wealth they had generated in their businesses. In this part of the book we leave all that behind as background to the contemplation of a different history: that of economic thinking as handed down to us by the acknowledged masters in the field. There are many valuable economic histories, such as Heilbroner's *The Worldly Philosophers*, which turn out to be a little hagiographic. A more sceptical survey will be conducted here on the basis that many economists come from professional classes with no experience of industry, and as Heilbroner's book title suggests, are prone to the intellectual habits of the philosophers. The grimy reality of the Quaker enterprises – encompassing the obduracy of materials like iron, the dangers of high-temperature workings and caustic chemicals, the limb-mangling potential of power-driven factories, the fickle realities of the free market, and above all the encounter with a workforce dependent on the very existence of employers to feed their families – will be the touchstone by which to examine the armchair theories of the writers we will encounter. The economic theories applied to the rise of industrial capitalism may at times be only the literary dalliances of the chattering classes; at other times they represent serious analysis. But the key question here, of ethical capitalism, has grim implications for those on the receiving end of the more dubious benefits of industrialisation. It is right then to examine economic theories as to whether their concepts and rhetorical expressions are usefully analytical or whether they serve the interests of one group over another.

By the late seventeenth century the prosperity of the Quakers had become well known,[1] hence it is rather baffling that this did not lead economists to examine their example. There is nothing but silence from them with only very rare remarks here and there: as we saw, Marx praises one Quaker, John Bellers, and indicts others who are mill owners. By Marx's time of writing *Capital*, in the mid-nineteenth century, Quaker products and banks were everywhere, yet he, like all the economists we consider here, remains uninterested in the phenomenon. We start our survey of economic thought earlier on, however, with a look at the Mercantilists and the Physiocrats, the classical economics of Adam Smith, Thomas Malthus, David Ricardo and John Stuart Mill, leading to the neoclassical economics of Alfred Marshall. We finish our survey with contemporary writers on economics, and along the way we shall make a digression into criticisms of economic justice from novels. Our key preoccupation in this rapid historical march is social justice and ethical capitalism. To what extent are writers on economics interested in the ethics of industrial capitalism? Are they indifferent to what could be called the collateral damage experienced by working people in the inescapable drive to industrialisation, and if not, do they propose measures to mitigate its worst effects? And where might their thought align itself in its *theory* with the *practice* of the Quakers in the economic sphere?

In other words we will ask: what in the works of the great thinkers might lead economic activity towards an ethical basis, and what might lead it away? For we must not doubt the impact of their writings. In an oft-quoted comment John Maynard Keynes said:

> The ideas of economists and political philosophers, both when they are right and when they are wrong, are more powerful than is commonly understood. Indeed, the world is ruled by little else. Practical men, who believe themselves to be quite exempt from any intellectual influences, are usually slaves of some defunct economist.[2]

The contemporary economist Paul Krugman helps us understand how this might work today, through the role of the 'policy entrepreneur': advisors to government, who, if not exactly slaves to defunct economists, are at the least partisan enthusiasts for one economic philosophy or another, often from decades previous.[3]

It is with these preoccupations that I have made the selection that follows. Many important thinkers in economics have naturally been left out in this brief survey, but the purpose here is to trace the arguments, often extreme versions of them perhaps, that directly impinge on the ethics of capitalism. Just as a reminder of what is at stake, here is a list of the evils of *unethical* capitalism as concluded with in the last chapter:

1. Unemployment
2. Subsistence wages
3. Health hazards
4. Environmental harm

Mercantilism and the Physiocrats

We start our survey in the obscurity of two economic principles of the eighteenth century: Mercantilism and the ideas of the Physiocrats. Mercantilism, the belief that foreign trade should be used as a tool for dominance in the international competition for wealth, was an economic doctrine that dominated much of the early Quaker period. This involved the use of tariffs on imported goods to support national industries and markets, and was criticised by most later economists who argued for free markets. The doctrine lead in Britain to the Corn Laws, which placed a high tariff on imported grain, and led to higher prices than would otherwise have existed for basic foodstuffs. We saw that Quakers, including John Bright, played a significant part in the abolition of those laws on the grounds that the higher grain prices impoverished working people and led only to the enrichment of the landed gentry.

François Quesnay (1694–1774) was a French economist of the Physiocratic school, remembered for his 'Economic Table' published in 1758. His work helps us focus on the role of food in the economy, and lets us consider land and water as basic means of production. Quesnay thought that 'productive expenditures' were those employed in 'agriculture, meadows, pastures, forests, mines, fishing, etc., to perpetuate riches in the form of grain, beverages, wood, cattle, raw materials for the handicrafts.' On the other hand he defined 'sterile expenditures' as those employed in 'handicraft products, housing, clothing, interest on money, servants, commercial expenses, foreign commodities, etc.'[4] No economist today believes in this distinction of course, but it does remind us that all economic activity must have its ultimate basis in food production, and that a significant part of economic injustice historically, today, and potentially more so in the future, is when a person is separated from this most basic means of production.

For subsequent economic writers their argument with Quesnay and his school is over the origins of 'value'. For Adam Smith it was not located in agriculture, but in human labour, and the 'labour theory of value' has had a long and interesting history since that time. The Quakers were not much concerned with economic *theory* of course, but their journey from agriculture into industrial commerce usefully places the argument between Quesnay and Smith in context.

Adam Smith

It is often said that Adam Smith (1723–1790) is the father of economics, or political economy, as a science. His book *The Wealth of Nations* is perhaps the first really substantial work of political economy, and the Quaker businesses of his period – which he never mentions – were well established by the time of its publication in 1776. Smith lived during the mercantilist period, and his work includes extensive arguments against its principles. He also disagreed with the Physiocrats, devoting Chapter 9 of his book to their shortcomings.

Smith's key contributions to economic thought are in two related theories: wealth as the result of the division of labour and wealth as a result of free trade. He is perhaps most famous for proposing that the market distributes goods in the best possible way, through the 'invisible hand':

> As every individual, therefore, endeavours as much as he can, both to employ his capital in the support of domestic industry, and so to direct that industry that its produce maybe of the greatest value; every individual necessarily labours to render the annual revenue of the society as great as he can. He generally, indeed, neither intends to promote the public interest, nor knows how much he is promoting it. By preferring the support of domestic to that of foreign industry, he intends only his own security; and by directing that industry in such a manner as its produce may be of the greatest value, he intends only his own gain; and he is in this, as in many other cases, led by an invisible hand to promote an end which was no part of his intention.[5]

This is a key passage and perhaps the most quoted of Smith's ideas now. He is suggesting that in the very nature of economic activity the individual entrepreneur is pursuing self-interest that is at the same time, and in perhaps a rather mysterious way, the public interest. This self-interest promotes the public interest despite it being in no part of the entrepreneur's intention. Does this square with Quaker business activity? To some degree, yes. The Quakers would take it as an article of faith that their individual flourishing meant the flourishing of the community as a whole, and that to some extent this was both mysterious – in religious terms *providential* – and had outcomes that could not be seen with any precision. But they would sharply disagree with Smith that they did not intend 'to promote the public interest' – this was as much their motivation as was profit. Cooking pots from Coalbrookdale were for the public interest; chocolate from Fry was medicinal, and for Cadbury and Rowntree an alternative to alcohol. For all of them a considerable proportion of profits were devoted to the betterment of the working poor.

Neither would Quakers agree with the way that Smith continues his passage on the 'invisible hand' with further thoughts on the self-interest of the entrepreneur. He says:

> By pursuing his own interest, he frequently promotes that of the society more effectually than when he really intends to promote it. I have never known much good done by those who affected to trade for the public good. It is an affectation, indeed, not very common among merchants, and very few words need be employed in dissuading them from it.

Smith believes it to be an 'affectation' to want public good out of private business, or to use modern terms, for a business to take on corporate social responsibility. For the Quakers this was simply not true: it was never an affectation, but rather at the core of their activities. When Quakers either fell from their own ideals, or quit the Society of Friends, or were expelled from it, it was not a case of being dissuaded from this 'affectation' – they rather just descended to the level that Smith advocates as the norm. When he says 'I have never known much good done by those who affected to trade for the public good' he clearly knew nothing of the Quaker tradition, or indeed of other contemporary philanthropic capitalists. But he anticipates the modern formulation of the same idea in the work of Milton Friedman, as we shall see.

In a passage as often cited as the one on the 'invisible hand', Smith says this: 'It is not from the benevolence of the butcher, the brewer, or the baker, that we expect our dinner, but from their regard to their own interest. We address ourselves, not to their humanity, but to their self-love, and never talk to them of our own necessities but of their advantages.'[6] I think the Quakers would regard this as a half-truth. As businesspeople they expected to be paid a fair price for their products or services, but they *continuously* addressed themselves to the humanity of everyone they met.

The general tenor of Smith's writing suggests a philosophy open to questions of economic justice – he was after all a moral philosopher – but in the extracts just quoted there is a certain bleakness regarding human nature. I think that he misses an essential element of economic activity, the *human* exchange bound up with it. Of course businesspeople have to make a profit, as a bottom line, but what in that would deny a proper friendship with the butcher, the brewer and the baker? And what in the fundamentals of economic exchange means that the butcher, the brewer and the baker, once their business is secure in its flourishing, are *not* addressable in their humanity? Why should we not speak to them about the broader necessities of the community? Or ask them about their grandchildren? It is a great loss to the discourse of economics that we forget that much economic exchange also involves the exchange of friendship.

Let us continue with a trawl through Smith's ideas on the general nature of economic activity. He is clearly enthusiastic about economic life in general and is interested in the increase of wealth or 'improvement', as he likes to call it. His basic understanding of the engine of economic life as it were – outlined in his introduction – is that 'capital stock' is what can put labourers to work, so if the former is increased then so are the number and good conditions of the latter.[7] Clearly, the Quakers would not disagree with this, having no socialist qualms about being the originators and deployers of 'capital stock'. Neither would the Quakers disagree with another essential insight of Smith's – that the division of labour is crucial in industrial production, and key to the generation of wealth. His famous example is that of making pins – commemorated as visibly on the British twenty pound note as Fry's reforms are on the five pound note – though he also mentions nail making, a trade familiar to the Quaker ironmasters. In his words: 'The division of labour, however, so far as it can be introduced, occasions, in every art, a proportionable increase of the productive powers of labour.'[8] He doesn't mention it, but watch- and clock-making in that era were highly divided in their stages of manufacture, and again Quakers were deeply familiar with this. But Smith's argument feels a little forced at times, for example when he describes a country workman who is obliged to turn his hand to many different trades, and hence frequently changes his tools. Smith believes that this leads to indolence, which is doubtful. One cannot imagine the Darbys made more indolent or 'incapable of vigorous application'[9] on account of them running a farm, a forge, a railway and a canal, and engaging in extensive public philanthropy. In the construction of their model towns and villages they were keen to provide workers with an opportunity to grow their own food in small gardens: did that lead to indolence?

Smith gives support to the Quaker brewers in this passage (should they be worried?): 'The employment of a brewer, and even that of a retailer of fermented liquors, are as necessary divisions of labour as any other.'[10] In other words an economy needs a full spectrum of activity.

Like most economists of the era Smith speculated on the wages necessary to sustain life, for example that a worker must earn double his own subsistence to bring at least two children into the world to reproduce labour, given that one will not survive. He insists that wages in general should be above the lowest subsistence 'consistent with common humanity' and declares:[11]

No society can surely be flourishing and happy, of which the far greater part of the members are poor and miserable. It is but equity, besides, that they who feed, clothe, and lodge the whole body of the people, should have such a share of the produce of their own labour as to be themselves tolerably well fed, clothed, and lodged.[12]

This passage indicates a concern for social justice, but one wonders quite how he hoped for its fulfilment, as he fails to suggest any route to this 'equity' – a typical stance of the right-of-centre economists, as we shall see. (We also now generally desire more than a working population 'tolerably well' fed, clothed and housed: in a meritocracy we demand the equal opportunities that education, amongst other things, brings.)

Perhaps rather naturally for the period, Smith thinks that there is very limited scope for public works: roads and other communications should be privately built. The early Quakers, as we saw, were just the kind of entrepreneurs to achieve the private building of roads, bridges, canals and railways. Smith concedes however that some things, such as the military defence of colonial trading, are naturally the realm of state provision.[13] We would now regard the idea of the private initiation and building of infrastructure as unworkable in the modern world: it has changed too much since Smith's time. But there are those who take the letter of Smith's legacy, rather than its rounded approach, as support for extreme free market policies.

Historically it is Smith's work that has perhaps had the most weight of ethical interpretation placed on it. His ideas were forged however just prior to the worst impact of industrialisation on the working poor, and at considerable remove from the experiences of a man like his younger contemporary Abraham Darby III. It was from the blast furnace of the latter that the metal flowed for the construction of the Iron Bridge, and which heralded the era of industrial capitalism. Hence I would suggest that Smith simply lacked both the data and the first-hand experience to leave us any definitive capitalist ethic for the modern world.

Thomas Robert Malthus

The Reverend Thomas Robert Malthus (1766–1834) was an Anglican clergyman who published his famous *An Essay on the Principle of Population* in 1798. The essay was so influential, particularly on evolutionary thinkers, that the term 'Malthusian' came into the English language to signify a belief that human populations will always outstrip food production, leading to continued misery. Of course this misery is to be experienced by the working people whose incomes will fluctuate about subsistence level, and not by people of the class of Malthus, Smith and, as we shall see, Ricardo. Malthus' real aim in the essay was to settle the argument between 'the friend of the present order of things' who condemns the idea of progress out of the fear that they will be made relatively worse off by it (for example through advances in social justice) and 'the speculative philosopher' who equally offends against truth by imagining the perfectibility of the human condition.[14] The latter, for Malthus, included Adam Smith.

Malthus' argument boils down to these two postulates: 'First, That food is necessary to the existence of man. Secondly, That the passion between the sexes is necessary and will remain nearly in its present state.'[15] He goes on to say:

> Assuming then my postulata as granted, I say, that the power of population is indefinitely greater than the power in the earth to produce subsistence for man. Population, when unchecked, increases in a geometrical ratio. Subsistence increases only in an arithmetical ratio.

The remainder of his essay is spent in proving these two points: that agricultural production can only increase in a linear fashion, while population will increase in an exponential fashion. The arguments appear convincing, and there have been times when his ideas have apparently received support, for example in the Club of Rome's *Limits to Growth* in 1972 which applied greater scientific and mathematical precision to similar forecasting. But on both his basic postulates technology and culture have intervened – for at least a hundred years – by which agricultural production has vastly increased and populations in Western-style economies have tended to stabilise. Agriculture, particularly after the so-called 'green revolution' in the 1960s, has led to massive increase in food yields and the steady decline in the proportion of household budgets spent on food (though that may be increasing again by small amounts). At the same time the invention of contraception and the aspirations of women beyond the home have ensured smaller families.

Historically, Malthus has been proved spectacularly wrong – up to now. But for the future the population and food production curves look less optimistic, perhaps, particularly if global warming and other environmental changes are to have the impact that most scientists predict.

David Ricardo and John Stuart Mill

John Stuart Mill (1806–1873) was perhaps the most influential English-speaking philosopher of the nineteenth century. His *Principles of Political Economy*, published in 1848, built on the work of previous writers in the field, in particular David Ricardo (1772–1823) who was a friend of his father, James Mill. Ricardo was something of a tutor to the young Mill, but a nervous breakdown at 20 led Mill to reject the strict utilitarianism of Jeremy Bentham and his father, and the purely 'scientific' approach of Ricardo. Instead he absorbed more romantic elements of thought, and this probably led to the much stronger interest in social justice in his political economy. And it is this which makes one regret most, amongst these early theorists, that the details of Quaker industrial and financial practice were not available to him as they are to us.

Before considering the work of Mill it is worth looking at the influential publication by his mentor David Ricardo, *On the Principles of Political Economy and Taxation* (1817). Ricardo was born into a Jewish family of Portuguese origins who disowned him on his marrying a Quaker. Ricardo became a wealthy stockbroker, and was inspired by reading Adam Smith's work to publish his own writings on political economy. His major contributions lie in the area of rent and 'comparative advantage' – an idea still used today by economists in the field of international trade.

It has to be said that Ricardo's *Principles* looks uncongenial to those with an interest in social justice. Where Adam Smith has a certain balance in his outlook, Ricardo is entirely on the side of capital, entirely against the poor laws designed for the relief of the destitute, and extremely reluctant to allow that taxation for poor relief, or anything else for that matter, could be a good thing. In him we find the true precursor to Milton Friedman – to jump ahead a little – and it is no surprise to find that of Marx's precursors it is Ricardo that Marx most wishes to oppose the arguments of.

Ricardo once wrote a letter to Malthus in which he said: 'Labour, like all other things which are purchased and sold, and which may be increased or diminished in quantity, has its natural and its market price. The natural price of labour is that price which is necessary to enable the labourers, one with another, to subsist, and perpetuate their race without either increase or diminution.'[16] This has been called the 'iron law of wages', but one unfortunate turn of Ricardo's phrasing surely stands out when referring to the 'natural' wage of labourers. He talks of the level necessary to 'perpetuate their race'. What 'race'? Are labourers somehow of a race to which Ricardo himself does not belong? This is an *appalling* idea. The Quaker factory owners at Coalbrookdale met with their workers in the company offices for Meeting for Worship in the certain knowledge that they were all of one race, enjoined by Fox 'to meet that of God in everyone'. This is totally missing in Ricardo's work, despite the fact that he married a Quaker and subsequently became a Unitarian, a tradition with a similar lack of hierarchy. He belonged to a world of privilege, culturally sanctioned in its certainty that the 'other race' – Disraeli's other 'nation' – was destined to forever live at a level just sufficient for its reproduction, a race, however 'who feed, clothe, and lodge the whole body of the people' – as Smith put it – including Ricardo himself. Hence his thought is largely a repudiation of Quakernomics.

With this in mind we now turn to Mill's work, interested to see if he rises above the indifference of his mentor on questions of social justice. It was a text more widely read than Ricardo's, becoming the standard work on economics at the University of Oxford until 1919 when it was replaced by the work of Alfred Marshall. While Mill's *Principles* might be of interest as a general and rather incremental development of economic theory in the classical school, of more importance are the posthumously published *Chapters on Socialism*. These brief notes were written in the years prior to his death and subsequently published in 1873 by Helen Taylor, his stepdaughter. Where his *Principles* are strongly free market, his later *Chapters on Socialism* opens the way to a considered debate on alternatives that could lead to greater social justice while preserving freedom.

But first, Mill's defence of capitalism in his *Principles*. It is written, unlike the works of his predecessors, in considerable knowledge of proposed socialist alternatives. Change is in the air. Put briefly, Mill wants to defend private property and entrepreneurial competition, and insists that this competition lowers prices and makes goods available for the greater benefit of working people. He sees socialism's greatest criticism of capitalism, the rejection of competition, as its weakest argument.[17] In fact there is little in this that the Quakers of the period would have argued with. They had no difficulty with competition, profit or the argument that industrial capitalism turned out affordable necessities for ordinary people. Hence it is more interesting to turn to the later *Chapters on Socialism* to see where there might be common ground on the question of social justice. Here it is immediately clear that the great change overtaking British society uppermost in Mill's mind is this: the impending universal male franchise. If all working men were to have the vote – and steps in that direction were being incrementally taken throughout this period – then, being such a vast majority, would they not vote against *all* privilege, and even private property?

Mill's chapters are written after the 1867 Reform Act, which extended voting to working men, but in practice brought change only very slowly. Mill is certain that the limited use of workers' new powers would be only temporary however: 'they will before long find the means of making their collective electoral power effectively instrumental to the promotion of their collective objects.'[18] In fact, one of the great political mysteries often put forward by socialists since that time is the obvious fact that working people have so often voted against their class interests. Mill of course detects a certain confusion in expressing those interests, created mostly by the extreme demands of the socialists for the end of private property and the end of usury – lending at any interest level at all.

But Mill has a conscience. He says the following about the workers, along lines very similar to Engels (and somewhat hedged around by Disraeli in *Sybil*):

No longer enslaved or made dependent by force of law, the great majority are so by force of poverty; they are still chained to a place, to an occupation, and to conformity with the will of an employer, and debarred by the accident of their birth both from the enjoyments, and from the mental and moral advantages, which others inherit without exertion and independently of desert. That this is an evil equal to almost any of those against which mankind have hitherto struggled, the poor are not wrong in believing.[19]

But what is the solution? Here Mill becomes highly speculative, and at the same time inevitably betrays his own fortunate birth and the inherited assumptions that go with it. We may note that he already considers the working person to be denied – by birth – both 'mental and moral advantages'. In contrast Quakers – being constitutionally outsiders to the world of privilege by birth – regarded working people as mentally and morally equal, though mostly denied education, and it is that which they sought to rectify amongst their workers. They certainly did not believe that anyone could inherit mental and moral advantages 'without exertion and independently of desert'.

   The Quakers were in fact practical optimists regarding working-class poverty – and it is 'Poverty' which Mill considers their chief evil – where Mill is something of a theoretical pessimist. He says, for example: 'The very idea of distributive justice, or of any proportionality between success and merit, or between success and exertion, is in the present state of society so manifestly chimerical as to be relegated to the regions of romance.'[20] Here Mill is effectively opposing the great tide of Enlightenment thought which was deeply optimistic that society was moving inexorably from aristocracy to meritocracy, a meritocratic tendency that the Quakers had greatly availed themselves of. To back up this pessimism Mill quotes the passage from Louis Blanc cited in Chapter 2 on how competition between workers would drive their wages down far below subsistence.

Alfred Marshall

Alfred Marshall (1842–1924) is known as one of the founders of the neoclassical school in economics. His *Principles of Economics* (1890) was the dominant economic textbook in England for many years, replacing that of Mill. The opening of Marshall's work spells out, like no similar work that we have so far looked at, what poverty means. He says for example: 'the study of the causes of poverty is the study of the causes of the degradation of a large part of mankind.'[21] It is clear that Marshall cares about this, and the context of his caring is his strong religious outlook. He is confident that 'affections towards God and man' in working people can lead to lives more complete than some of those with wealth (I believe this is both observably true and one of the most compelling arguments against the accumulation of riches), but mostly poverty is a 'great and almost unmixed evil' to the poor. He insists that it matters that people's lives are 'incomplete' through poverty, because, apart from actual physical suffering, they have no chance of developing their higher faculties. Here he is in complete agreement with Mill and the liberal tradition – and also with Marx. Marshall continues by commenting that industrial progress – including the steam-engine as relieving men from 'much exhausting and degrading toil' – has brought great improvement, and its potential is to continue that improvement of the working classes. But to achieve the goal of a 'cultured life' for all raises questions that 'cannot be fully answered by economic science.' Once again we have a clear goal but no clear route yet envisaged to it.

Like Mill, Marshall is keen to defend competition, presumably because socialist theories demanding its end were much debated at the time. For Marshall, competition is an accident of modern industrialism which involves in fact much cooperation, as I have commented on earlier. He admits that 'competition' is an unsavoury term but argues that: 'It is deliberateness, and not selfishness, that is the characteristic of the modern age', and goes on to defend not only the basic idea of competition but to argue that trust in business is also a key aspect of modernity.[22] However he does agree that: 'If competition is contrasted with energetic co-operation in unselfish work for the public good, then even the best forms of competition are relatively evil; while its harsher and meaner forms are hateful.'[23] In the history of socialistic ventures, he adds, ordinary people are not capable of pure altruism for any long period, unless they are perhaps deeply religious (or, I would add in the Soviet context, unless forced to by a police state.) But his crucial comments for an ethical economics are these:

> No doubt men, even now, are capable of much more unselfish service than they generally render: and the *supreme aim of the economist* is to discover how this latent social asset can be developed most quickly, and turned to account most wisely. But he must not decry competition in general, without analysis: he is bound to retain a neutral attitude towards any particular manifestation of it until he is sure that, human nature being what it is, the restraint of

competition would not be more anti-social in its working than the competition itself.[24] (My emphasis.)

Socialists who decry competition itself will probably see in this extract only a defence of what they loathe, but the key – and remarkable – element in it is the idea that the 'supreme aim' of the economist is to discover how the latent social asset of altruism can be developed and wisely applied.

Marshall thinks that Ricardo achieved great things in economic thinking but in a very narrow scope. So how does Marshall extend that scope? Does Marshall live up to his opening remarks? The answer to these questions lies in the term 'microeconomics' – the study of individual markets and industries, as opposed to the study of the whole economy – the rigorous pursuit of which Marshall introduced. Here is the problem for us however: Marshall's motives are known in his life and set out early in his text, but the ethical basis and the quest for economic justice then gets rather lost in the sober development of microeconomics as a science. About halfway through his text he does turn again to the question of economic justice, framed, as so often, as a question of the *distribution* of wealth: 'What', he asks, 'are the general causes which govern the distribution of this surplus among the people?'[25] He is concerned about subsistence wages and thinks that when Adam Smith talked about the 'natural' rate of wages he inclined 'careless readers to suppose that he believes the mean level of the wages of labour to be fixed by an iron law at the bare necessaries of life.' He disagrees with Malthus, adding: 'This law has been called, especially in Germany, Ricardo's "iron" or "brazen" law: many German socialists believe that this law is in operation now even in the western world; and that it will continue to be so, as long as the plan on which production is organized remains "capitalistic" or "individualistic"; and they claim Ricardo as an authority on their side.'

Marshall's optimism on economic justice is perhaps epitomised in this statement which he then makes: 'highly paid labour is generally efficient and therefore not dear labour; a fact which, though it is more full of hope for the future of the human race than any other that is known to us will be found to exercise a very complicating influence on the theory of distribution.'[26] Quakers recognised the truth that well paid labour is efficient, but the history of low wages, right into the twenty-first century, suggests that Marshall's qualification is right: whatever the 'complicating' effect on the *theory* of distribution, the fact is that the reality of low wages remains as the greatest question of global economic justice. I have suggested that highly paid labour may well be efficient, and that Quakers understood this, but that their high levels of industrial welfare were prompted by motives far beyond such enlightened self-interest. And beyond this Marshall does not go.

Ethical Capitalism: First Assessment

Having looked at key early works of political economy, writings that span the classical and begin the neoclassical period, we are in a position to make some early generalisations about theories of ethical capitalism within the emerging discipline. We have to conclude that in this group of thinkers, comprising the Mercantilists, Physiocrats, Adam Smith, Thomas Malthus, David Ricardo, John Stuart Mill and Alfred Marshall, we have at best a desultory engagement with such a concept. At one extreme we find that Ricardo regards working people as a separate race bound by a law that would be named after him and characterised as 'iron' or 'brazen', and which presumed them condemned forever to subsistence wages. There is nothing to regret in this: it is the natural order. At another extreme we find that Marshall wants to eliminate the 'great and almost unmixed evil' of poverty amongst working people and regards the supreme aim of the economist to be the encouragement of unselfish service from all. Smith, perhaps in the middle, believes that the best result will come from the 'invisible hand' and that it is futile to encourage the businessman to trade unselfishly or for the common good. Indeed it is only by the time of Marshall that 'capitalism' as a concept distinct from economic activity had gained much currency, and that any possible alternative might exist. Marshall, it seems, was making a positive response to the idea of an ethical capitalism, but it was based on the possibility of encouraging a different kind of behaviour rather than on any prescriptive economic theory. This may well be because his contribution lies in the field of microeconomics and that it is perhaps in the field of macroeconomics where the real ethical questions and economic policies lie. We will bear this in mind with later, macroeconomic, thinkers.

So far then we have a discipline called 'political economy' – segueing perhaps into just 'economics' in Marshall – which either fails to demonstrate in its remit any necessity for an ethical capitalism, or which demonstrates it but fails to propose a solution. It is true that all are interested in the general human flourishing that wealth creation brings but they propose no precise mechanisms to militate against unemployment, subsistence wages, and health and environmental hazards. We now turn to Marx to examine, if not a theory of ethical capitalism, at least a theory of unethical capitalism.

Chapter 15

KARL MARX

We have briefly surveyed the major early economists, taking us up to
1890. It is now time to go back a little to *Capital*, the key economic
work by Karl Marx (1818–1883), to discover the major early expression
of socialist opposition to mainstream economic theory. *Capital* was first
published in 1867. Marx was considered by the later economist Joseph
Schumpeter to be, as an economic theorist, a 'pupil of Ricardo',[1] but
Marx's work is nothing like that of John Stuart Mill who really was
his pupil. One of Marx's life-long interpreters, the British historian
Eric Hobsbawm, tells us that early reactions to *Capital* actually gave
no indication of the later polarisation of thought in the field that it
would create: for example an American professor in the late nineteenth
century placed the work 'on par with Ricardo'.[2] Others took its major
propositions in their stride, though generally gave it no great status:
Marshall for example mostly made remarks in footnotes on it. Marshall
found *Capital* to have little to offer, saying of socialists in general: 'what
they regarded as the scientific foundation of their practical proposals
appears to be little more than a series of arguments in a circle to the
effect that there is no economic justification for interest, while that
result has been all along latent in their premises; though, in the case of
Marx, it was shrouded by mysterious Hegelian phrases, with which he
"coquetted", as he tells us in his Preface.'[3]

It is impossible in a short section to cover the history of Marxist
thought and its development in the later thinkers. All that can be done
here is to briefly see how the *practice* of Quakernomics contrasts with
the *theories* of Marx in *Capital*, leaving aside the practice of Marxist
economics in Soviet Russia and elsewhere, claimed by many socialists
to have anyway failed to put the theory into practice. Or, putting it
another way, we are interested in how *Capital* adds to our understanding
of unethical capitalism, and what measures it proposes to ameliorate
those shortcomings.

Marx's *Capital* can be seen as doing three things: firstly documenting the appalling conditions of workers in the factories of the Industrial Revolution; secondly analysing 'capitalist' economics and its failings; and thirdly – here and there – dropping hints about the revolution and what society would look like after the inevitable collapse of capitalism 'under its own contradictions'. Where the Quakers and Marx – and for that matter Engels, Disraeli, Mill and Marshall – are united is in their interest in social justice. However, I am not at all sure that Marx's *Capital* of 1867 adds anything to Engels' *The Condition of the Working Class in England* of 1848 as an exploration of working-class poverty, though there is no doubt that Engels and Marx, with their revolution-inclined works, predated the studies by Charles Booth (focussing on London) and Seebohm Rowntree (focussing on York) by some decades. The contrast is enormous however: Engels and Marx thought the only solution was the end of private ownership and the 'expropriation of the expropriators' (workers taking over the factories), while the reports of Booth and Rowntree, along with the Fabian Society, suggested a 'gradualist' approach and led indirectly to the British welfare state. A central element of Marxist thought is that of class war. Marxist economic theory alleges that the capitalist system exists to funnel capital to where it can exploit labour. The workers have their surplus labour stolen from them, and the inevitable outcome is war between the working classes and the capitalist, in which the proletariat is destined to win. Leaving for now the validity or otherwise of Marx's prognosis, it will be obvious from the Quaker tradition that anything resembling 'war' is against their deeply held principles of peace. What the Quakers did, within a paternalistic framework, was to create a partnership with workers, where the enterprise was conceived of as a collaborative effort, and management did everything to provide those incremental 'Fabian' improvements.

Let us return to *Capital*. Its presentation of the sufferings of the working class may add nothing to that in Engels' early work, and its theories of revolution are detailed elsewhere in the works of Marx. What, then, of its economic analysis, its real claim to fame? In the chapter titled 'Ten (or so) Famous Economists' in *Economics for Dummies*, the authors excuse the fact that Marx gets more space than, for example Ricardo or Marshall, but they need it to discredit his theories. The implication is that he is more wrong than the others, all of whom put forward theories that are also disputed, or perhaps that Marx is totally wrong.[4] Is he, as an economic thinker, totally wrong? As Schumpeter points out, Marx inherited many of Ricardo's theories and set out to develop or disprove them, the most important of which is the labour theory of value. I would suggest in fact that *Capital* stands or falls on this. There is not space here to go into the convoluted development by Marx of the labour theory of value, other than to say that he insists that the entire value of a commodity lies with the labour 'congealed' in it, and that the capitalist, with raw materials and machinery, adds nothing. Indeed the lengthy exposition of this in the first volume of *Capital* can be summed up by a little equation that Marx slips into the text: '$c = 0$'.[5] The term 'c' stand for 'constant capital', which is everything the capitalist brings to production, in contrast to the labour that the workers bring, termed 'v' to stand for 'variable capital'.

With this little equation Marx, without drawing on any empirical evidence, asserts to the world his prejudice: that capitalists contribute nothing, zero, '0'. The fact that it appears so suddenly in this equation is what makes his work little more than pseudo-science, though in fairness, quite a bit of mainstream economics is hardly more rigorous. Marx asserts that workers are cheated of 50 per cent of their labour. There is no empirical basis to this either; clearly Marx plucked the figure out of the air, and repeated it so often that he came to believe in it. This idea gave rise historically to the demand that workers should receive the full value of the products they make. If we translated this into either the ironworks at Coalbrookdale or the Bryant & May match factory, this would entitle the workers to share the entire *gross* profits of the enterprise. Even in the sane version of this, where we talk about *net* profits, how would this work? If the workers had simply taken ownership of those enterprises and set their wages to an equal division of the net profit, then two things would absent themselves immediately: the availability of profit as capital for future development either in those firms or elsewhere, and the innovative mind of the entrepreneur.

However, we are interested, as with all the economists under consideration here, as to how Marx views subsistence wages, that is wages so low as to bring the worker and his family to the edge of starvation. On this it cannot be doubted: Marx is magnificent in his concern, if not his analysis. We saw that while a thoughtful economist like Marshall set out his goal to be the liberation of the worker from poverty, from 'exhausting and degrading toil', there is little or nothing in Marx's following analysis that directly pertains to that goal. Everything Marx writes is fuelled by his anger at the social injustice of labour exploitation, *as he sees it*. It makes it inevitable, perhaps, that he accepts the basic premise of Malthus that population growth would outstrip economic growth, or at least the miserable share in the growth of wealth allotted to the worker. It also drives perhaps his certainty that profits in competitive capitalism would perpetually shrink, and therefore force employers to continuously reduce wages, the so-called 'perfect competition' of economic theory. It also drives his theories of productive and unproductive work. He is cynical of classical definitions of productive work, for example that of Smith, because he sees work so labelled because it creates profit for the capitalist. And so there is no hope for capitalist production: it must be overthrown.

What Marx's theories cannot entertain therefore is the concept of a fair wage under capitalism. Because he is concerned to show that capitalism is essentially an evil, and its demise inevitable, he is not interested in exploring its moderation. Hence Quakernomics would be, it seems, of no interest to the Marxist tradition, which could not accept the idea that a group of employers may have paid a fair wage to their workers, or investigate what it would mean, or how to legislate for it. After all, $c = 0$. But the question remains: what guarantee is there at all that capitalism can raise wages sufficiently above bare subsistence to allow for the full human development of the worker? We saw that John Stuart Mill was greatly exercised by the vote for working people, and imagined that this gave them a power they would eventually deploy for these ends. At the same time trade unions were emerging, and in Disraeli's *Sybil* their existence was surrounded by mystification if not absolute horror on the part of the Establishment. But neither of these developments – which are two major factors in the historical rise of welfare for working people – interested Marx.

The economic analysis in *Capital*, in summary, presents us with this: Marx believes that the capital deployed in building a factory and paying costs, including wages, has the sole purpose of extracting wealth as congealed labour from the workers, and such profits are used solely to build more factories to further this exploitation. All this ignores whether the by-product of this activity, the 'goods', are in fact any good to the workers or made available to them at affordable prices. Indirectly *Capital* implies that there is no such thing as a fair wage and that labour unions and the vote will never achieve the end of exploitation. I don't believe that any of this makes sense. As Marshall says, the conclusions of Marx's prodigious writings in *Capital* are not the development of a rational exposition, but were simply latent in its premises.

We saw earlier that although Marx admired the Quaker John Bellers, he was generally scathing of prominent Quakers in his day, particularly

Samuel Gurney. But I will leave Marx with the contrast between the Coalbrookdale Quakers and their display at the Great Exhibition – some of which, as we saw, attracted aesthetic criticism – and Marx's rejection of the whole thing. Marx thought the Exhibition would be a modern 'Roman pantheon of bourgeois idols erected with pride and happiness by man,' as he put it with his usual sarcasm.[6] As the brainchild of the Prince Consort it certainly epitomised the British Establishment, or 'bourgeois' society, if you like. But it contained within it all the goods that brought a better life to working people; 'goods' being a term that Marx could not mouth, preferring the dismissive 'commodities'. I would suggest that all significant contributions to the discipline of economics start with at least some enthusiasm for economic activity itself, and the Great Exhibition was perhaps the first time in history in which that enthusiasm was brought together under one – 'crystal' – roof. A Quaker entrepreneur could not fail to resonate with it, and indeed we saw that the Coalbrookdale Company and Clarks exhibited there to good effect. The contempt that Marx showed for it is, I think, simply a good indicator of the unbridgeable distance between his theories and Quaker practice.

A brief contemplation of Marx's work is always useful however in a debate on the ethics of capitalism. He helps us see perhaps that there is no necessary imperative in a work on unethical capitalism, or on the negative impact of capitalism on the working poor, to consider what an ethical capitalism should entail. For writers like Marx who have already made up their minds that capitalism is irredeemable, the question cannot arise. He simply cannot ask: what does it take to make capitalism ethical? It is for this reason that a further consideration of Marx's thought will not help us here.

Chapter 16

GEORGE, VEBLEN AND SCHUMPETER

We now look at three economists who have some common ground with Marx: Henry George (1839–1897), Thorstein Veblen (1857–1929) and Joseph Schumpeter (1883–1950). None of them are particularly well known now, but all three in different ways have arguments with capitalism as classically defined. Schumpeter, an Austrian, was even known as the 'bourgeois Marx', and had in common with the other two that his mature work was carried out in America (where it turned more conservative). George and Veblen are truly American economists, and are important influences on the work of Kenneth Galbraith.

Henry George

Henry George's most famous book, *Progress and Poverty*, was published in 1879, only 12 years after Marx's *Capital*, and makes the same basic point: industrial capitalism was producing extreme poverty amidst wealth. George says, 'All over the world, we hear complaints of industrial depression: labour condemned to involuntary idleness; capital going to waste; fear and hardship haunting workers. All this dull, deadening pain, this keen, maddening anguish, is summed up in the familiar phrase "hard times".' Dickens of course used just that phrase as the title of one of his novels (which we look at later). George's rather sober point is that this hardship seems to be the case under democracy as much as under tyranny, under free trade as much as under tariffs, and under the gold standard as much as under paper currencies. He equates the greatest poverty with the longest established industrialisation: 'Beggars and prisons are the mark of progress as surely as elegant mansions, bulging warehouses, and magnificent churches.'[1] Progress, to George, brought no reduction in poverty; indeed poverty is produced by progress.

An immense wedge, it seems, is being driven between those elevated by industrial capitalism and those crushed by it. How can that be? What is the remedy? As he puts it: 'This relation of poverty to progress is the great question of our time. It is the riddle that the Sphinx of Fate puts to us. If we do not answer correctly, we will be destroyed.'

George is essentially pursuing the question of subsistence wages, as we have done here. He asks the question in this way: 'Why do wages tend to decrease to subsistence level, even as productive power increases?'[2] This gives us a clue as to his direction: he needs to refute Malthus. His arguments then take an unexpected turn, perhaps: he insists that wages are not paid out of capital. It is absurd, he thinks, that 'labour cannot be employed until the results of labour have been accumulated.'[3] At times George sounds like a more reasonable version of Marx, but in the end there seems to be a similar naivety about capital. For George, as capital is the surplus produced by the collective, it belongs to all. This is a fair point, but that accumulation is what is essential to pay for the forge, the furnace, the foundry, or the chocolate factory. None of the Quaker enterprises could have begun without capital, the profits of previous productive industry, which largely came from within the Quaker network. The question of *ownership* of those profits – what proportion should be taxed, for example, and so made truly collective – is different to the question of its necessity for enterprise. Without that capital no workers can be hired. George's rejection of this simple reality is baffling.

Returning to Malthusianism, George devotes a whole chapter to refuting it, commenting on its bolstering from Social Darwinism, the doctrine that 'survival of the fittest' applies to human society. He says:

> But the real reason for the triumph of the theory is that it does not threaten any vested right or antagonize any powerful interest. Malthus was eminently reassuring to the classes who wield the power of wealth and, thus, largely dominate thought. The French Revolution had aroused intense fear. At a time when old supports were falling away, his theory came to the rescue.[4]

This is a key realisation: that much economics of the Ricardian and Malthusian type is in fact unconsciously designed to support and justify the owning classes – with less or more hand-wringing according to temperament. George's arguments against Malthus are very good as there appears to be no correlation historically between poverty and population growth. Instead, he says, 'vice and misery spring either from ignorance and greed, or from bad government, unjust laws, or war.'[5] The starvation of millions in Soviet Russia and Maoist China, long after George's death, are examples that confirm his ideas. But we slowly discover that George is perhaps looking backwards rather than forwards, to an agrarian ideal rather than an industrial reality. America in his period was certainly a land occupied by the small independent farmer, a version of the British yeoman, and furnishing an image of stout American independence from government and the centres of production. That cannot simply cancel out the development of industrial capitalism however. Hence by the time we reach Chapter 11 on the 'Law of Rent' George reads rather like the Physiocrats. He seems to have overlooked the industrialisation of the economy, and perhaps this is the key to his almost complete dismissal of capital machinery in the creation of wealth. (It's almost 'c = 0' again.) 'Increasing rent is the key that explains why wages and interest fail to increase with greater productivity', he offers instead.[6]

While there is much to admire in George's thought, even the slightest triangulation of his ideas on capital with Quaker industrial practice show serious points of departure. He is simply blind to the very essence of industrialisation: the dull but economically explosive *efficiency* of modern methods. He compares for example the output of a mechanised woollen factory and that of the spinning wheel, saying that the difference in output gives the factory owner no entitlement to the difference in profit. 'The march of knowledge has made these advantages a common property and power of labour.'[7] When such a claim is laid next to the Quaker practice at Coalbrookdale, Cadbury's Bournville plant or Bryant & May's match factory it seems unrealistic. George might think it unethical for patent holders to make big money on sand casting, or to pursue innovations like the use of steam-engines to grind cocoa, or electrical machinery to make matches, but new knowledge is never common property *to start with*, and the lengthy and costly experimentation and capital investment in the equipment that produces and embodies that knowledge is certainly not common property. Of course, the profits may be huge. But the entitlement, *in the first instance*, of a Darby, Cadbury or Crosfield to the profits (after costs and taxation) of their industry is theirs, shared of course with the original capital providers. But George insists that prior capital is unnecessary, and that workers are paid effectively out of the wealth they create for the factory. This is a denial of the fundamentals of capitalism, driven however by a genuine anger at poverty.

In summary, George's thinking was agrarian, and failed to accurately characterise either industrial processes or industrial capital. He was a genuine rival to Marx, each considering the other's ideas wrong to some extent, but George was a home-grown American, and later American economists would often pay homage to him.

Thorstein Veblen

Thorstein Veblen's *The Theory of the Leisure Class* of 1899 is not a treatise on economics like Alfred Marshall's *Principles of Economics* of 1890, for example, but is instead one of the first detailed critiques of consumerism, and hence is of general interest regarding economic justice, and specifically as an antecedent to Galbraith's *The Affluent Society*, which we look at shortly. Veblen's work popularised the term 'conspicuous consumption', as opposed to aristocratic or inherited *rentier* wealth which was traditionally more discreet. One of his key ideas was the distinction between industry run by engineers, which actually makes useful things, and what he saw as the parasitism of businessmen who made profits for a leisure class whose chief activity was conspicuous consumption. He took as examples of earlier leisure classes those in feudal Europe or Japan who didn't labour but were confined to 'honourable' occupations such as in government, warfare, sport or the priesthood.[8] He says:

> The leisure class is in great measure sheltered from the stress of those economic exigencies which prevail in any modern, highly organised industrial community. The exigencies of the struggle for the means of life are less exacting for this class than for any other; and as a consequence of this privileged position we should expect to find it one of the least responsive of the classes of society to the demands which the situation makes for a further growth of institutions and a readjustment to an altered industrial situation. The leisure class is the conservative class.[9]

This remains as true today as then, but is also interesting because of how it does *not* describe the Quakers, even by and large the wealthiest of them. They were not conservative in the sense of clinging to old systems, but on the contrary were at the forefront of innovation in industrial capitalism, including its engineering, science, business and banking. Neither were they conservative politically.

In a later book, *The Engineers and the Price System* (1921), Veblen proposed a 'soviet' – meaning something like a technocracy – of engineers. His persistent – and, it might be said, cynical – distrust of the business community makes him sound like Marx at times, but he has no idealistic faith in the workers either: rather it is the engineers who might lead the revolution.

Joseph Schumpeter

Though Joseph Schumpeter was born in what is now the Czech Republic, taught in an Austrian provincial university and was briefly an Austrian finance minister, he is not part of the so-called 'Austrian School' of economists, no doubt because of his unusual thinking on capitalism and socialism. Schumpeter was possibly referred to as the 'bourgeois Marx' because of his agreement with Marx over the inevitable collapse of capitalism. In one of his books he has a section titled 'Can Capitalism Survive?' which opens with the answer 'No. I do not think it can.' Another section titled 'Can Socialism Work?' is answered with: 'Of course it can.'[10] Schumpeter is best known for his idea of 'creative destruction' in capitalism – the idea that the perpetual renewal and innovation in industry and commerce requires the destruction of previous plant and processes.

Most interesting to us is that Schumpeter was the first economist to really consider the nature of the entrepreneur as a character type. Marx generally failed to distinguish the entrepreneur, the one with the idea, from the capitalist, the one with the capital, and where he did make reference to those innovations in industrial or commercial practice pioneered by entrepreneurs it is usually with a sarcastic tone. He says for example in a footnote in the first volume of *Capital* that, 'The more or less extensive application of division of labour depends on length of purse, not on greatness of genius.'[11] Schumpeter however paints a convincing portrait of the type of person who becomes the entrepreneurial captain of industry. He thinks that entrepreneurial leadership is both special and 'only in rare cases appeals to the imagination of the public.'[12] If we take contemporary cases, such as Steve Jobs of Apple and Richard Branson of Virgin, one would have to agree that such individuals are the exceptions of the type that otherwise rarely impinge on the general consciousness. And here perhaps is the reason: Schumpeter goes on to say that for the success of the entrepreneur 'keenness and vigour are not more essential than a certain narrowness which seizes the immediate chance and *nothing else*.'[13] This captures perhaps the intensity and isolation of the entrepreneur; the narrowness is also of a non-romantic type, and George Cadbury, for one, exemplified all of this, as we saw. Schumpeter could be describing any of the Quaker entrepreneurs when he adds: 'To act with confidence beyond the range of familiar beacons and to overcome that resistance requires aptitudes that are present in only a small fraction of the population and that defines the entrepreneurial type as well as the entrepreneurial function.'[14] You could say that the entrepreneur is therefore rather unique, something of an outsider, and inclined to be a loner.

The entrepreneur is certainly a leader, but does not lead by convincing anyone other than his creditors: he does not persuade, for example, like a politician. He acts. But Schumpeter is a little wary, almost Marxist, when he says: 'what may be attained by industrial or commercial success is still the nearest approach to medieval lordship possible to modern man.'[15] This 'lordship' is of course exactly what Marx attacks as the basis of the exploitation of the worker, and at the same time is what gave the great industrial philanthropists, including the Quakers, both their air of paternalism and their capacity to do good. Schumpeter adds that the entrepreneur has the will to conquer, 'to succeed for the sake, not of the fruits of success, but of success itself.' Marx acknowledges of course that capitalists often do not seek to spend their profit in personal consumption: the 'virtuous' capitalist reinvests for a yet greater return. In fact Schumpeter's entrepreneur is not interested in profit per se, and it is here that his description fits that of the Quaker industrialist so well, including his discovery amongst the motives of the entrepreneur distinctly 'anti-hedonist' tendencies.

Where Schumpeter would have benefited enormously from the material we now have to hand concerning the Quaker enterprises – and what he would have been astonished by – is the observation that Quaker entrepreneurs operated as a collaborative group, in particular in networking and the provision of capital. Schumpeter says: 'Because being an entrepreneur is not a profession and as a rule not a lasting condition, entrepreneurs do not form a social class in the technical sense, as, for example, landowners, or capitalists or workers do.'[16] He is right of course that entrepreneurs did not and still do not form a profession even though, as we saw, Veblen effectively thought they should and, as we will see, Richard Tawney proposed they do, but he is wrong that they have to be necessarily isolated. The Quaker entrepreneurs were interconnected, and also linked with those with capital as, in fact, at a less visible level, are all entrepreneurs who have to, as part of their success, extensively interact with other entrepreneurs and bankers. Many of the Quakers we have looked at would also provide the exception to his other rule, or assumption, that after a while the entrepreneur stops innovating and simply runs his business as a manager. The Darbys for example continued to innovate over five generations, but at the same time kept grounded in their insistence on the production of cooking pots.

On another note, we have to say that Schumpeter has the rather unorthodox idea that capital for entrepreneurs cannot be found out of existing savings, and has to be created ex nihilo by the banks, thus fuelling inflation.[17] A close study of a goldsmith banker like Freame, and of the other Quaker bankers, would probably show this to be unfounded. However it remains a contested idea with occasional support from heterodox economists of both the right and left, as mentioned earlier.

Finally, we must ask of Schumpeter's work its concern for poverty, particularly wages that hover around basic subsistence. The answer is that he appears completely uninterested in this aspect of capitalist economic activity. His response to Marx is simply not at this level.

Chapter 17

THE AUSTRIAN SCHOOL

The Austrian School of economic thought originated with a number of economists, though we shall only be interested here in two of its principal exponents: Ludwig von Mises (1881–1973) and Friedrich Hayek (1899–1992). The school is considered heterodox, that is outside of mainstream or orthodox economics, for several reasons, principally its concern with money and its 'non-neutrality' in economic exchange and in the business cycle. With the move to America of some of its principal thinkers, and the establishment there of the Ludwig von Mises Institute, it became a deeply American phenomenon, providing the intellectual basis for radical free market politics.

Ludwig von Mises

Ludwig von Mises was an economist, philosopher and classical liberal who moved to New York in 1940 fearing Nazism, and this fear was undoubtedly central to his thinking. He was a prominent critic of socialism, using the term to mean state ownership and planning of the economy, and won the 1974 Nobel Prize in Economics. Von Mises' book *Socialism*, first published in 1922, revised in 1932, and again in 1951, is an attack on the economics of socialism, but went much further and became a sourcebook for American libertarianism. He influenced such figures as Ayn Rand and Alan Greenspan, culminating perhaps in the triumph of the Chicago School economics of laissez-faire which has dominated world economics since the 1980s. Hence this is an important book for understanding the contemporary context for the reception of Quakernomics. It owed its publication to Lionel Robbins, head of the LSE, who brought von Mises' pupil, Friedrich Hayek, to London.

Von Mises' *Socialism* states that Nazism was a form of socialism, and therefore socialism, with its apparatus of state ownership and control, leads to political forms that resemble Nazism. This is not found in the pre-war versions of the text, but in a short epilogue in the later editions where he says: 'The philosophy of the Nazis, the German National Socialist Labour Party, is the purest and most consistent manifestation of the anticapitalist and socialistic spirit of our age.'[1] He believed that for over seventy years German university intellectuals had imbued their students with a 'hysterical hatred of capitalism'.[2] Mises adds that the Nazi plan went further than the Marxist one: 'It aimed at abolishing *laisser-faire* not only in the production of material goods, but no less in the production of men.'[3] He was referring of course to eugenics, and is making a fair point.

It was Friedrich Hayek who further developed the idea that state control of the economy for socialist reasons is effectively the same as Nazism, as we shall see. But who gets to define what 'socialism' means? Von Mises declared: 'The essence of Socialism is this: all the means of production are in the exclusive control of the organised community. This and this alone is Socialism. All other definitions are misleading.'[4] Perhaps for Americans it was von Mises who defined socialism in this rather threatening way. In Britain the Labour Party's Clause Four, which demanded 'the common ownership of the means of production, distribution and exchange', would have supported this definition of the term 'socialism' right until Tony Blair abolished this goal in 1995. But the socialism of Britain is best characterised as Fabian, or democratic socialism, a socialism of the mixed economy – and that, very roughly, is where Quakernomics seems to locate itself. It seems that the definition of socialism can depend on how much you want to scare people.

Von Mises is interested in the relationship between Christianity and socialism and devotes a short chapter specifically to the subject. He is certain that 'Christian Socialism, as it has taken root in the last few decades among countless followers of all Christian churches, is merely a variety of State Socialism.'[5] He is keen to point out that the 'communism' of the early disciples, that is their shared life together, is definitely not socialism, and that Jesus was no social reformer. But apparently Jesus has 'resentment' towards the rich. Von Mises says:

> Later revisers have tried to soften the words of Christ against the rich, of which the most complete and powerful version is found in the Gospel of Luke, but there is quite enough left to support those who incite the world to hatred of the rich, revenge, murder and arson. Up to the time of modern Socialism no movement against private property which has arisen in the Christian world has failed

to seek authority in Jesus, the Apostles, and the Christian Fathers, not to mention those who, like Tolstoy, made the Gospel resentment against the rich the very heart and soul of their teaching. This is a case in which the Redeemer's words bore evil seed.[6]

Von Mises, it seems, is against Christianity because it incites a hatred against the rich. I think few would agree that the Gospels offer any support to those who preach hatred of the rich, let alone revenge, murder and arson. But von Mises continues: 'The Gospels are not socialistic and not communistic. They are, as we have seen, indifferent to all social questions on the one hand, full of resentment against all property and against all owners on the other.' In the example of the Quakers however we find Christians with plenty of distrust of riches, but no hatred of anyone; a perfect acceptance of private property, but no hesitation to use the wealth it brings for social ends. In conclusion one has to say that the works of thinkers like von Mises are as extreme on the right as Marx's are on the left.

Friedrich Hayek

Friedrich Hayek is perhaps the most important of the Austrian School in terms of his economic legacy. Born in Vienna, he worked for Ludwig von Mises, and inherited von Mises' idea that the move towards state socialism leads inevitably towards Nazism. Indeed it was von Mises' book *Socialism* that led to Hayek's shift from a form of democratic socialism to the libertarianism we now associate him with. Hayek was invited to the LSE in 1931 by its then head, Lionel Robbins, and from there observed the descending racism and chaos of Nazi Germany. Hayek's most famous book, *The Road to Serfdom*, sold more than three hundred and fifty thousand copies in the United States alone, and became an inspiration to Margaret Thatcher. He was awarded the Order of the Companions of Honour on the advice of Thatcher for his 'services to the study of economics', received the US Presidential Medal of Freedom from the first President Bush, and the Nobel Prize for his work in economics. Hayek was in fact at the centre of a revolution in economics that ended the post-war 'Keynesian' consensus, of which more shortly. Here we focus on the thesis of von Mises and Hayek, that state control over economic life leads to totalitarianism.

The essential thesis of *The Road to Serfdom* is that totalitarian regimes of the left and of the right at the time of the Nazis had the same source in Hegelian historicism: that is a belief, respectively, that either the international 'proletariat' or the German 'Volk' represented the future of humanity and all other social groupings were destined to succumb to that power or be swept away (let's be honest: murdered). Hayek's thesis at its best is sobering because it shows how many of the German intellectuals who shaped Nazism did indeed start as Marxists or socialists of some kind. But Hayek himself succumbs to a pessimism – perhaps quite natural in 1943 – that the dreaded collectivism demonstrated in Communism or Nazism was also gaining ground over liberal traditions in the UK and the US. For Hayek and his successors collectivism spells the end of the most precious of all human gifts: freedom. Hayek's book ends with dire predictions that Britain in 1943 was going down the same road to serfdom that Germany had in the twenties and thirties, with the complete destruction of personal freedom, and the assimilation of the individual into the state.

We now know that his pessimism was completely unfounded, because the post-war nationalisation in the UK – certainly of a socialist impetus – built up both an unprecedented standard of living *and* freedoms unknown to previous generations. We will see that it fulfilled more the vision of another LSE economist, Richard Henry Tawney. Hayek's pessimism was perhaps kindled by the war-footing economies of the UK and the US, where – as always happens in times of war – collectivism of a relatively benign kind does take precedence over individualism, and the entire economy begins to look more like a command economy than traditional capitalism. But perhaps Hayek couldn't see that the British and Americans would abandon such total centralisation as soon as war was over.

Hayek's appeal is enduring however, and Thatcher's enthusiasm for his ideas shows the power they have over politicians of the right. At root it is an extremism which sets itself against the mixed economy that in practice nearly all developed nations have pursued: a balance of private competitive enterprise and state control, or, in other words, a moderated capitalism. Hayek doesn't believe that this balance can work. In his words:

> Both competition and central direction become poor and inefficient tools if they are incomplete; they are alternative principles used to solve the same problem, and a mixture of the two means that neither will really work and that the result will be worse than if either system had been consistently relied on.[7]

Hayek sets up a basic conflict between 'planning' and 'competition', saying: 'What in effect unites socialists of the Left and the Right is this common hostility to competition.'[8] We may find it odd to hear the phrase 'socialists [...] of the Right', and wonder that 'planning' should strike us with such terror. After all is not the 'planned' and state-owned French national railway, the SNCF, generally superior to the privatised British railways in technology and rail safety? And did not Cadbury's town planning in Birmingham shape it for the better? But the fears that Hayek raises strike a chord with the right today, and the views of the Tea Party in America are a natural expression of this tradition.

Hayek's thought is so driven by the fear of collectivism that it cannot resolve or begin to work through the central contradiction that he keeps stating. He *does not* in fact want social injustice. He *does not* in fact want poverty to blight people's lives. He *does not* in fact want the collective to stand back with arms folded when a hurricane strikes or a man is injured or taken so ill that he cannot work any more. He says, 'there can be no doubt that some minimum of food, shelter, and clothing, sufficient to preserve health and the capacity to work, can be assured to everybody.' He adds that 'there is no incompatibility in principle between the state providing greater security in this way and the preservation of individual freedom.'[9]

But *how?* This is the central question of social or economic justice. If 'collectivism' and 'planning' are evils that are the inevitable prelude to Nazism, then *how* can the state provide the security that Hayek insists is a good thing? If *either* competition *or* central direction is to be pursued, then how can *both* be combined in making such provision? Adam Smith equally failed to answer this question. The European nations after the war experimented with various forms of mixed economy in which planning and competition were brought into balance, each nation according to its temperament. If Hayek's thought had won the day, then unmoderated free enterprise would have brought wages back down to subsistence and a society that stood with folded arms at the prospect of hurricane, unemployment, accident, sickness and inequality. Put bluntly, Hayek's thesis, and the entire tradition built on it, has never resolved this conflict of principles.

Here also lies the contradiction to Quakernomics in all this: *fear of the collective*. It is the fear that attempts by the collective to moderate competitive capitalist enterprise will lead to the horrors of fascism. It is the fear that attempts to harness capitalism for the greater good will destroy all freedoms. It is the fear that 'social ends', as Hayek puts it, will be seized on by ideologues and maniacs for power and lead us all to serfdom.[10] It is also the certainty that there is no civic or public life, no public spiritedness, no honest government. It is the classical Tea Party stance: an adoration of 'democracy' in theory and a loathing of government in practice.

Hayek agrees that industries should not pollute, that social security is within our grasp, that some monopolies like transport are inevitable, that people need hurricane relief. Everywhere he lays down the necessity for a mixed economy, but in the same breath insists that it is not possible. But Quakers, good individualist Schumpeterian entrepreneurs that they were, had no fear of the collective. Their Quaker Business Method ensured that the community as a whole entered into decision making, and the Meeting was accepted as the arbiter of commercial probity. Above all they moderated their capitalism to serve social ends. Neither were they ideologues: George Cadbury avoided party politics in his pursuit of social justice in the public sphere precisely because the political parties of his day pursued simplistic ideologies. And clearly the Quakers were no maniacs.

It is important to explain why Hayek's was a *failed* futurology. Prophets of future doom gain ready audiences amongst the anxious, and, in the classic psychological bind, when the doom fails to arrive at the due date, an infinite number of rationalisations are found. The essence of Hayek's predictions lies in the role of the state: if it were to even begin to impose a 'central direction' on the economy then 'competition' would be finished. This is the antithesis he sets up. But the post-war consensus in most Western nations involved a huge growth in 'central direction' – in particular in the nationalisation of many key industries, or at the very least stricter regulation of them, and a Keynesian determination to intervene when slump or recession threatened jobs. According to Hayek all of this should have quickly led to massive reductions in personal freedoms. Yet any analysis of the sixties and seventies – in general the high Keynesian period prior to Reagan and Thatcher – shows the absolute reverse. I grew up in that era and there was an explosion of personal freedom and expression at every social level: Mods, Rockers, the Beatles, the Beat Generation, Abstract Expressionism, satirical film, TV, radio, theatre and novels, and the cultural pluralism of melting-pot urban life. Citizens of the European nations had unprecedented freedoms at exactly the same time that the railways and health provision were collectivised, to name just a few aspects of the economy that came under state control. It is certainly true that right-wing politicians and thinkers wrung their hands in horror at all this freedom, because it so often expressed a left-wing perspective: the events of 1968, 'the year of revolt', brought such ideas to a head. (You can take any number of events in that year to symbolise the mood of liberal protest and imaginative freedom: student barricades in Paris or the Beatles' *Yellow Submarine*; take your pick.) It is also true that a handful of entrepreneurs were shut out of industries that they had dominated since the start of the Industrial Revolution: steel, coal, transport, communications, and so on. But what is absolutely false is the idea that the later privatisation of these industries led to more 'freedom' for the population as a whole.

Any careful consideration of the post-war period shows that with the ebb and flow of collectivisation, as industries were first nationalised and then privatised again, personal freedoms were little affected by either. It will also show that mixed economies are the reality, whatever the exact nature of the mix, and that personal freedoms continued to reach historically unprecedented highs. In fact these personal freedoms grew out of movements that had little to do with economics in the first place: the civil liberties movement finding the realisation of its goals through the Supreme Court in the 1960s in America, and in the less structured approach of British civil life in the same period.

In many ways, the legacy of von Mises and Hayek represents the antithesis of the Quaker tradition: the 'kryptonite' to Quakernomics perhaps. It drives a wedge between economic activity as initiated by the entrepreneur within a broadly free market, and any consideration of social consequences, and it does so by raising the spectre of Nazism. We may find this absurd when stated so starkly, and there is no doubt that *The Road to Serfdom* looks immensely dated from our present perspective, an exercise in failed futurology. It may not have been very charitable of Keynes to characterise some economists as 'defunct', but it may well be fair to label some of their ideas as such. Despite this the ideas of von Mises and Hayek have a lasting appeal to the right, and found their economic leverage on the entire global economy through the work of Milton Friedman and the Chicago School. Before considering their work we examine some other important influences on the economic sphere.

Chapter 18

KEYNES, TAWNEY AND GALBRAITH

John Maynard Keynes (1883–1946) was a British economist who worked as a civil servant for a while before teaching at Cambridge, including on a lectureship funded by Alfred Marshall. He was a giant in his field, having invented an economic theory from which an extensive school developed. For the extreme left, their God was Marx, while for the moderate left, it became Keynes. For the right, once the threat of Marx had waned, the threat of Keynes became all-consuming. He shaped the post-war economies up until the Thatcher and Reagan revolutions swept aside his ideas in the 1980s, though state intervention in the global economy during the Credit Crunch again followed basic Keynesian principles to some extent.

For almost all economists of the left of centre Keynes is a hero. Why? Because, in an economic downturn he insists that the role of government is to step in and be the spender of last resort. By borrowing money or even by printing it, and then engaging in public spending programmes, particularly on infrastructure, government can reverse a vicious downward economic spiral, and prevent the evils of unemployment visiting the worker. That's about it, though this distilled essence of Keynesianism can't even hint at the huge influence and long reach of his ideas. It is far removed from anything in the practice of the Quaker businesses, because it is part of what Keynes pioneered: *macroeconomics*. This is the study of large-scale economic patterns, and particularly the impact on them of the fiscal and monetary policies of government. But where the Quakers would agree, and where I think the admiration for Keynes derives, is in the idea that unemployment is the worst of all economic ills and it is the role of government to eliminate it or reduce it to an absolute minimum.

Having said this, for most people, and even for most economists, Keynes is as unreadable as Marx – and at times almost as prolix. His major work, *The General Theory of Employment, Interest and Money*, published in 1936, created the 'Keynesian revolution'. The left-wing economic commentator Will Hutton writes admiringly of Keynes in his important work *The State We're In*, and in the Credit Crunch another admirer, Robert Skidelsky, published a book-length tribute called *Keynes: The Return of the Master*, as mentioned earlier. Indeed, most Western governments adopted a Keynesian approach in the early part of the 2008 financial crisis, buying out banks and firms that hovered on bankruptcy, and engaging in massive rounds of quantitative easing. At a different point in economic history the phrase 'we are all Keynesians now' circulated, and its message was proclaimed by Richard Nixon.

Whatever the status of Keynes today, there is not much common ground between his thinking and Quakernomics. His writings reveal little interest in the reality of economic life, and also reveal many of the assumptions of his class. He was an asset speculator who lost two personal fortunes and gained three (as he liked to boast), and whose economic thinking tended to revolve around pre-existing assets and not so much around the basic production of goods.

Keynes said: 'Consumption – to repeat the obvious – is the sole end and object of all economic activity.'[1] It is hard to think of something the Quakers were less likely to agree with. This line is from *The General Theory*, in which other, frankly bizarre, statements are to be found. Here is one:

> If the Treasury were to fill old bottles with banknotes, bury them at suitable depths in disused coalmines which are then filled up to the surface with town rubbish, and leave it to private enterprise on well-tried principles of laissez-faire to dig the notes up again (the right to do so being obtained, of course, by tendering for leases of the notebearing territory), there need be no more unemployment and, with the help of the repercussions, the real income of the community, and its capital wealth also, would probably become a good deal greater than it actually is. It would, indeed, be more sensible to build houses and the like; but if there are political and practical difficulties in the way of this, the above would be better than nothing.[2]

Following this he suggests that the fabled wealth of Egypt was partly a *consequence* of building pyramids – also hardly a 'sensible' activity. Any careful analysis of the real-world economics of ancient Egypt shows that its wealth was due to the fertile flood plains of the Nile in which grain was grown, and it was the surplus of grain that was used to feed the conscripts that enabled pyramid building. A real-world economics always starts with food production.

It may be that Keynes did enormous good in the world by persuading governments to spend their way out of recessions. But the thinking of Keynes often just reinforces the vague anxiety I have – and others share – that economists can become confused about cause and effect. A community cannot become rich by burying something and digging it up again – let alone banknotes – and it cannot become rich by building pyramids. Both of those activities require pre-existing surpluses. Quakernomics as a sober discipline of actually making things knows this: the *foundations* of wealth start elsewhere, with providing goods or services that the bulk of people need, starting with food.

Tawney

If Keynes shaped the post-war consensus on economics up to the 1970s he gave only modest impetus to the nationalisation of the industries in most European countries in this period: that was more down to Richard Henry Tawney (1880–1962) mentioned earlier as appreciative of the Quaker tradition. Tawney was an English economic historian and a Christian Socialist: just the sort of person that von Mises was opposed to. In fact I don't think Tawney is much remembered in economics, but two of his books have a bearing on Quakernomics: firstly *The Acquisitive Society* (1921) and secondly *Religion and the Rise of Capitalism*, which we looked at earlier. From 1917 to his retirement in 1949, Tawney taught economic history at the LSE, and was in fact an influential thinker in his period. He joined the Fabian Society in 1906 and served on its executive from 1921 to 1933. His fellow Fabian Beatrice Webb described him as a 'saint of socialism' exercising influence without rancour; he in turn wrote a book about her.

What link is there between Keynes and Tawney? Tawney argued for the 'extinction of the Capitalists'[3] while Keynes, in another memorable phrase, looked forward to the 'euthanasia of the *rentier*'.[4] But the nagging doubt must lie over the life of Keynes: did he himself not belong to the *rentier* class? His background was one of insider privilege, a far cry from the Quaker outsider tradition, while Tawney as a Christian is closer in spirit to Quakernomics. Tawney's *The Acquisitive Society* was highly influential amongst socialists; the Labour cabinet minister Richard Crossman referring to it as the 'socialist bible' – reflecting perhaps the instinct of English left-wing politics to prefer its tone of Christian reasonableness to the angry Hegelian polemic of Marx's *Capital*. But it is also probably true to say that as religion continued its retreat into the private sphere Tawney's influence waned and Marx was left standing as the only significant anti-capitalism theory to hand for the British left.

Tawney's *The Acquisitive Society* does not mention the Quakers, and is equally innocent of any mention of Marx, which is more perplexing, given its interest in socialism. It is in Tawney's *Religion and the Rise of Capitalism* where we find an acknowledgement of the special history of the Quakers. Tawney mentions first that Robert Owen hailed the Quaker John Bellers as 'the father of his doctrines', and then goes on to praise the good conscience and forbearance of the Quakers in their economic transactions and their 'duty to make the honourable maintenance of the brother in distress a common charge.' (I quoted this earlier.) But Tawney concludes his brief mention of the Quakers with: 'The general climate and character of a country are not altered, however, by the fact that here and there it has peaks which rise into an ampler air.'[5] I think this is pessimistic: the Quakers took hold of a significant part of the country's output, and philanthropy amongst industrialists spread far beyond them, as we have seen.

In fact Tawney helped usher in a defining period in British post-war socialist modernity: the welfare state, and in particular the nationalisation of major industries. His basic view of any industry is that it is 'a body of men associated, in various degrees of competition and co-operation, to win their living by providing the community with some service which it requires.'[6] He goes on: 'Because its method is association, the different parties within it have rights and duties towards each other; and the neglect or perversion of these involves oppression.' Tawney is not vituperative about capitalism but observes, as Quakernomics does, the duties of those in the 'association' which makes up industry towards each other. Tawney clearly occupies a middle ground between Communism and free market radicalism. His approach is therefore as sceptical of the conservative English tradition of economics as it is of far-left socialism. He saw in the English tradition an organised inequality. He suggests that compared to the vision of freedom of the French thinkers the English school preached resignation 'to the monotonous beat of the factory engine' and to the 'melancholy mathematical creed' of Bentham, Ricardo and James Mill.[7] He also targets property rights, and in effect criticises Smith's 'invisible hand'. True, he says, individuals exercising their rights over their own property – and here he means the captains of private industry such as Darby, Crosfield and Cadbury as much as *rentier* landowners – render services to society in pursuit of their own interests. But this service seems to be secondary rather than primary. It is a triumph of rights over obligations. It leads him to give a new term to a society in which the acquisition of wealth made possible by such rights is 'contingent upon the discharge of social obligations': a 'Functional Society'. Instead, he argues, we have allowed the converse, the development of an 'Acquisitive Society'.[8]

While Quakers up to now would find everything to agree with in Tawney, in particular his ethics of the economic life as deriving from Christian morality, their history would suggest a divergence of opinion. As Tawney prepares his argument for the nationalisation of industry and the removal of the rights of those owning capital to dictate the nature of industry, Quakernomics in its historical development falls silent. It is not the method whereby non-acquisitiveness was practiced by Quakers, and it is not, directly at least, what their history suggests as the way forward. Tawney insists that 'nationalisation' as a method of moderating property rights involves, again, a spectrum of possibilities. 'Properly conceived, its object is not to establish State management of industry, but to remove the dead hand of private ownership, when the private owner has ceased to form a positive function.'[9] By 'positive function' I take him to mean a service to the community as a whole, as indeed Quaker owners insisted on. Tawney's eventual prescription turns out to be rather like Veblen's 'soviet of engineers' – it is to the engineers as a class that industry should be handed over. For Tawney, the liberation of industry lies in the professionalisation of the engineer – and in the process capital should cease to employ labour, but rather the other way round.

Schumpeter noted that the 'entrepreneur' has not the status of the professional; Tawney the same for the 'engineer'. Veblen wanted to rid the entrepreneur-businessman of the businessman element. But we have seen that the core of industrial capitalism in the Quaker microcosm lies in the entrepreneur who is *both* engineer *and* businessman, owner of capital and director of works. The lesson of Quakernomics here seems to be that this type of person is the one who needs to be fostered for flourishing industries – but that they need yet one more characteristic: that of the devoted, perhaps even religious, servant of humanity.

Galbraith

John Kenneth Galbraith (1908–2006) was a Canadian-American Keynesian economist, writing a number of bestsellers on economic topics.

He had a year-long fellowship at Cambridge in England where the ideas of Keynes dominated, and travelled at times to the LSE to hear the lectures of Hayek – who he profoundly disagreed with. He was reputed to have had a close personal rapport with President Kennedy, but Paul Krugman, an economist we shall consider before long, seems to have a low opinion of Galbraith, considering him more of a 'policy entrepreneur' than an economist.[10] There may be some truth in this and it may also be true that Galbraith's *The New Industrial State* left little mark, but I want to consider another of his works: *The Affluent Society*. Galbraith had a Guggenheim Foundation grant for a study in poverty – which might have developed along the lines of Engels', Booth's or Rowntree's studies – but, as Galbraith remarks: 'such grants often go astray; this one was no exception. What emerged was not a treatise on the poor but one on the affluent.'[11] The book opens with this passage:

> Beyond doubt, wealth is a relentless enemy of understanding. The poor man has always a precise view of his problem and its remedy: he hasn't enough and needs more. The rich man can assume or imagine a much greater variety of ills and he will be correspondingly less certain of their remedy. Also, until he learns to live with his wealth, he will have a well-observed tendency to put it to the wrong purpose or otherwise to make himself foolish.[12]

I am not sure that I have found this sentiment better put. My own experience of the rich is that they put their wealth to mostly trivial purposes, very few of which even bring them any happiness, never mind the good it would do if diverted to the poor. Galbraith's phrase 'wealth is a relentless enemy of understanding' seems to me to be true not just of the mega-rich, but even for the middle-classes right down the scale.

We have seen however that for the majority of Quaker entrepreneurs their wealth seemed to create little obstacle to their understanding, an exception to Galbraith's rule. Most of them placed a ceiling on their personal affluence, sometimes quite severely. Above all they seemed to have 'learned to live' with their wealth in precisely Galbraith's terms: they neither put it to the wrong purpose nor made themselves foolish. But Galbraith's thesis – originally put forward in the 1958 publication and elaborated on in its 40th anniversary edition – is remarkable for its time: that essentially the post-war boom had done its job. It had created sufficient wealth, in aggregate, so what was this relentless drive for more? It is an astonishing idea to come from an economist, and I can't think of any other mainstream thinker on the subject who questioned the idea of growth so eloquently or so early – or so in tune, it happens, with Quaker thinking.

Galbraith is conscious of the historical issue of subsistence in the early economists, quoting Adam Smith: 'We have no acts of Parliament against combining to lower the price of work; but many against combining to raise it.' Galbraith comments:

> This was the beginning of perhaps the most influential and certainly the most despairing dictum in the history of social comment, the notion that the income of the masses of the people – all who in one way or another worked for a living, whether in industry or agriculture – could not for very long rise very far above the minimum level necessary for the survival of the race. It is the immortal iron law which, as stiffened by Ricardo and refashioned by Marx, became the chief weapon in the eventual ideological assault on capitalism.[13]

Galbraith points out that while this iron law was held with qualifications, 'the notion of massive privation and great inequality became a basic premise.' He adds that it was to Ricardo and Malthus that Carlyle was referring when he talked of the professors of the 'dismal science'.[14] Galbraith summarises the work of Smith, Malthus and Ricardo as: 'a formidable interpretation of, and prescription for, the world as they found it.'[15] This is a precise echo of Henry George when he suggested that the pessimism of Malthus and Ricardo came to the rescue of the status quo, not just a theory of, but a prescription for, systems of exploitation. The lives of people then were harsh, and possibly the Industrial Revolution made things no worse, but could make them better. To do that freedom from feudal and mercantilist restraints was essential, and that is what the Quakers relied on, having themselves shaken free from the many restraints placed upon them. But Galbraith's point is that this classical economics *was of its time*: in the late twentieth century economics had to be rethought, and certainly Keynes had made a start.

Galbraith draws on Henry George and Thorstein Veblen in his work, though barely mentions Tawney, and disregards *The Acquisitive Society* completely – perhaps Galbraith too wanted to distance himself from religion. Veblen, as we saw, introduced the idea of 'conspicuous consumption', and painted contemptuous portraits of the leisure classes that certainly met popular approval. But Galbraith, in commenting on

Veblen's failure to put faith in the working classes or to suggest any real way forward, points out that this is simply a disbelief in the possible progress of economic justice. Galbraith says: 'Veblen thus precipitated the doubts and pessimism which lurked in the central tradition.'[16] Indeed the central tradition of economic thought as pursued in America does seem to have little faith in the possibility of economic justice, and this pessimism reaches its depth I believe in Friedman, as we will see. Galbraith considers that the tradition of Social Darwinism initiated by Herbert Spencer (1820–1903) found its best disciples and reception in America, another strand of entirely pessimistic thinking, though resisted, as we saw, by Henry George. Galbraith points out that the rise of Social Darwinism in America coincided with the rise of prominent new wealth.[17]

Galbraith's thesis is that all of these early economists were Malthusian pessimists, and that history has proved them wrong: there was clearly now affluence for all. This was his view at the end of the 1950s, going so far as to say that the decline of interest in inequality was one of the most evident features of social history at that time. Galbraith says that it was the increase in post-war output, not redistribution of income, that took the masses out of poverty; that growth therefore became the obsession just as much of the left as the right; that despite all this there was still a 'self-perpetuating margin of poverty at the very base of the income pyramid'; and that this minority was voiceless because the liberal tradition *expected* poverty for the masses.[18]

As Galbraith points out, economic theorists are keen to demonstrate how economic insecurity is the spur to hard work and risk-taking entrepreneurship, but in reality this economic insecurity is always good for *other* people, not oneself. As he says: 'Restraints on competition and the free movement of prices, the greatest source of uncertainty to business firms, have been principally deplored by university professors on lifetime appointments.'[19] Material comfort undreamt of by workers of fifty years previous meant there was much more to lose as one climbed the income ladder. And I would add this: the pessimism within American culture towards economic justice creates a vicious circle in which the ordinary person's economic insecurity is stoked, making them, as they grow wealthier, even less likely to support social safety nets.

The Quaker experience is different. From the start as a persecuted minority economic security came not from personal affluence but from membership of the Society of Friends. It's not socialism in the usual sense, but rather a freedom from insecurity based on mutual ties – mutual obligations extending all the way up the earning scale to the wealthiest Quaker industrialist or banker.

I'll leave Galbraith, as a broadly left-of-centre economic thinker, with a quote from him that perhaps sums up the conundrum faced by the left in the second decade of the twenty-first century: 'Increased real income provides us with an admirable detour around the rancour anciently associated with efforts to redistribute wealth.'[20] Quakernomics, I would suggest, is a rancour-free determination to redistribute wealth, though its exact methods, seen now as paternalistic and philanthropic, may not be appropriate today. The *determination* to redistribute wealth is what matters. And, as Galbraith points out, it cannot be ducked by a call for endless growth.

Ethical Capitalism: Second Assessment

We can now recapitulate the additional panorama of economic thought just covered to consider how George, Veblen, Schumpeter, von Mises, Keynes, Hayek, Tawney and Galbraith help us think about ethical capitalism. Since our consideration of Marx we can break this down into two questions rather than one: (a) how do each of these thinkers analyse the outcomes of unethical capitalism?; and (b) how would they correspondingly make capitalism more ethical? It is clear that Schumpeter, von Mises and Hayek at no point consider either question, however framed. Their economic debates are purely technical. George, Veblen, Tawney and Galbraith however form a continuum, even if they do not all reference each other, in their unsparing critiques of capitalism. The key ethical question for them is inequality. The working poor are for them the road-kill of unmoderated capitalism, while its true scandal is conspicuous wealth and unbridled acquisitiveness. However none of them have much enthusiasm for the entrepreneur, the person at the heart of industrial capitalism – at least as revealed through Quakernomics – and so their responses to unethical capitalism are rather to sidestep its fundamental issues. George barely acknowledges the industrial side of capitalism; Veblen has no real empathy for the worker; Tawney advocates the nationalisation of industry; and Galbraith, well, it is not clear what Galbraith advocates, despite the acuity of his analysis. Despite these caveats this group of authors must be counted as essential reading for any debate on ethical capitalism, however.

This leaves Keynes as bequeathing us perhaps the most complex legacy in its implications for ethical capitalism. Skidelsky sums him up like this: 'his knowledge of the business of "making things" rather than "making money" was slight.'[21] This is not a good augur for an economist when it comes to industrial capitalism and its ethics. But single-handedly he seemed to have initiated the most important ethical buffer to raw capitalism yet to have emerged: a call to government to mitigate unemployment in a downturn. By the year 2013 two of the most important central banks in the world, the Federal Reserve System and the Bank of England, had come to adopt – in the teeth of a philosophy I shall call Friedmanism – policies that placed unemployment as a trigger for central bank action. In this the first evil of capitalism – the loss of the individual's personal means of production – is recognised. Keynes may have been at one level an aristocratic playboy asset speculator, but perhaps the basic English sense of fair play worked in him to acknowledge that 'their race', as Ricardo would have it – the workers – deserved better than to be repudiated by the bourgeoisie when the going got tough.

Macroeconomics as a discipline has no choice but to factor in the role of government. Elected politicians are rarely economists, and turn to individuals like Keynes as advisors on economic matters, but even then they only pursue the art of the possible. And what is possible is what voters can stomach, and that in turn is culturally determined. Hence we turn away from economists for now to explore how ethical and unethical capitalism is dealt with in literature.

Chapter 19

ECONOMICS IN FICTION

In the late nineteenth century Henry George's *Progress and Poverty* was a bestseller (with over three million copies sold) – now it is largely forgotten. Marx's *Capital* barely shifted off the shelves in George's day, but now has status as a sacred text. Keynes's *General Theory* was highly popular, Galbraith's work sold well, and, as we shall see, Friedman's *Capitalism and Freedom* sold in huge numbers, sales no doubt supported by the two runs of his TV series. Since the Credit Crunch books on economics have soared up the Amazon charts. Mostly, however, people don't read economics books, popular or otherwise. They do however encounter ideas about economics in fiction, and so here we look at some novels with enduring appeal that put forward either left-wing or right-wing economic views. We will look first at a spectrum of broadly socialist novels because the legacy of their concern for social justice does at times far outstrip the impact of the worthy studies that we have encountered by the likes of Engels, Marx, Booth and Rowntree. All this is by way of background to Ayn Rand's *Atlas Shrugged*, a single right-wing novel of free market economics that has probably swayed more minds than all the socialist novels put together.

Where are the novels that accurately portray the reality of the working class faced with unemployment and subsistence-level wages? I have not made a comprehensive survey but these four recommend themselves in rather different ways: Dickens' *Hard Times*, Robert Tressell's *Ragged Trousered Philanthropists*, Upton Sinclair's *Oil!* and John Steinbeck's *Grapes of Wrath*.

In Dickens' *Hard Times* – criticised by Thomas Macaulay as conveying a 'sullen socialism' – the author invents two marvellous capitalists: Gradgrind and Bounderby. Von Mises regrets that *Hard Times* caricatures Bentham's utilitarianism, suggesting that Dickens had little understanding of economics, which is probably true.[1] However, the very term 'Dickensian' has come into the language to describe the horrors of working people on the edge of subsistence, contrasted with the wealth of the middle classes. Dickens is perhaps an essential part of our response to poverty, but I think that von Mises is right to suggest that Dickens, as a romantic, is confined by the unworldliness of that tradition. The fact is that the caricatures of the capitalist entrepreneur in *Hard Times* tell us little about the reality of business leaders, including Quakers. Worse still, Dickens – perhaps to avoid any offence to his middle-class readership – dwells very little on the *real* problems of the working people in his novel. The trades unions are satirised (as in *Sybil*) and the working-class hero, Stephen Blackpool, has made an inexplicable vow to shun union membership. Any description of Blackpool's actual industrial hardships are scrupulously avoided, apart from the loss of his job and his subsequent romantic martyrdom by falling into a large hole in the ground. Gradgrind's son Tom is instrumental in Blackpool's unhappy end, but evades justice through family intervention. Again this can only be explained as sparing the feelings of the middle-class readers who would identify with Tom rather than Stephen, but to a Quaker it would represent a monstrous injustice. It is an indictment of Dickens that he so feared to alienate his middle-class readers that he could not have a middle-class young man face the law for ruining a working man's life. Or perhaps it was simply part of Dickens' cynicism about all public institutions, including the justice system.

The novel's real polemic is against Benthamite 'rational' education, which distorts the true expression of a person's emotional life: this is shown through the impact on Sissy Jupe, an adopted daughter of Gradgrind, as well as on his own children. There is a great deal of truth in this romantic attack on rationalism, but for the Quaker founders of technical colleges for working people it would obscure the greater truth: that education in technical subjects was essential for improving the lot of working people. When the Darbys set up the Coalbrookdale Literary and Scientific Institute they initially planned to call it an 'Institution for the Acquirement of Useful Knowledge'[2] – had Dickens known of it the name would have been a perfect vehicle for his satire.

In contrast Robert Tressell's *The Ragged Trousered Philanthropists* – some of whose characters seem directly modelled on those in *Hard Times* – delivers a vivid account of just exactly the nightmare of subsistence wages held low under the twin forces of capitalist competition and the threat of unemployment. It does what Dickens entirely fails to do: show in all its starkness what a working man endures when his children go hungry. It is set in the decorating trade in an English town called Mugsborough, modelled on Hastings, and its 'philanthropists' are the workers who so generously provide their corrupt employers with wealth. One of the decorators, a man named Frank Owen (in an obvious reference to Robert Owen), is a socialist who delivers a series of vaguely Marxist lectures to his less literate colleagues. In fact the novel presents a good analysis of how the English working classes were generally suspicious of socialism and mostly tolerated the social injustices of their position. It well illustrates the difficulties that Edward Reynolds Pease would have had in his failed attempts to convert the workers of Newcastle to socialism. But in the novel's presentation of the Marxist alternative to unchecked capitalism we find it hard in fact to see how the workers could possibly have been persuaded of it. That is not the strength of the novel, which lies instead in the portrayal of the relentless shadow that poverty casts over family life, where parents cannot provide enough food for their children, never mind a few toys or basic education, and where the passage from Louis Blanc rings with such force in our ears, in which workers forced to compete for jobs undercut wages even further.

But the real failing of Tressell's work is this: while his working people are often vividly real, Owen's employer is a Dickensian caricature with the company name Sweater, Rushton, Didlum & Grinder. The other decorating firms in Mugsborough are called Pushem & Sloggem, Bluffum & Doemdown, and other similar titles. By inventing names in this satirical vein Tressell invites the suspicion that his mind is already made up: they are all crooked. In terms of economics he has succumbed to Malthusian certainties, in which the history we have examined of Quaker employers, of decent and philanthropic capitalists, is impossible. And ultimately the workers too are a little two-dimensional, despite the wonderful attention to accent, banter and the usual failings of ordinary people: there is a missing warmth, indicating in Tressell a rather pervasive pessimism. Raymond Williams, an important socialist cultural theorist, said of the novel: 'There is no finer representation, anywhere in English writing, of a certain rough-edged, mocking, give-and-take conversation between workmen and mates.'[3] This is possibly true – and anyone who has worked in similar circumstances even today will recognise the typical Englishness of it – but nonetheless, the warmth is missing. Although Tressell does document the occasional generosity of the poor to each other, particularly Owen's, too often the working characters are unmoved by the plight of others.

It is widely believed however that the novel won the 1945 election for Labour.[4] Hence it would be wrong to focus on the novel's occasional failings if we are interested in the question of social justice. It is just that there are better novels that document the same poverty, and with less economic naivety.

Upton Sinclair's *Oil!* for example is better balanced on both sides of the employer–employee divide. It concerns an industrialist called James Arnold, a decent man made rich in the oil business, and his son Bunny who is set to inherit from him. As a teenager Bunny accompanies his father, much as a Quaker son would learn about the family business. Arnold is happy to see good pay and conditions for his workers, but is placed under increasing pressure by his peers in the oil industry to reduce wages after WWI, resulting in terrible deprivation for the working community. In the end Bunny is so disgusted with the workings of industrial capitalism that he becomes a socialist, a 'red' in the slang of the day. Sinclair's aim was to show that however well-meaning an industrialist may be, the forces of profit, competition, peer pressure and cartelisation will drive down wages to subsistence. Arnold in the story had neither the Quaker Testimonies to guide him, nor the Quaker network to give him the collective power to resist his peers. But the oil industry is portrayed as not so different from any other new venture in the history of industrialisation, and the wells sunk in the Teapot Dome area of Wyoming are as remote and sparsely populated as the Teesdale operations of the Quaker Lead Company. Villages of workers spring up around the wells, and are initially humanely resourced by Arnold, descending into pure exploitation later on. Arnold does not start out corrupt like the boss of the decorating firm in Tressell's novel, but is slowly changed through the increasing scale of his business ambitions. This is what makes Sinclair's novel more realistic: the slow change of Arnold in one direction, and the matching change in the other by his son.

For Sinclair capitalism cannot be redeemed however, and neither can socialism provide the answer. Galbraith was right: the economic pessimism that he detected in the American mainstream of economic thought is pervasive in American society, and well reflected in this novel. However, along the way Sinclair provides much food for thought and many interesting contrasts between the rich and the poor which are sympathetic to both. Amongst Bunny's high society friends for example are a group of ladies who decide to help the poor during the Depression. One gives all her clothes to the Salvation Army, thus giving her an excuse to re-outfit herself in the costliest possible manner. The group as whole decide on their main duty however: 'they would purchase only the most expensive kinds of food, so as to leave the lard and cabbage and potatoes for the poor.'[5] Sinclair's novel *The Jungle* is an equal indictment of raw capitalism, this time set in the meat-packing industry, but gives no insight into the employer side of the story.

It is John Steinbeck's *Grapes of Wrath*, I believe, that does the best job out of this group of novels in conveying what subsistence really means in a capitalist economy. Unlike Dickens he was not concerned with protecting the sensibilities of his readers. Indeed he says:

> I've done my damndest to rip the reader's nerves to rags. I don't want him satisfied. [...] I tried to write this book the way lives are being lived not the way books are written. [...] Throughout I've tried to make the reader participate in the actuality, what he takes from it will be scaled entirely on his own depth or hollowness.[6]

I believe that Steinbeck lives up to this rather Whitmanesque claim, perhaps something rare in any artist's self-appraisal. The story concerns a farming family, the Joads, driven off their land in Oklahoma by the banks, though more literally by the huge tractors now capable of cultivating in an hour what the family had taken weeks to do through older means. In an unconscious parallel with the 'Trail of Tears', in which Native Americans were driven from the land because their methods yielded so little and therefore sustained so few, the Joads are displaced by yet more modern methods of agriculture. In terms of economics this is highly significant, because the collapse of farm prices – due in a large part to the new mechanisation of cultivation – was a factor in the Depression. The Joads set out for California where they believe they will find work amongst the peach and orange trees, though along the way the family is already reduced in numbers through the hardships of travel. Once in California they discover that work is scarce, fought over by other 'Okies', and subject to rampant exploitation, particularly in the form of the 'company store' where credit is granted against wages on inflated prices. We saw that the Quakers operated such stores – 'truck shops' in the English system – with integrity, and drove out exploitative credit shops amongst their lead miners, but here we find the practice in its most malignant form. 'I sold my soul to the company store' goes the song, deriving from the bitter experience of migrant workers, effectively indentured by poverty. State intervention at the Federal level is what gives the Joad family a little respite; it was also what was most loathed by many Californians in their growing resentment of the Okies.

Steinbeck's novel is too majestic in its sweep to be amenable to any further summary however, so it is best to mention a single passage from late in the story, where the anger of the writer over this shameful chapter in American capitalism spills over. He describes how the skills of the grower and grafter of vines and fruit trees create produce that then have to be destroyed to keep up prices. He says:

> The people came for miles to take the fruit, but this could not be. How would they buy oranges at twenty cents a dozen if they could drive out and pick them up? And men with hoses squirt kerosene on the oranges, and they are angry at the crime, angry at the people who have come to take the fruit. A million people hungry, needing the fruit – and kerosene sprayed over the golden mountains.[7]

Coffee is burnt for fuel in ships, corn to keep warm. Potatoes are dumped in the river and guards posted to prevent hungry people fishing them out.

Industrial capitalism has largely avoided such over-production and simultaneous starvation since that time, but Steinbeck's classic portrayal of subsistence lives in the American mind, and it must surely be possible to tap into this memory to resist the march of the untrammelled free market. Poverty amidst plenty was the experience of the Joad family, but is again the experience of many in the Great Recession since 2008.

Fiction has a greater power over the eventual voting patterns of a society than worthy academic studies – even those of 'defunct' economists – so it is no surprise that von Mises writes bitterly about such works as Steinbeck's, declaring them 'tendentious art' peddling the idea that capitalism is evil, but with no alternatives to offer other than a vague hope for socialism.[8] The socialist novel may be tendentious and boring, according to von Mises, but what of the capitalist novel? We now turn to contemplate that very thing, a masterpiece of that genre.

Chapter 20

AYN RAND

Ayn Rand (1905–1982) was a novelist, playwright, screenwriter and philosopher, born and educated in Russia, who left in 1926 for America. She is famous for her two bestselling novels, *The Fountainhead* and *Atlas Shrugged*, and for her philosophy called Objectivism. She has been largely dismissed by intellectuals, universities and philosophers as the peddler of pulp fiction and a naive philosopher: a typical term of criticism flung at her work being 'sophomoric', while a less generous term is 'claptrap'.

But I think her work needs to be taken seriously. If Hayek's theories are kryptonite to Quakernomics it is because they declare that collective attempts to secure social and economic justice lead directly to Nazism or Stalinism. They paralyse attempts to establish social justice at the very outset by raising the spectre of industrial serfdom, but at least those fears can be demonstrated as unfounded in the post-war period. Rand shares those fears, having experienced Stalinism at first hand, where Hayek was merely a distant onlooker. But Rand's work – equally opposed to collectivism of any form – presents a *positive* archetype alongside the purely negative message that is Hayek's, and hence has an enduring appeal to the mainstream American who admires self-reliance and is suspicious of officialdom. That archetype is the heroic entrepreneur, and at first glance this Randian entrepreneur looks a little like a Quaker industrialist. This is not, however, the main reason to take her seriously. Instead it is the growing evidence from America that her work, largely dismissed by the mainstream as crankish in the early days, now commands enormous public respect, and aligns itself to mass political movements on the right, particularly the Tea Party. A business journalist called Gary Weiss has documented her resurgent popularity in the Great Recession in a book called *Ayn Rand Nation*. Weiss exposes the core madness within her thinking, but also demonstrates how seductive her ideas are to the mainstream in America (and even to himself).

There is no doubt that Rand's bitter hostility to socialism must have been formed by her early experiences under Stalin, and her writings form one of the most influential pro-capitalist free market canons of all time. During the Credit Crunch, as ordinary Americans attempted to comprehend the nature of the recession and its origins in the banking world, sales of her works surged – most of which had been around half a century in print.[1] The social activist Naomi Klein branded Rand's economic thinking as 'pulped-up Adam Smith',[2] but this is to miss the impact of Rand's work on American politics, and indirectly on the power of free market ideas in the UK as well. In other words I think it important for the left to answer her doctrines instead of ignoring her. Her influence is not just on the grass roots of such movements as the Tea Party, but also on people like Alan Greenspan, chairman of the Federal Reserve, and economist Milton Friedman (who I discuss in the next chapter).

Greenspan contributed an essay to *Capitalism: The Unknown Ideal*, a collection mostly written by Rand, in which her essay 'What is Capitalism?' sets out her basic position. As a critique of what she had left behind in Russia it is compelling – and so she has won the first round in terms of persuading the average American. It is also perceptive, saying, for example, concerning Western intellectuals: 'material production was regarded as a demeaning task of a lower order, unrelated to the concerns of man's intellect, a task assigned to slaves or serfs since the beginning of recorded history.'[3] This is accurate because the entire history of Western philosophy – originating in Plato (whose 'Republic' would have been built on slavery) and Aristotle (a slave-owning playboy), who both published lengthy justifications for slavery – is permeated with this lack of interest or even hostility to 'work'. These ideas have also tinged the entire Marxist tradition, including such authors as Hannah Arendt, having arrived there via Hegel. Quakernomics would have to agree with Rand here.

Rand is building up a defence of capitalism: that the surplus invested in production has a unique private owner, and that for the political economists of the left or right to call this a 'social' surplus is wrong. For Rand this surplus is not social, or tribal, or collective: it is entirely owned by individual entrepreneurs to be disposed of productively by them alone. For her the entrepreneur must have total freedom to deploy this surplus (i.e., to invest capital) because only they are capable of *thinking*, while the ordinary man, the labourer, is not. For her the very survival of the species is down to those she calls 'intransigent innovators', a description close to that of Schumpeter. The entrepreneur must above all be free, and for her capitalism is the only political system that guarantees this freedom. We have here the beginnings of the basic equation put forward by libertarians of all stripes: that capitalism *is* freedom. But I would suggest that the patient Quaker, listening with an open mind to Rand, begins to part company with her as she develops her theme:

> The moral justification of capitalism does not lie with the altruist claim that it represents the best way to achieve 'the common good.' It is true that capitalism does – if that catchphrase has any meaning – but this is merely a secondary consequence. The moral justification of capitalism lies in the fact that it is the only system consonant with man's rational nature, that it protects man's survival *qua* man, and that its ruling principle is: *justice*.[4]

For Rand the essence of man is rationality. But for the Quaker the humanity of man lies in exactly what Rand rejects: altruism. For the Quaker, capitalism needs no justification because productive work needs no justification in the first place, but if it had to be justified then certainly the 'common good' is precisely where it would lie. For Rand the 'common good' is a deceit or a fiction, a meaningless concept. We learn why, of course: because that very phrase in Soviet Russia was the excuse for the absolute destruction of freedom. As to her other point, no Quaker would agree that capitalism's 'ruling principle' is justice: the enslavement of blacks and the great trading triangle that ensued between Africa, America and Europe was entirely capitalist for example, and capitalist forces resisted every attempt at justice for the enslaved people. But Rand's ideas about capitalism in her non-fiction writing have had less impact than in her fiction, which we now turn to.

Atlas Shrugged

Rand's *Atlas Shrugged* (1957) is perhaps the most ambitious attempt yet to explore an economic philosophy in fiction. By a nice irony it sets out to consider what was proposed only in jest in Robert Tressell's novel *The Ragged Trousered Philanthropists*: that the capitalists should go on strike for once, instead of the workers. At the end of Chapter 11 in his book Tressell reminds us of a common saying: 'The men work with their hands – the master works with his brains'. The masters here are the capitalists, and at the end of Chapter 14 Tressell repeats the saying, adding sarcastically: 'What a dreadful calamity it would be for the world and for mankind if all these brain workers were to go on strike.'[5] Rand's novel imagines this literally, showing just what a socialist catastrophe would take place in America if the capitalists withdrew their labour.

Naomi Klein is right to call *Atlas Shrugged* 'pulp' – there is plenty of bodice-ripping in its romantic sections, and, very significantly, there are never any babies produced. The family is not the centre of the human world for Rand, but merely the irritating microcosm of a society which endlessly produces dependents parasitical on the entrepreneur. But the story of two 'masters' of industry is told engagingly enough: that of Dagny Taggart who is the female heir to a railway dynasty and Hank Rearden who is the brains behind a steel mill. Their love affair is a meeting of like minds: people committed to their work to the exclusion of all else, including any interest in wealth for its own sake. It is this that makes Rand's novel an interesting parallel to the Quaker tradition. Both are testimonies to the power of the entrepreneur and both declare such individuals to be unmotivated by wealth or luxury per se. Hank Rearden is a driven man, a technologist in love with molten steel and committed to innovation in his field, while Dagny Taggart, convinced by his new 'metal', orders enough for a whole new line. Rearden could be Abraham Darby II – or for that matter Andrew Carnegie – while Taggart's father who founded Dagny's fictional rail company could be the 'Father of the Railways' in Britain: Edward Pease.

But an enormous difference remains between Rand's entrepreneurs and the Quakers. It is not just that Rand herself is a committed atheist and has her characters believe in nothing of the world of faith, but that they are indifferent to the sufferings of others. Their response is: *I owe you nothing*. In effect they believe that the idea of a 'common humanity' and the obligations it places on one are lies. Rand's entrepreneurs are noble to this extent however: they declare that they would rather starve than steal, rather starve than accept charity. They are the ultimate armoured solitary individuals of competitive American free enterprise fantasy. And they never consider the question that is uppermost in the mind of the working man hovering at or below subsistence wages: how can I feed my hungry child? Children do not belong in Ayn Rand's world.

Rand paints state socialism as a creeping *incompetence* that lays waste to all the industries it nationalises and ruins everything it touches. Rand's entrepreneurs are totally self-reliant, and if they are corrupted, as in the case of Taggart's railroad dynasty relations, it is either through indulgence in luxury or adopting quasi-socialist values themselves.

Taggart and Rearden are of course model employers who stand up for and admire an honest working man or woman. In Rand's view, if there was an untrammelled free market then every such honest worker would have a well-paid job, and there would be no need for the state in any form, no need for any safety net. Rand is in good company with many economists who are simply not interested in the problem of subsistence wages – as we have seen – the impact of which on the working classes is portrayed so vividly by Tressell, Sinclair and Steinbeck. She is in good company with those who are not interested either in the question of full employment. But her ideal world degenerates very fast into science-fiction fantasy. The men and women of brains, the masters, really do withdraw their labour and retreat to a mountain fastness where they maintain an entire economy by themselves. No workers. Who needs them. This is the ultimate absurdity of Rand's vision. It is this that makes Rand the perfect opposite extreme to Marx. He thought – and Tressell followed him – that workers do not need the entrepreneur. Rand thinks that the entrepreneur does not need the worker. Both represent a foolish extreme that Quakernomics as a middle way rejects. There is obviously an utter interdependence between entrepreneur and worker, and, because of their naturally competing claims in their 'method of association' – as Tawney puts it – a system of economic justice has to be discovered that mediates between them, creating an ethical capitalism.

The story of *Atlas Shrugged* builds up the mystery of a man called John Galt who finally speaks his philosophy on national radio in the climax of the novel. The speech – essentially a summary of Rand's politico-economic philosophy – takes up 55 pages. Galt explains why the entrepreneurs have gone on strike: 'We are on strike against self-immolation. We are on strike against the creed of unearned rewards and unrewarded duties. We are on strike against the dogma that the pursuit of one's happiness is evil. We are on strike against the doctrine that life is guilt.'[6]

Rand has identified socialism and mysticism as the two great evils that declare one's obligation to others ('mysticism' here can be understood as religion). And the socialist dictator – Stalin is never mentioned by name because *Atlas Shrugged* is determinedly non-historical – combines both evils. Galt's rant would be incomprehensible however without knowing the history of Hitler's and Stalin's regimes. To grow up with one's individuality subsumed under the collective of 'the Volk' or 'the proletariat', particularly for an artistic personality like Rand, is to suffer a nightmare. But the extremes which she identifies with both socialism and religion become easy targets, straw men for Galt to knock down. And of course she, through Galt, advocates an equal extreme, which has as little basis in the real-world economy as the most extreme of socialist utopias. Indeed it turns out that Galt's whole entrepreneurial genius lies in the discovery of a perpetual motion machine that creates energy out of nothing. I was also keen on developing such machines, but stopped sketching out designs for them around the age of 14. Such ideas undermine Rand's pretensions to economic competence, which, if it is not based in real-world physics, becomes a romanticism as ineffective as Dickens'.

Yet one cannot deny the immense appeal of the Randian entrepreneur, personified in *Atlas Shrugged* through the characters of Rearden, Taggart and Galt, and personified in her earlier and equally influential novel *The Fountainhead* through the architect Howard Roark. Both novels have sold in the millions. In the first instance, when these entrepreneurs are set against the great Quaker entrepreneurs and scientists, the common ground is extensive. Quakernomics as a history of enterprise would be attractive enough to Tea Party enthusiasts, especially those repelled by Rand's extreme atheism and anti-family stance. But the real question that Quakernomics puts to all of Rand's followers is this: why stop at the Randian entrepreneur? Look at Andrew Carnegie, a real steel giant like the fictional Rearden. He insisted on what Rand loathed: on altruism, on philanthropy. Did that undermine American freedom? He was born in a one-room Scottish hovel, and, starting as a telegraph boy, seized the opportunities within American industry to become a billionaire. Is his life any the less because of his philanthropy? And if so why stop there? Why not consider Abraham Darby II, a man whose family initiated the whole modern story of iron and steel, and who epitomises Quakernomics, a capitalism determined to create wealth and social justice at the same time? Is not a Darby, or a Cadbury, or a Rowntree, or a Clark exactly twice the entrepreneur of a Rearden or a Roark?

To see and admire the entrepreneur as the key individual in modern civilisation is to understand the real economy. Rand is right to say that theorists within philosophy and even within economics have neglected this figure. But, restating my previous question, why settle for the Randian entrepreneur, which is exactly half the Quaker entrepreneur? Why settle for a vision of the genius entrepreneur who only cares about himself and his kind when you could have a vision of the entrepreneur who cares for the whole of society? What loss to freedom does this vision possibly represent?

Rand and Marx

When Quakernomics looks to its left and considers Marx, it finds a utopian extremism in which the entrepreneur has become the evil capitalist, source of all social injustice. When Quakernomics looks to its right and considers Rand it finds a utopian extremism in which the entrepreneur has acquired heroic stature but is utterly indifferent to questions of social justice. Where Marx cries out in rage at the injustice done to the working man and woman, Rand cries out in rage at the injustice done to the entrepreneur. Their equal and opposite rage attracts millions of angry people to their rhetoric, but I would suggest that the quiet Quaker finds them equally lacking in *truth*. As pointed out before, if Coalbrookdale had been taken over by its workers and the Darby and Reynolds families sent to Siberia as class enemies, who would have made the genius breakthroughs in iron making celebrated by Danny Boyle? And how would the capital for further development have been amassed? In Stalinist Russia it was extracted by diktat, instead of allowing capital markets – in this case often Quaker-led – to generate finance on an elective risk-taking basis. Conversely, how could Abraham Darby – however big his family and Quaker connections – have produced the smallest scrap of iron without workers? Both Marx and Rand are utopian dreamers. And, historically, Rand is a reaction to Marx: his extremism has begot hers.

The post-war consensus in economics, which was broadly pro-state and Keynesian – and probably deriving from the collective witnessing in the US of the Okie phenomenon and also the collectivisation of effort through the war – broke down in the 1970s and allowed the Randian vision to come to the fore. While Rand is worth rebutting, as Weiss points out, it is Milton Friedman who acted within his own lifetime on the world economic stage, effectively attempting to make real what Rand only fantasised.

Chapter 21

MILTON FRIEDMAN

We now turn to look at the work and legacy of Milton Friedman (1912–2006). It is in this section perhaps that I am able to present the starkest contrast between the theories of a highly influential mainstream economist of the right, and ethical capitalism as found for example in the entrepreneurial practice of the Quakers. It is here that economic theories reach a pitch of indifference to the question of how industrialism impacts on the poor and how one might construct an ethical capitalism. It is here that capitalism, as in Rand, actually becomes an ethics in itself. More than that, it becomes the overarching ethic which sweeps away all other considerations.

Capitalism and Freedom (1962) is a major popular work of Friedman's that sits happily on the bookshelf of the conservative American alongside Rand's *Atlas Shrugged* and Hayek's *The Road to Serfdom*. Friedman wrote the introduction to the 50th anniversary edition of the latter. All this might suggest that Friedman is only of importance in the American context, but, as we will see, his programme was rolled out world-wide. On the right, thought of von Mises, Hayek and Rand was initially confined to a small group of enthusiasts and Friedman himself laboured many years as an obscure academic before his ideas began to find favour. The aim of this section is to show that when the Freidmanite revolution did get underway, however reasonable its exterior, it was an extremism as great as the Marxist one.

The heritage of Friedman's economic thought is traced through his long-time associate Friedrich Hayek back to von Mises, and starts out relatively moderate. Friedman's career began as a mathematical statistician working on weapons design for the Division of War Research at Columbia University. He then took up a teaching post in economics at the University of Chicago where he worked for thirty years and built a community of economists who were eventually to have more influence on global economics than perhaps any other in history apart from the Keynesians.

Friedman's economic thinking began within the Keynesian mainstream of his day, while his research focussed on monetary issues, leading to several influential academic works on the monetary history of the US and recommendations for monetary policy. Chief of these was the proposal that the Federal Reserve System abandon attempts to mitigate the business cycle, and simply increase the money supply at a steady rate to match economic growth, a policy in fact never adopted. His monetary research gave him a strong platform for the assertion that government interference had caused the Great Depression.

Whatever his research in economics Friedman's philosophy was simple: reduce government. Here is the real divide between the economists of the left and right in the USA: on the left are the Keynesians who believe that government intervention – the New Deal – rescued America from the Depression, while on the right are the Friedmanites who believe that incompetent intervention – or lack of it – by the Federal Reserve System caused it in the first place, and that the New Deal, as a form of socialism, made things worse.

Whatever the truth of depression economics, Friedman's position on it is now universally adopted by the right in America. Ayn Rand used it in her day as the simplest and most direct argument against government involvement in the market. Once the idea takes hold that the US government caused the Depression a powerful case for reducing government is made, though Friedman's view has only gradually become widespread in America. Friedman commented, for example: 'However, government's responsibility for the depression was not recognized – either then or now. Instead, the depression was widely interpreted as a failure of free market capitalism.'[1] This is a quote from *Free to Choose*, the book published in 1980 that accompanied his highly influential TV series of the same name. In 2006 Ben Bernanke, a scholar of Depression economics who appears to agree with Friedman on its causes, was appointed chairman of the Federal Reserve. By this time Friedman's argument was largely won.

Free to Choose set out to further popularise the ideas of small government found in *Capitalism and Freedom*, arguing above all that capitalism is an essential prerequisite for freedom. To the extent that these two books are a critique of Soviet economics, written during the Cold War, there is little to disagree with in them. In fact socialists would do well to read *Free to Choose* because it deals with a historical period in which socialist goals in the US and UK had indeed driven the economies of both countries into a form of stagnation which was bound to provoke a reaction from those seeking a more dynamic enterprise culture. The extremes of socialist intervention in Russia in the economy and people's lives were clearly indefensible, and Rand and Friedman were on the side of social and economic justice in attacking Communism in that form. But the whole history of this is that one extreme provokes an opposite extreme.

Capitalism and Freedom is a short and readable book. It offers views on a range of economic issues, some of which are long outdated, others of which are continuously revived. Its essential message is that government is a bad thing, tolerable only to perform some minimum role beyond which it is an evil bound to become the 'Road to Serfdom'.[2] The book's first chapter sets out Friedman's stall, in which he makes the link between capitalism and economic freedom, and between economic freedom and political freedom. He bemoans the fact that most intellectuals hold socialist views and have contempt, as he sees it, for the 'material aspects of life'. This is indeed a valid criticism, made by Rand as well, that the intellectual, particularly the tenured university academic, is divorced from the real economy of making things; ignorant of the entrepreneur; and inclined to demand that the state pay for everything. Friedman continues: 'For most citizens of the country, however, if not for the intellectual, the direct importance of economic freedom is at least comparable in significance to the indirect importance of economic freedom as a means to political freedom.'[3]

It is not difficult to understand what political freedoms are: they are the right to vote, to form associations, to travel, to criticise government, to be free from racial, religious or sexual prejudice, and so on. But what exactly are 'economic freedoms'? For Friedman these are the freedoms to conduct business without government interference in such things as prices, wages, quotas, tariffs, taxation, regulation, and so on. Crucially, perhaps, economic freedom for Friedman is freedom from taxation. The more that the government spends, the greater the taxes it levies, and the less free we become to spend our dollars as we would like. He concedes that some regulation is needed, to stop the factory furnace dumping soot on the neighbours, for example, but the less government control over the economy the better. Hence economic freedom demands small government both in terms of its overall tax take, and in terms of its regulatory controls over enterprise.

But why should increased economic freedom as so defined bring *political* freedom? He insists: 'The kind of economic organisation that provides economic freedom directly, namely, competitive capitalism, also promotes political freedom because it separates economic power from political power and in this way enables the one to offset the other.'[4]

The separation of powers is essential to a fair, democratic society. But does competitive capitalism actually separate economic power from political power? If we imagine a transition from a democratic economy where most large industries are nationalised, and hence unfree from political power, to an economy where they are returned to private hands and hence free, do those industries then offset political power? Is there an increase in political freedoms for the ordinary citizen? Do the captains of those industries use their new economic powers to lobby government to protect the political rights and freedoms of the citizen? George Cadbury, amongst other Quaker industrialists, did, though his contemporary John Bright was sceptical of the role of government. But Cadbury, as we have shown, was an island in a sea of unethical capitalism where economic power lobbied government at every step to *reduce* political freedoms for the ordinary citizen. It was not Victorian business interests on the whole that lobbied for shorter working hours, trades union rights and the universal franchise; far from it. Competitive capitalism since the dawn of the Industrial Revolution has thrown up economic power that instantly slips its tentacles around political power, and no phenomenon better demonstrates this today than the role of corporate funding in US presidential elections and in corporate lobbying power over Congress.

Privatised industries are unlikely to increase political freedoms for any but the few who run them. Deregulation of those industries again only increases political freedoms for the few. But regulation of industry is costly, and needs tax dollars. What about Friedman's more general claim that reducing taxes increases both personal and political freedoms? If regulatory bodies are dismantled and the tax dollars they absorb are returned to the citizen, they have increased freedom to exercise personal choice over those dollars. We should not doubt this, not the desire of the citizen for this. But the deregulated food industry, for example, will now poison more people. Deregulated automobile manufacture will increase road deaths. Deregulated financial services will bankrupt more citizens. Friedman does not discuss this trade-off. But the more radical claim that Friedman makes is that reduced government, both in reduced regulatory interference with enterprise and in reduced taxation, increases political freedom. Economic power, he argues, will hold political power in check. But whose economic power? The ordinary citizen with a few more dollars in their pocket is no more free to express their political leanings than before. The ordinary citizen with more dollars in their pocket is no more free of political corruption than before. Even if they have made an informed decision about the increased risks of poisoning, automobile accidents and bankruptcy, what political freedoms have their increased dollars bought them? Instead, I would suggest, it is the wealthy citizen, now relieved from substantial redistributive taxation, who might care to spend that new money in the political arena, and has the wealth to make a political difference. The poor citizen, on the other hand, who had been the net beneficiary of redistributive taxation, may actually lose dollars. Their economic freedom is reduced even from what low level it had been, and their political freedoms – other things being equal – are not enhanced at all.

Hence I would suggest that the intellectual incoherence of Friedman's assertion – that economic freedom is a means to political freedom – lies in this: that economic freedom for one person is economic servitude for another. The Joad family, confined to low wages that could only be spent at the company store, were in servitude to their exploitative employers. Economic freedom for the employers is no guarantee of economic freedom for the workers, or of political freedom: attempts to unionise in Steinbeck's story were met with company violence backed up by the police. The intellectual incoherence in Freidman's idea therefore lies not in the concept of political freedom – which is an ongoing compromise between the various adversarial sectors that constitute society – but in the concept of economic freedom itself. It is simply not comparable to political freedom, and to compare them is a category mistake. Billionaire industrialists intervene in the political process because they are free to spend their money. That is their economic freedom. Poor people may be equally free to spend their money, but don't have any. Economic freedom is therefore never equally enshrined in law for all – you can't pass legislation that makes everyone rich – whereas political freedom is – and its very basis is 'one law for all'. And where it is not it is usually because the economic freedom of the billionaire has bought votes in the legislature.

The incoherence of Friedman and his followers on economic and political freedom would not be possible without its counterpart: the extremism that declares government inevitably incompetent, and worse, a threat to liberty. Friedman's argument goes like this: freedom is a 'rare and delicate plant', as he puts it, and few would disagree. And the greatest threat to freedom is the concentration of power. Again this is reasonable. But now he insists: 'Government is necessary to preserve freedom; yet by concentrating power in political hands, it is also a threat to freedom.'[5] What happened to democracy and its adversarial separation of powers? There is at least as much enthusiasm for the concept of democracy in America as there is for the concept of the free market. But one searches Friedman's writings in vain for any enthusiasm for democracy, and there is less still confidence, hope, or faith that democracy is what makes good government or that democracy is what guarantees freedom, or that the separation of powers underpins all this. Galbraith is right: the tradition of economic writing in America is a pessimistic one.

It is Friedman's job to convince us that competitive capitalism is the guarantor of economic freedom, which is the guarantor of political freedom. He is aware however that he has an uphill task, conceding in fact that capitalism is a necessary but not sufficient condition for political freedom. He cites fascist Italy and Spain as examples, but today China would better represent a contemporary state in which capitalism is the economic order but democracy is not the political order. He also notes that 'Welfare rather than freedom became the dominant note in democratic countries.'[6] Again all this rather weakens his argument. Clearly post-war Western democracies tended to vote for welfare. Voters turn out to be rather unaccommodating to Friedman's ideas. But why *does* Friedman think that the citizen faces an exclusive choice between either more welfare or more freedom?

I pointed out from personal experience that Britain in the 1970s, under the most generous welfare arrangements yet experienced in its history, allowed an almost infinite range of personal freedoms to its citizens, again unprecedented in its history. America was no different: think Haight-Ashbury, hippies, Woodstock, and so on. On the other hand it is perfectly true that there was economic stagnation in the 1970s, at least if growth figures were compared to the immediate post-war boom. There was also a certain endemic torpor in the nationalised industries: as a typical student summer job I worked at British Leyland for a day and worked for several weeks valeting British Leyland cars in dealership showrooms. Its products were no doubt mediocre. All of these problems are well documented by Friedman and are sobering factual histories for socialists to contemplate. Few now argue for a return to nationalised industries of that sort. But where in all of this was freedom snatched from me, or the great bulk of British citizens, by the 'concentration of power' allegedly exercised by a bloated government sector? I was perfectly free to choose a Renault car over a British Leyland car – equally products of nationalised industries – and I was free to buy subversive papers, choose my university course, and free to choose where I lived and what political party I would support. And free of course to grow my hair long, wear flairs and play the saxophone in a funk band. Non-hippies were equally free to join the Young Conservatives.

Friedman says: 'As liberals, we take freedom of the individual, or perhaps the family, as our ultimate goal in judging social arrangements.'[7] So just what freedoms are lost when governments get big, or when they attempt to intervene on any scale in the economy? Hayek's answer was vague but simple: the next step is Nazism. But Friedman cannot argue that, because no Western post-war state even remotely resembled such a thing. He has to catalogue instead a series of choices denied to the citizen. Some of his examples are historical accidents of the period, such as constraints on Churchill speaking on the radio, or restrictions on travel because of the Cold War or because of currency exchange controls, all long gone. But other examples are worth examining: for instance, lack of choice over schooling, health insurance or pensions. Under a welfare state citizens are forced to contribute to state education, health and pension arrangements. These restrictions of economic freedom are, according to Friedman, the basis on which political freedom is slowly withdrawn from the citizen. Friedman shows indeed that if the average citizen is forced, through taxation, to subscribe to state schools, state health provision and state pensions, then they are not free to devote those same dollars to their private choice of schools, healthcare and pension. We should, apparently, be horrified by this.

But Friedman omits the question of poverty. What about people who could afford none of those things in the first place? He is adamant that there should be no minimum wage, so who is to say that people on low wages could afford schooling for their children, healthcare or a pension? Every Quaker employer was exercised over exactly those issues. Friedman's concern for economic freedom, then, is a concern for the well-off sector of the population, and not for all of it. But the argument for economic justice presented by Quakernomics is this: should not the well-off sector of the population give up some small economic freedoms so others have basic provision? After all, does not Hayek argue for this basic provision? In fact so does Friedman. But in both cases there remains an unresolved contradiction: the basic provisions, annoyingly, require large government. And even more annoyingly, citizens seem to vote for those provisions, suggesting perhaps it is not just a minority who are protected by them.

More economic freedom for the reasonably well off would allow more choice, that is clear. Granting them that would reduce the standards of living of the poor, but then, they are free to be poor. But would all this increase political freedoms for the two groups? Would there be a rise in the right to vote, to form associations, to travel, to criticise government, to be free from racial, religious or sexual prejudice, and so on? It is hard to see why. But it is clear to see that the wealthier group, now paying less tax, can more easily mitigate the impact of existing unfreedoms. A rich person can choose to live away from the unsightly dwellings of the poor for example; that, no doubt, is a freedom of a certain sort. But, if we can find any kind of metric by which to measure the aggregate freedom of a nation – the average freedom expressed in the number of free choices open to all citizens – then that metric is unlikely to show that increased freedoms for the rich also increase the average freedoms for all. The opposite is more likely in fact.

These are the general arguments, I suggest, which make Friedman's thesis incoherent, politically naïve and effectively an extremism of the right.

I now want to focus on an element in Friedman's thought, introduced in a chapter titled 'Monopoly and the Social Responsibility of Business and Labor'. It is here that Friedman expresses views about the role of the company that are the most opposed to everything the Quaker tradition stands for. He says that the businessman in a competitive market has little power to 'alter the terms of exchange', i.e., influence prices, and hence 'it is hard to argue that he has any "social responsibility"'.[8] Friedman contrasts the small entrepreneur with the monopolist, who is 'visible and has power', and of whom he says: 'It is easy to argue that he should discharge his power not solely to further his own interests but to further socially desirable ends. Yet the widespread application of such a doctrine would destroy a free society.'

I don't believe that Friedman has made *any* logical connection here between, firstly, an entrepreneur who cannot dictate prices to the market and the obligations or otherwise to society, and secondly, between a monopolist who does further socially desirable ends and the destruction of a free society. In the first case competitive entrepreneurs, as we have seen, can make huge profits in very competitive markets, or may take losses for many years, regardless of their capacity to influence the market as a whole – it depends more on what stage of development the company is in, and on the state of the economy. But the Cadburys, while making losses and failing to dent Fry's dominance in the early days, still placed their obligations to society at the forefront. These obligations began with the workers and extended from raising wages above subsistence to later providing a garden village for them. Had Cadbury been able to dictate prices to the market his advantage would have made no difference to his obligations as he saw them. In the second case, were a monopolist to further social ends because they faced no competition and could therefore guarantee higher levels of profit, how exactly would this destroy a free society? If an electric monopoly practiced welfare on the scale of a George Cadbury, how exactly would this erode our freedoms?

But Friedman's objection is the crux of the new free market philosophy, and appears to be inherited directly from von Mises and Hayek. For a capitalist, whether a competitive one or a monopolist, to pursue socially desirable ends would allegedly 'destroy' a free society. Friedman returns to this theme a little later, and I would have the following passage etched in stone so as to make free marketeers consider the absurdity of what they stand for:

> Few trends could so thoroughly undermine the very foundations of our free society as the acceptance by corporate officials of a social responsibility other than to make as much money for their stockholders as possible. This is a fundamentally subversive doctrine.[9]

Friedman expanded this theme in a famous 1970 essay for the *New York Times Magazine*, which includes this statement:

> The businessmen believe that they are defending free enterprise when they declaim that business is not concerned 'merely' with profit but also with promoting desirable 'social' ends; that business has a 'social conscience' and takes seriously its responsibilities for providing employment, eliminating discrimination, avoiding pollution and whatever else may be the catchwords of the contemporary crop of reformers. In fact they are – or would be if they or anyone else took them seriously – preaching pure and unadulterated socialism. Businessmen who talk this way are unwitting puppets of the intellectual forces that have been undermining the basis of a free society these past decades.[10]

Was George Cadbury the 'unwitting puppet' of intellectual forces that undermined the basis of a free society? Was this 'pure and unadulterated socialism'? Not unless you call the Quaker tradition a subversive movement whose followers were bent on locking up those who fought for political freedom. Actually I can't find a way of constructing an absurdity to parallel Friedman's here. His arguments have a rigorous veneer, but when triangulated against Quaker entrepreneurs, or for that matter the entire tradition of philanthropic capitalism represented by, say, Andrew Carnegie or William Lever, they rapidly reveal themselves as incoherent.

Quakernomics still has to defend this objection of Friedman however: how exactly can the social conscience of a man like Cadbury transfer from the family firm to the corporation? Where corporate executives, it is argued, have a moral responsibility to the owners of the corporation, i.e., to the shareholders? Let us grant that incorporation does change the stakes, at least to some degree. The Quaker entrepreneurs who raised capital through the Quaker network – and through Quaker banks from the wider world – had an obligation to their investors. So far so simple: they had to be repaid with the agreed amount of interest. But stockholders who expect a dividend, and who are anonymous, are different, perhaps. This may indeed be one of the major ethical questions in contemporary capitalism: is it not morally correct to say that the prospective recipient of the dividend has the moral right over the use put to of that profit, rather than the corporate official? Surely the small shareholder can donate some proportion of their dividends to charity if they wish – as very many of them likely do in the normal course of charitable giving – thus leaving the choice to the consumer rather than the capitalist? Isn't that precisely the kind of freedom that raw capitalism is famously good at endowing?

I believe that the answer to that is no, however. The stockholder who receives a smaller than otherwise dividend, or watches a smaller than otherwise growth in the value of their stock, is free to sell up and buy other shares. A stockholder by definition is a *gambler* because they have bought stocks rather than government or corporate bonds – on the statistical argument that in the long term they give a better return – and they hope for the share value to rise. Many serious economic works have exposed the sheer fantasy world of the speculator when, sheep-like, they place their savings in bubbles doomed to burst like a chewing-gum balloon and leave only a sticky mess on their faces. What moral obligation is the honourable corporation under to provide the gambler with the *maximum* dividend, when an average dividend is possible? What obligation does any sector of society have to the something-for-nothing intoxicated speculator? The margin between a maximum dividend and a realistic one is exactly what transforms a corporation from a machine indifferent to its workers, community and the environment into one which becomes socially responsible – *at the same time* as delivering its beneficial goods or services. Quakernomics proves not just the possibility of that dual ambition, but its desirability. If Friedman's logic is pursued far enough – and no doubt many companies would do so if they could – then not only is corporate social responsibility withdrawn beyond the factory gates, but it is abandoned within them. What is to stop the industrialist from withdrawing all those concessions to the worker which make the difference between dignified and undignified labour, between good and lousy wages? All in the name of maximising profit destined as dividends? Dividends destined to fuel more fantasy speculation? Making profit the *sole* responsibility of the corporate executive would be a license to regress to subsistence wages and environmental irresponsibility – because who is to say that market forces on their own can deliver living wages and unpolluting factories? Making profit the *sole* responsibility of the corporate executive would be a license to promulgate the four evils of industrial capitalism on a yet greater scale.

The economist Ha-Joon Chang makes another argument against Friedman's theory. He points out that the stockholder or shareholder is the person with the least stake in the long-term viability of the company. All the other stakeholders, including management and the workforce, have everything to lose if the company does badly, but the shareholders, at the first sign of trouble, sell their shares and walk away. As Chang puts it: 'the very ease of exit is exactly what makes the shareholders unreliable guardians of a company's long-term future.'[11]

Surely Friedman's doctrines are absurd. What on earth is there in making provisions for welfare and the environment that could 'destroy a free society' or be an embodiment of 'a fundamentally subversive doctrine'? If the corporation chooses to endow a university, build a model village, or conserve a local woodland, what freedoms does this destroy or what subversion of the social order does this represent? If the shareholder is disgusted with all this, they can sell their shares. After all, they are the haves, while the have-nots can hardly be said to labour under this unfreedom of lower dividends.

Friedman further believes that a businessman setting out to undertake what he or she feels are the obligations of social responsibility faces an impossible question: what are those obligations? In his own words: 'If businessmen do have a social responsibility other than making maximum profits for stockholders, how are they to know what it is? Can self-selected private individuals decide what the social interest is?'[12] This is typical of Friedman, as we shall see shortly: a rather defeatist approach to *any* questions of the greater social good. But the Quaker example shows that such businessmen find no difficulty at all in identifying the social interest: it lies with low wages, inequality, the poor, the underprivileged, the sick, the young and the old, and in protecting the environment. It's not rocket science.

Here I want to make a few more comments about Friedman's economic vision and how it stands in stark contrast to Quakernomics. In a newspaper article on the 2012 US primaries, a journalist commented on the fact that the only thing that united the Republican presidential hopefuls was their equal hatred of government.[13] Friedman demonstrates this continuously in his book, where his notion of 'freedom' is devoid of its social counterpart, 'responsibility'. In fact the conundrum of the American right is how to reconcile an alleged love of democracy with a profound distrust of government. It is here that Friedman is open to the charges of political naivety and extremism, as I have shown. The former he readily admits to in many passages in his works where he effectively says that politics is beyond his expertise, after all he is just an economist, while the extremism, admittedly, is low key, somewhat hidden, and perhaps an extremism of omission.

The impression he gives is of a rather forlorn vision, and nothing is more forlorn than his chapter in *Capitalism and Freedom* on discrimination. He says:

> The development of capitalism has been accompanied by a major reduction in the extent to which particular religious, racial, or social groups have operated under special handicaps in respect of their economic activities; have, as the saying goes, been discriminated against.[14]

He even cites Jews and Quakers as beneficiaries in the reduction of discrimination, and there is no doubt that both groups were able to seize the opportunities of new economic developments for their general progress towards emancipation. That may be true, but under Communism in most cases the reduction in discrimination was far more immediate and widespread, and on the collapse of Communism many ancient prejudices, whether racial, religious or sexual, re-emerged under burgeoning free market capitalism. Any claim that capitalism is the key factor in the reduction of such prejudices has little historical support. But Friedman wants to explain just how capitalism might achieve reductions in prejudice, saying that a man, for example, who refuses to buy from, or work with, a 'Negro' (his term) limits his choices, and therefore raises his *costs*. Those free from such prejudices can buy things more cheaply as a result. He concludes:

> As these comments perhaps suggest, there are real problems in defining and interpreting discrimination. The man who exercises discrimination pays a price for doing so. He is as it were, 'buying' what he regards as a 'product'. It is hard to see that discrimination can have any meaning other than the 'taste' of others that one does not share.[15]

Friedman appears to be saying that racism is merely a matter of taste but has a discouraging economic cost, and those with the money to do so should be free to exercise it, to 'buy' the right not to work with or purchase products from a member of a racial minority. You can see the shrug of his shoulders. It's a matter of taste isn't it? He certainly regards state legislation in such things as employment discrimination as unacceptable: 'Such legislation clearly involves interference with the freedom of individuals to enter into voluntary contracts with each other. Thus it is directly an interference with freedom of the kind that we would object to in most other contexts.'[16]

This is bad enough, but I think Friedman is at his most forlorn in this passage where he effectively denies the very *possibility* of social justice:

> As a general rule, any minority that counts on specific majority action to defend its interests is short-sighted in the extreme. Acceptance of a general self-denying ordinance applying to a class of cases may inhibit specific majorities from exploiting specific minorities. In the absence of such a self-denying ordinance, majorities can surely be counted on to use their power to give effect to their preferences, or if you will, prejudices, not to protect minorities from the prejudices of majorities.[17]

This is perhaps his strongest expression of disbelief in democracy. Who knows: perhaps it derives from his family experience, however distant, of the Holocaust where the majority slaughtered a minority. For him democracy, as majority rule, cannot hope to protect minorities; only capitalism can do that by imposing costs on those who discriminate.

Indeed it is perhaps one of the enduring mysteries of democracy that its progress has been measured by precisely the degree to which majorities *have* voted to protect minorities. Here lies in Friedman, not so much naivety, but lack of interest. What of the US constitution and the work of the Supreme Court? What of the slow but steady march of civil rights, gay rights and women's rights? Friedman is simply not interested. Capitalism will sort all that out, and if it doesn't? Shrug.

Given that the truly impoverished, the disabled, the immigrants and most other minorities are to receive no support from either the state or corporation, things look bleak indeed in Friedman's vision. The little protection that the Okies had in California, as shown in Steinbeck's novel, came from Federal sources. If majorities can be counted on not to protect minorities from their prejudices, then what hope is there for any minority? The actual history of the US shows something that Friedman, it seems, cannot envisage: a growing consensus over human rights, as embodied in the constitution and interpreted by the Supreme Court. Quakers were concerned for such rights and embodied those principles in their capitalist enterprises as far as their human limitations permitted. At the same time they grew wealthy. In *that* lies the real rebuke to Friedman.

The Friedmanite Legacy

Friedman happened to be in the right place at the right time and so he became the visible symbol of an entire economic theory, particularly for Americans who watched his TV series. In a *Telegraph* article after Friedman's death in 2006 Margaret Thatcher was reported as saying: 'Milton Friedman revived the economics of liberty when it had been all but forgotten. He was an intellectual freedom fighter. Never was there a less dismal practitioner of a dismal science.'[18] Friedman was a regular advisor to the Thatcher government, but it was perhaps Hayek's books, including *The Constitution of Liberty* and *The Road to Serfdom*, that were the greater influence on her. It doesn't matter: the point is that for both Reagan and Thatcher the neoliberal free market thinkers including von Mises, Hayek, Rand and Friedman had seized the intellectual high ground. In the economic revolutions instigated under the two leaders, the post-war Keynesian consensus was swept away and the state abandoned whole swaths of control over capitalist economic activity. In addition, as

Joseph Stiglitz says: 'The former communist countries generally turned, after the dismal failure of their post-war system, to capitalism, but some turned to a distorted version of a market economy: they replaced Karl Marx with Milton Friedman as their god.'[19]

Friedman's work is seductive because he writes and argues well (at first sight at least) and appears moderate, though I have suggested that many of his 'arguments' are in fact non-sequiturs, as examined above, and that his moderation is illusory. When it comes to difficult political issues, he metaphorically shrugs and tells us that such things lie beyond his expertise. Is it fair then to call him both politically naive and also extremist, albeit more by omission than by direct recourse, as Hayek does, to fears of Nazism and other terrors? This is not a question about a single academic and his books. What matters, as with the Quakers, is the impact on the world. And that impact is huge.

Friedman's most vociferous critic perhaps is Naomi Klein in her book *The Shock Doctrine*. In it she documents how the 'Chicago Boys' – Friedman's pupils – set out to implement his economic principles around the world in a variety of regimes inclined towards socialism during the Cold War, and hence a matter of deep anxiety for the US administration. The countries that she lists as affected by this mix of economic entrepreneurialism and US State Department intervention include: Chile, Argentina, Brazil, Bolivia, Poland, Russia, South Africa and Indonesia. Thatcher introduced Friedmanite reforms into the UK more directly, and without the horrific 'disappearances' that took place for example in Chile. There is not space here to explore Klein's controversial thesis in depth, and it is not correct to lay all the consequences at the door of Freidman (or even the Chicago School): he just happened to become one of the more visible faces of a growing right-wing reaction to post-war socialist policies. But one case is worth comment: that of Friedman's support for General Pinochet, extending to a meeting with him in 1975. After the extent of Pinochet's brutality became known Friedman was hounded by protestors asking him to explain his willingness to meet with the dictator. Effectively his response was that he was only a mere economist, and of course he condemned the violence. It is a shrug of the shoulders, a quick concession that his expertise does not lie with politics, and a comfortable return to the belief that economics and politics are thus separable.

But we may recall that the Galtons of Birmingham were summoned to their local Quaker Meeting to explain their continued manufacture of arms. Their response was that the manufacturer was not to blame for the violence – that was down to those who used the weapons. This did not wash with the Quakers who proceeded to disown them. Economists create policy instruments not guns, but they can no more disown the results of implementing them than can arms manufacturers. Klein argues that in every country where the Chicago Boys were parachuted in the short-term outcome was a massive funnelling of wealth from poor to rich and a suspension of democratic organisations, in particular the trade unions. State benefits to the poorest were abandoned, and foreign capital bought up national resources and local companies. Those opposing deregulation were kidnapped and murdered: the 'missing' across South America are a scar on all its societies that will not heal until every single death is accounted for. The International Committee of the Red Cross is still working in Argentina, Chile, Colombia, Guatemala, Mexico and Peru to discover the fate of loved ones who underwent 'forced disappearance' (the legal term for it in international law) under reforms like those of Pinochet. Chile's own official reports later concluded that well over two thousand people were killed and over thirty-eight thousand people had been imprisoned for political reasons, most of them tortured. Economic freedom of the kind advocated by Friedman had, it seems, brought little immediate political freedom.

It is interesting to set Friedman's philosophy alongside that of the neoconservative Francis Fukuyama. As we have seen, the core of Friedman's work is the proposition that capitalism is an essential prerequisite of freedom. However economic 'freedom' in Chile was bought at the cost of political oppression, even if, as many assert, in the long run Chile's economy developed faster than its neighbours and democracy was eventually restored. Fukuyama says in his famous book *The End of History*: 'Chile put liberal economic principles into practice earlier in the 1980s under Pinochet, with the result that its economy was the healthiest of any in the Southern Cone as it emerged from dictatorship under the leadership of President Patricio Alwyn.'[20] This is again approval by omission: Fukuyama is not prepared to mention the 'forced disappearances' and torture that were required to implement those liberal economic principles. Indeed he is impressed that: 'There is considerable empirical evidence to indicate that market-oriented authoritarian modernizers do better economically than their democratic counterparts.'[21] The idea that authoritarian leaders, in other words dictators or fascists, are better at supporting capitalism than democratic leaders again rather contradicts Friedman's idea that capitalism has some necessary connection with freedom.

Fukuyama dismisses the idea of redistributing wealth from the rich to the poor in socialist Latin America 'in the interests of "social justice"' as mercantilism.[22] It is telling that he puts the term 'social justice' in scare quotes (and odd to compare it with mercantilism). Social justice *is* scary – for the free market fundamentalist. Fukuyama insists: 'Market-oriented authoritarians, on the other hand have the best of both worlds: they are able to enforce a relatively high degree of social discipline on their populations, while permitting a sufficient degree of freedom to encourage innovation and the employment of the most up-to-date technologies.'[23] A man like Pinochet, he is arguing, has the 'best of both worlds'. That may have been rather nice for Pinochet. But the union officials who Pinochet tortured and murdered did not have the best of anything at all. In all of Fukuyama's theorising there is no recognition that the increased freedoms of entrepreneurs to make profit for themselves were bought at the price of dramatically reduced freedoms of ordinary people to live without fear of kidnapping, torture and murder.

Klein does not of course deny that countries under the 'shock' of Friedmanite economic liberalisation may have done better in raw economic terms, in the long run. But 'raw' economics – which measures gross domestic product – does not measure either its social distribution or the cost in human suffering on the road to growth. And one case study in her book has convinced me more than anything of the need for economic justice, and also the difficulties in thinking about it: that of South Africa. All those who cared about social justice were exhilarated at the release of Nelson Mandela and his election under universal franchise to the presidency of South Africa in 1994. The peaceful transition to majority rule and the perceived dignity of the Truth and Reconciliation Commission – a 'restorative' body – boded well for democracy everywhere. But Klein shows a different side to the story: the simultaneous Friedmanisation of South Africa's economy, enthusiastically adopted by the incoming black government as part of its reconciliation with white power. She claims that Thabo Mbeki, effectively Mandela's economic advisor, leant over backwards to reassure the white business community that the ANC had no Communist policies in its economic plan. As Klein says: 'In June 1996, Mbeki unveiled the results: it was a neoliberal shock therapy programme for South Africa, calling for more privatization, cutbacks to government spending, labour "flexibility", freer trade and even looser controls on money flows.'[24] Mbeki in London, it seems, was keen to be called a Thatcherite, despite the obvious irony that Thatcher had declared the ANC to be a typical terrorist organization. The real point is this however: that the achievement of a high-profile goal of *social* justice for the blacks of South Africa did not include in it any advance in *economic* justice: indeed, Klein claims that on many indicators living standards for blacks stayed still or went into reverse. Winnie Mandela, for one, agrees with her. And Klein lays the blame for all of this at Friedman's door.

When I read Klein's book some years ago I was inclined to think it shocking but perhaps overstated. I thought the analogy of economic shock therapy with electroshock treatment for mental patients a journalistic exaggeration. I still think it shocking, but now better understand her arguments. But let the opinion of one of the world's most respected Nobel prize–winning economists, Joseph Stiglitz, sum it up:

> Klein is not an academic and cannot be judged as one. There are many places in her book where she oversimplifies. But Friedman and the other shock therapists were also guilty of oversimplification, basing their belief in the perfection of market economies on models that assumed perfect information, perfect competition, perfect risk markets. Indeed, the case against these policies is even stronger than the one Klein makes. They were never based on solid empirical and theoretical foundations, and even as many of these policies were being pushed, academic economists were explaining the limitations of markets – for instance, whenever information is imperfect, which is to say always.[25]

This is a passage from Stiglitz's review of Klein's book in the *New York Times* in 2001. It is noteworthy that he claims that the case against Friedmanite policies is stronger even than Klein's. We return to Stiglitz shortly, and to what he means by the 'imperfection of information' and why that matters for economic justice. But he gives us perhaps the best single term by which to characterise the economic philosophy of the von Mises–Hayek–Rand–Freidman tradition. It is the title of his review: 'Bleakonomics'. Is not Quakernomics the middle ground that avoids extremes of left and right, and stands as the best alternative to Bleakonomics on the right and the police state on the left? I discussed earlier Hayek's belief that the collectivism implicit in state welfare was the road to Nazism, and that this was perhaps kryptonite to Quakernomics because it halted the smallest move to industrial welfare in its tracks. But perhaps Quakernomics in turn is the kryptonite to Bleakonomics.

When the latter is confronted with questions of social justice it just shrugs. It doesn't even try, it is *determined* not to try. We have seen that the efforts of Quakers to try were sometimes unsuccessful, never more so than on the island of São Tomé. But the kryptonite to Bleakonomics within Quakernomics is this: it *tries*, again and again.

Chapter 22

QUAKERNOMICS AND THE CREDIT CRUNCH

One might say that the post-war period in economics belonged to Keynes and the post–Cold War period belonged to Friedman. Robert Skidelsky thinks that Keynes was the greatest persuader in twentieth-century economics though he concedes that some allow Friedman to share that place with him.[1] But the Credit Crunch has shown that, if stagflation was the outcome of the post-war mixed economy, then unfettered capitalism of the Friedmanite revolution has brought corruption to banking on a scale that almost brought down the entire capitalist order, rescued only by government intervention. Vast public resources were used to bail out private bankers' gambling, costing the citizens of the worst affected countries perhaps more than the allegedly 'failed' social programmes ever did. However, vast wealth still remains in private hands: the average riches across the world go far beyond the conceptions of the Friedmanite dream. Indeed if Veblen castigated 'conspicuous consumption' in 1899, Tawney chastised us for the 'acquisitive society' in the 1920s, and Galbraith sounded warnings over the 'affluent society' in the late 1950s, what on earth should we call the wealth amassed in the private hands of today? In 2012 a British Sunday paper ran the headline '£13 Trillion: Hoard Hidden from Taxman by Global Elite'.[2] At that time the cumulative British government debt was around the £1 trillion mark, showing that public debt, however mountainous it is trumpeted as being by the right-wing press, is small in comparison with private hoarding. And this £13 trillion hidden away in tax havens represents only the *liquid* portion of this private wealth, the ready cash, whereas the private stocks, bonds and material assets of the wealthy must reach astronomical figures.

The key feature of the growing wealth unleashed by unfettered capitalism since the 1980s has been inequality. Klein accuses the regimes of all the economically liberated developing nations of overseeing a massive upwards funnelling of wealth, but the same is true in the developed economies, and nowhere more so than in America. The standard of living at the bottom has barely increased since Friedman wrote *Capitalism and Freedom*, while those at the top have rocketed away. All this leads us to see that where subsistence was the issue haunting economics through the emergence and peak of Quakernomic history, inequality is the core issue today.

Did the crash of Lehman Brothers in 2008 indicate that the Friedmanite legacy had run its course, having almost blown up the world economy? In the immediate aftermath there was plenty of talk: bring back Marx, bring back Keynes, as we saw. But, perversely, the bankers who brought the global economy to the edge of ruin mostly received phenomenal bonuses, and, despite the disappearance of some behemoths of the banking world such as Lehman Brothers, business as usual appears to be the outcome. For the wealthy, the Credit Crunch and the Great Recession have merely been a hiccup; perhaps like the wealthy ladies in Upton Sinclair's *Oil!* they are generously refraining from eating lard, cabbage and potatoes. For the poor of Greece it has meant queues for food handouts and violence directed at immigrants, while in Spain unemployment has reached the levels of the US Great Depression. Recessions always accentuate economic injustice, indeed Keynesian economics is the acknowledgement of this. So where do we find the most compelling analysis of inequality, the very inequality that trailed in the wake of global Friedmanism? The answer is: in an academic study called *The Spirit Level*.

Inequality and *The Spirit Level*

Richard Wilkinson and Kate Pickett, the authors of *The Spirit Level*, are professors of social epidemiology and epidemiology respectively. Epidemiology is the study of health in populations, including epidemics (whence its name), and social epidemiology looks at the distributions of health and the factors affecting it across society. As a *Guardian* reviewer summed up their work: 'On almost every index of quality of life, or wellness, or deprivation, there is a gradient showing a strong correlation between a country's level of economic inequality and its social outcomes.'[3] While the right-wing press generally dismissed its arguments, it was a book however very much taken up by contemporary Quakers, and in many ways its message is close to the vision presented here of Quakernomics, that the absolute levels of wealth, now we are long past subsistence, are far less important to the wellbeing of society as a whole, than the fair distribution of that wealth. George Cadbury created wealth for the sole purpose of redistributing it – a saintly example we cannot expect all entrepreneurs to follow. Andrew Carnegie created wealth because he could, but insisted that it should be distributed before death rather than left to family inheritance. Again we cannot force individual billionaires to follow this noble example, though a notable group of them do today. But why should we not agree with *The Spirit Level* that redistribution should be a shared goal, given that all the evidence points to a better society for all social groups within it? For that is the message of the book: societies which have a more equitable distribution of wealth serve *all* their citizens better, the wealthy included.

In the introduction to the 40th anniversary edition of *The Affluent Society* Galbraith tells us that much of what he wrote still stands, but that he would have placed greater emphasis on inequality if he had known how things would develop. In particular he did not foresee just how great that inequality would become in the United States, and worse perhaps the degree of 'political eloquence' by which that inequality would be defended.[4] In the Great Recession following the Credit Crunch of 2008 one might expect that the political right in America would concede the issue of inequality, and welcome, however grudgingly, measures by the Obama administration to ameliorate poverty, extend healthcare and toughen regulation of the economy relaxed so greatly in the Friedmanite revolution, in particular of the banks. In an interesting study called *Pity the Billionaire: The Hard-Times Swindle and the Unlikely Comeback of the Right* by journalist Thomas Frank, he shows how, in the aftermath of the Credit Crunch, the far right actually landed up calling for *less* state intervention, not more. The phenomenon is a continuation of the defence of inequality, argued persuasively – to some at least – as Galbraith observed. Its American epicentre is in the Tea Party which pursues a vision of capitalism more extreme even than Friedman – and has anything from twenty to thirty per cent of the vote.

Given this background, it is time to consider the *sane* views put forward by three Nobel prize–winning economists, all broadly Keynesian, whose thinking in different ways aligns itself to Quakernomics and the vision of *The Spirit Level*: Paul Krugman, Joseph Stiglitz and Jeffrey Sachs.

Paul Krugman: Not Free to Die

Paul Krugman (born 1953) is a Keynesian economist, 2008 winner of the Nobel Prize in economics, and an op-ed columnist for *The New York Times*. He is among a handful of economists who predicted the Credit Crunch. In one of his early books he made the useful distinction between economists and policy entrepreneurs, the latter directly employed by politicians for expounding economic policies that suit them rather than being based on rigorous economic theory. (We saw earlier that he had placed Galbraith in this category, perhaps a little unfairly.)

In 2011 Krugman wrote a piece for the *New York Times* called 'Free to Die', a reference to Friedman's TV series and book, *Free to Choose*. Krugman's article was prompted by an interview in which three-time presidential candidate Ron Paul, a Republican, was asked what should be done in the case of a 30-year-old man who had chosen not to purchase health insurance and suddenly found himself in need of six months of intensive care. Mr Paul replied: 'That's what freedom is all about – taking your own risks.' He was pressed whether society should just let him die. The crowd erupted with cheers and shouts of 'Yeah!'[5] Although Mr Paul attempted to show that no doubt charities would step in, Krugman's point is that many low-income Americans, including their children, are in the position of the hypothetical 30-year-old. Krugman concludes: 'So the freedom to die extends, in practice, to children and the unlucky as well as the improvident.'

This is a good illustration of what we could call the 'Okie Syndrome': the presence in the midst of affluence of a group of people with such low resources as to face death from sickness or starvation, a death that would be entirely avoidable. Krugman sees the contemporary indifference to the relative suffering of the American poor as a shift in attitudes. He says in his article: 'In the past, conservatives accepted the need for a government-provided safety net on humanitarian grounds. Don't take it from me, take it from Friedrich Hayek, the conservative intellectual hero, who specifically declared in *The Road to Serfdom* his support for "a comprehensive system of social insurance" to protect citizens against "the common hazards of life," and singled out health in particular.'

This position, that Hayek was actually a moderate, in a Keynesian economist who broadly opposes the Freidmanite revolution, is interesting and we will find versions of it with Stiglitz and Sachs. We have seen that it is perfectly true that Hayek wished for a 'comprehensive system of social insurance', but that – just like Friedman who was also capable of striking an apparently moderate note – he shrank from recommending the slightest policy step in that direction, a hesitation going all the way back to Adam Smith. It is, as I have suggested, an extremism by omission. Leaving this aside, Krugman's account of the Credit Crunch in a book called *The Return of Depression Economics and the Crisis of 2008* aligns itself with Quakernomics in a Keynesian kind of way.

He says: 'What does it mean to say that depression economics has returned? Essentially it means that for the first time in two generations, failures on the demand side of the economy – insufficient private spending to make use of the available productive capacity – have become the clear and present limitation on prosperity for a large part of the world.'[6] (This is exactly the failure of capitalism that led Tressell and Steinbeck to write their novels.) He adds: 'The truth is that good old-fashioned demand-side macroeconomics has a lot to offer in our current predicament – but its defenders lack all conviction, while its critics are filled with passionate intensity.'

Decoding this a little, what Krugman means by 'old-fashioned demand-side macroeconomics' is precisely the Keynesian interventions governments have been pursuing in order to revive demand, on the basis that the government has to be the spender of last resort – or perhaps the optimist of last resort. But it is also true that the Friedmanite legacy makes it embarrassing to do so. Krugman tells us of an earlier crisis in Hong Kong where its supremely free market government actually intervened in the market to save its economy in 1998, bringing down the wrath of Friedman – who called their actions 'insane' – and prompting the Heritage Foundation, a conservative US think tank, to 'formally remove the city-state's designation as a bastion of economic freedom.'[7] Krugman is right that, although largely Keynesian measures were adopted globally to counter the Credit Crunch, they were weakly defended (or even not explained to the public at all, as Frank comments about Obama) and passionately attacked (as in the Tea Party).

Krugman's analysis of the Credit Crunch concludes that deregulation was part of the cause, but that it was the so-called 'shadow' banking system – organisations such as hedge funds – that operated outside of bank regulation, which created the real problems. He says: 'As the shadow banking system expanded to rival or even surpass conventional banking in importance, politicians and government officials should have realized that we were re-creating the kind of financial vulnerability that made the Great Depression possible – and they should have responded by extending regulation and the financial safety net to cover these new institutions.'[8]

Krugman is arguing, as are many other moderate economists, for a return to greater regulation. But in his 'Free to Die' essay he touches on questions of economic compassion that exercise all Quakers. Friedman, writing in the 2002 introduction to his *Capitalism and Freedom*, bemoans the fact that in 1956, when he and his wife were preparing their original book, US government spending was 26 per cent of national income, had risen in 1982 to 39 per cent, and had only dropped in 2000 to 36 per cent. In other words – and this is the eternal frustration of the right in America – the 'Leviathan' of state – as Friedman puts it – keeps growing. Krugman, I would suggest, shows us why: none of us are free to die. It doesn't matter how many people believe in Ayn Rand's philosophy in *theory*, in practice we are incapable as human beings of standing with folded arms while people die, or are made unemployed, or are otherwise made vulnerable in a modern economy. People simply don't have, at a personal level, their own means of production: we are all bound together within the capitalist industries which the Quakers played such a prominent role in establishing. In Tawney's words we are all bound together in this particular 'method of association', and this translates slowly and inexorably into government spending on social safeguards. It should not be deplored but celebrated; we *should* pity those who still face low or even subsistence wages in the midst of plenty – and we must be mad to pity the billionaires.

Joseph Stiglitz: Pervasive Externalities

Joseph Stiglitz (born 1943) is an American economist and a professor at Columbia University. He was the 2001 recipient of the Nobel Prize in economics and former Chief Economist at the World Bank. Stiglitz is a known critic of the Friedmanite legacy and also of aspects of globalisation, the IMF and the World Bank. His technical contributions to the field of economics lie in the issue of 'information asymmetry' – the implications of situations where economic agents have information advantages over their counterparts. For example a person taking out a mortgage may know full well that they face possible redundancy and fail to let their mortgage lender know: in this case they are placing the bank at an unfair risk (though few would see it that way). Alternatively a mortgage salesman might know full well that interest rates will rise but fail to inform the client as to the likely impact on their ability to repay: in this case they are placing the client at risk. The free market philosophy traditionally has two responses to this: firstly '*caveat emptor*', meaning buyer beware, and secondly a fundamentalist belief that these information asymmetries are unimportant and do not impair the efficiency of the market. Stiglitz's Nobel Prize was for work on these asymmetries. He is convinced that these are not trivial but that they are pervasive features of free markets and that economic policy should address them. Or in other words 'free' markets are not free at all: they are mostly rigged. In particular they create many situations that impact on the less well off.

In 2012 Stiglitz visited the UK at the height of the Libor banking scandal – the discovery of the 'fixing' of the London interbank lending rate – and didn't mind telling journalists that the only way that banking corruption of this sort would be ended was if bankers were jailed. There is something of a steely determination in his writings which confirm a long-standing rejection of the extremes of the free market. In his analysis of the Credit Crunch he is adamant: 'The reason why banks are regulated is that their failure can cause massive harm to the rest of the economy.'[9] We saw that early Quaker soap factories were fined for allowing hydrochloric acid build-ups in the surrounding fields and homes. Toxic chemicals are intensively regulated by government: so should toxic finance. Stiglitz points out that Lehman Brothers evaded regulation by moving significant tranches of risk off their balance sheets so auditors could not assess the overall status of the company: it reported a net positive worth of $26 billion shortly before it crashed, but actually had a hole in its balance sheet of $200 billion.[10] Here was an information asymmetry rather similar to that of Overend & Gurney's before it crashed: the company knew that is was in dire straits but continued trading. Hence investments were made in the company by those thinking it solvent, but lost everything. 'Information asymmetry' sounds technical, neutral and non-judgemental, but in ordinary language it means fraud, or at least a market in which the buyer, however aware, is taken advantage of. Prosecuting for it is hard, however, making regulation even more vital.

Stiglitz says: 'In many areas, we have come to recognise that the presumption of *caveat emptor* does not suffice. The reason is simple – buyers are poorly informed, and there are important information asymmetries. That's why we have, for example, government food safety regulation and government regulation of drugs.'[11] Needless to say, amongst Friedman's targets for criticism are just such government agencies.

Stiglitz, in contrast, believes that greater regulation of the banks is needed just as it has been accepted that food and drugs need regulation. Stiglitz would like to see the return of laws like the Glass–Steagall Act, introduced after the Great Depression, to prevent the kind of credit crunch seen in 2008. More than that, and here is an example of his uncompromising stance, he says that 'if banks are too big to fail, they are too big to exist.'[12] This is because governments simply cannot let banks of a certain size go under because of the knock-on effects on the entire economy – as with the RBS – and this encourages such banks to take unacceptable risks. The outcome so often commented on in this period is that profits become privatised, but risk socialised, meaning that the taxpayer is forced to pay for the mistakes of the private banker. Stiglitz also points out that banks of this size are also probably too big to be well managed, and even by traditional free market doctrines too big for competition to work properly. Other commentators suggest that they also become too big to be prosecuted.

In 2005 the US Congress passed a new law which created a greater obligation on borrowers to repay in situations like bankruptcy. This was greatly in favour of the banks, Stiglitz argues, creating a situation in which predatory lending by the banks was accompanied by tougher penalties on the poor for not repaying. Coupled with low interest rates provided by Greenspan this situation meant that many ordinary families took on unrealistic and dangerous levels of debt. Stiglitz quotes a bank, subsequently bailed out by the American taxpayer, which advertised its willingness to lend to absolutely anyone with the slogan 'Qualified at birth'.[13] We have seen that Quaker children were brought up to fear only two things: eternal punishment and debt, of which it was eternal punishment that faded from their world view. The history of Meeting oversight of business demonstrated an ethic in which individuals have to *prove* themselves capable of dealing with debt. But in America the passage of the 2005 bill resulted in a stronger legal basis for demanding repayment of the toxic mortgages being issued: punishment was for one side and not the other in this game.

Perhaps the most compelling point made by Stiglitz is in a simple remark: 'In competitive markets, wages are determined by the intersection of demand and supply, and there is nothing that says the "equilibrium" wage is a living wage.'[14] I can think of no more eloquent case for the need of a regulated market than this. It says that whatever the doctrines of the free marketeers, they have no evidence at all to suppose that wages determined by the market, particularly at the bottom, will provide a dignified level of existence above subsistence. In boom times perhaps it is not so significant, but in the Thatcherite-style 'liberation' of labour markets wages dive down again, and in a recession even that little is taken away in the plague of unemployment that visits a nation. A janitor who is sacked from his or her cleaning job in Canary Wharf – as employers pursue 'out-sourcing' – may find no work in a recession, will be forced to live off diminishing unemployment benefits, and may walk amongst the gleaming towers staring in fury or incomprehension at the bankers having steak and champagne lunches by the dock basin (I have often walked past them, with neither of those emotions, but sobered by what the scene represents). It is poverty amidst plenty, an example of Okie Syndrome long after the Great Depression.

Like Krugman, however, Stiglitz thinks that Hayek has been falsely elevated to the status of a god among conservatives, saying: 'Hayek argued that government had a role to play in diverse areas, from work-hours regulation, monetary policy, and institutions to the proper flow of information.'[15] We have seen that this is probably too optimistic about Hayek's thought.

We leave Stiglitz with another remark of his: 'Today the challenge is to create a New Capitalism.'[16] It's neatly put, and I am hoping of course that Quakernomics may make some contribution to thinking on the subject.

Jeffrey Sachs: The Mixed Economy

Jeffrey Sachs (born 1954) is an American economist, director of the Earth Institute at Columbia University, and has twice been named as one of *Time Magazine*'s '100 Most Influential People in the World'. According to Melanie Klein he was instrumental in the adoption of Friedmanite free market policies in a number of broadly socialist countries, including Bolivia, Poland and Russia – making acceptable what had become tainted in Chile by the link to the repressive tactics of Pinochet. It is certainly true that he advised in Bolivia, applying what Klein calls 'economic shock therapy', and succeeded in bringing inflation down from over 10,000 per cent to a mere 15 per cent per annum. In Poland he created the economic transition plan for the anti-Communist Solidarity movement, and worked on a similar basis for Slovenia and Estonia. During 1991–93 he worked for the Russian presidents Mikhail Gorbachev and Boris Yeltsin. In each case Klein disputes the claims for success, pointing out the widespread hardship that the transitions brought to ordinary people. Whatever the truth of this, Sachs has been a leading economist in the fight against poverty in Africa, and became Special Advisor to the UN Secretary-General on developmental economics in 2002.

We find in Sachs, as in Krugman and Stiglitz, the same assertions acknowledging Hayek's willingness to accept the need for state intervention in the market[17] – a willingness that I have shown to be deeply compromised by the spectre adamantly raised of collectivism as the immediate path to Nazism. Neither is it easy to agree with Sachs that Hayek and Friedman 'recognised the need for public action to protect the environment' for example.[18] At best Friedman reluctantly concedes that parks in city centres have to be publicly funded because of what he calls the 'neighbourhood effect', but he is opposed to public funding of the National Parks.[19] If National Parks really were privatised, it is hard to imagine this as anything less than an environmental disaster, and the overwhelming evidence of Friedmanite policies as pursued by George W. Bush is that their legacy opens the doors to environmental plunder.

But these are quibbles when it comes to the many pertinent insights that Sachs offers. Whatever commitment Sachs may have had to the untrammelled Friedmanite market in his transitional plans for Bolivia, Poland and Russia, his most recent work, *The Price of Civilization: Economics and Ethics after the Fall*, dealing with the aftermath of the Credit Crunch, presents a powerful advocacy for a middle way. As Klein points out, Sachs, though a Keynesian, nevertheless admired Friedman's free market principles and thought them sounder than 'fuzzy structuralist or pseudo-Keynesian arguments' he discovered as prevalent in the developing world.[20] If this was his position in 1985, it was much modified in 2011 when *The Price of Civilization* was published. It takes its name from a remark found in a biography of a US Supreme Court justice. Sachs tells us:

> As the great Supreme Court Justice Oliver Wendell Holmes Jnr. wrote, 'I like to pay taxes. With them I buy civilisation.' It is a sentiment utterly unrecognisable in America today, where an ongoing thirty-year tax revolt predominates. Without adequate taxation we can't live in a civilized country.[21]

Sach's point is that the price of civilisation is paying taxes. The free market generates wealth, but a substantial part of that is needed to create the basic structures of civilisation, and as *The Spirit Level* points out, equality is part of that basic structure. Once inequalities reach a certain level, civilisation – in the form of community spirit, low crime, longevity and all the other indicators of wellbeing – is placed in serious jeopardy.

I took away three key phrases from reading Sachs's book: 'the price of civilisation', 'the mixed economy' and 'the race to the bottom'. The price of civilisation is in fact the taxation that allows for a substantial role for government, expressed in the idea of the mixed economy – as argued for by Tawney – and the enemy of which is an unfettered free market which creates the 'race to the bottom' in terms of wages, working conditions, environmental standards and honest government, which all otherwise wilt under the competitive onslaught. Sachs, as an economist of the developing or transitional states, is in a particularly good place to show how this race to the bottom operates at its most pernicious in the global context.

But first, let us look at how Sachs develops his thesis on the mixed economy. His book starts out with an unfashionable idea: 'civic virtue'. If Americans have lost all belief in taxation as the path to civilisation, then only a revival of civic virtue can halt that slide. In fact Sachs's ideas are a little unusual for an economist: he is one of very few commentators on the predatory lending that led to the Credit Crunch of 2008 who puts the blame squarely on *both* sides of the lending game. Blaming banks is easy, but the loss of civic virtue has extended to irresponsibility on the side of the borrower citizen as much as the lender banker.

Sachs looks back to the period of the 1940s to the 1970s – in which most European countries nationalised many of their industries – and gives it, for the American context, the name: 'The Age of Paul Samuelson'.[22] Sachs says that 'More than any other economist of his time, Samuelson provided the intellectual underpinnings of the modern mixed economy created in the United States and Europe after the Second World War.' This is perhaps what is now entirely missing: a powerful argument for the economics of the middle way, an argument for the mixed economy in which the free market and government have equally valued roles in creating and maintaining civilisation. If Quakernomics is to be relevant to the modern world, it has to provide material for that argument. But here is the difficulty, I think: it is hard to find enough imaginative thinkers prepared to argue for such a middle way, hard to find the powerful knock-down arguments in favour of something as bland as a mixed economy.

A mixed economy needs tax and spend. And the surprising fact that Sachs uncovers is this: that the public actually wants it (those pesky voters again!). He says: 'The compromises made with the rich are consistently out of line with public opinion. The public desires to tax the rich more heavily, cut military spending and develop renewable energy alternatives to oil, gas and coal.'[23] Sachs explains why politicians cannot listen to the voters however; it is corporate lobbying that provides campaign funds and hence shapes policies, as Thomas Frank shows so well in *Pity the Billionaire*. And Sachs makes another vital point, so rarely heard: 'The supposition that there is a massive waste to be cut in the civilian budget is simply a myth.'[24] He works through the figures, showing that there really is little to be gained in extensive welfare cuts: 'thin gruel', as he says, but of course there is enormous political mileage in denouncing the welfare 'scrounger' or 'skiver'. Quakers are, I think, sceptical that there is overspending on welfare, and it is very welcome to see a serious economist show that the figures do not support the popular myth. In a similar vein the Fabian Society published findings in 2012 confirming the same fact: that citizens of the UK have been led to vastly over-estimate government spending on welfare.[25]

Sachs does a good job of showing what the Friedmanite legacy, operating in a global context, leads to: the 'race to the bottom'. It undermines all balanced attempts at the mixed economy. Klein accuses Sachs of having perhaps accelerated that very race when he guided socialist states into the free market system in the 1980s. But Sachs's 2011 arguments are perhaps all the better for his earlier experiences: he, if anyone, knows what he is talking about with globalisation. His argument is this: in a globalised economy capital flows to where production costs are cheapest. However enlightened the labour practices, for example, might be in a European country or American state, factories tend to be set up where the costs are lower, and these will be in countries, or even different states within America, where wages and working conditions are worse. This applies to just about every economic factor, including environmental standards, levels of taxation, regulation of worker safety, product safety, product sourcing, and regulation of the financial sector.[26] For example, he says that London and New York were in a dramatic race to the bottom to deregulate their financial markets, resulting eventually in the Credit Crunch. Yet one always hears the argument from Wall Street or the City that tighter regulation will damage their competitive edge. Tax havens are another example of the damaging effect of the global race to the bottom. Here, incidentally, we can thank the Quaker economist Richard Murphy for relentlessly exposing tax havens and other evasions of the duty to render to the state that proportion of corporate revenue essential for the maintenance of civilisation.[27]

This race to the bottom reproduces at a global level the experience of early industrial capitalism in the UK, where competition could drive down wages below subsistence and led to the gloomy Malthusian certainties of endless starvation for the working classes. The huge struggle to moderate the harmful effects of capitalism within Britain, through successive legislation – very often supported or even proposed by the Quakers – leads the population to now imagine that capitalism is tamed perhaps. But the apparent moderation of it on the domestic front hides the global competition that so far has provided little historic parallel to the moderation of industrial capitalism undergone in developed nations.

And Sachs's recommendation? He says: 'There is one overarching solution to the race to the bottom: international cooperation.' In other words, he is proposing the very idea that causes American libertarians to spit blood: some kind of effective world government. If the mixed economy in the developed nations requires national government to regulate domestic industrial capitalism, then the mixed economy on a global scale requires a global 'government' to regulate global industrial capitalism. And so far all we have are the institutions of the United Nations, an organisation that is nothing less than the anti-Christ for the more extreme American libertarian. (If you doubt this, watch a film series called *Left Behind*, produced for the religious right in America, in which the Secretary-General of the UN actually *is* the anti-Christ, bent on such horrifying things as world government, a world currency and world peace. It has a huge following.)

We saw that Quakers have been at the forefront of supporting the institutions of the United Nations. Quakernomics *is* a philosophy of the mixed economy; it *is* a philosophy of the global regulation of industrial capitalism; and it *is* a philosophy of internationalism. And Sachs provides some very useful pointers in the direction that economic justice has to take, effectively an establishment of civic virtue at the global level.

Niall Ferguson

For the sake of balance it is worth including a voice from the economic right, one who disagrees with Krugman, Stiglitz and Sachs on the origins of the Credit Crunch. Niall Ferguson was invited to give the

2012 BBC Reith Lectures, which he titled *The Rule of Law and Its Enemies*, and in the second broadcast made a defence of the *deregulation* of banks. He says: 'The financial crisis that began in 2007 had its origins precisely in over-complex regulation.' He naturally points to US legislation that encouraged the sub-prime lending in the first place, aimed at bringing more low-income families into home ownership, and recognises that there was bound to have been mis-selling of mortgages in this market. However this confuses regulation on the one hand with signals or other interventions by a vote-hungry administration on the other. They are not the same thing at all. The US government certainly must be blamed for too optimistic an approach in encouraging home ownership, but a strong regulatory framework could have mitigated its impact. Commentators in 2013 were concerned that the British government's 'Help to Buy' scheme would trigger yet another housing boom with an inevitable bust to follow. At the same time the banking sector was experiencing tighter regulation. If there is another banking crash it will be because regulation is not tight enough to counter the political desire to please voters with easier access to the housing market. We may wish for less vote-seeking political intervention, but it makes no sense to wish for less regulation, especially if the former looms.

Ferguson indicates the historical thinkers he admires, including Thomas Malthus, and the inspiration that Darwin drew from him. Commercial banks, according to Ferguson, should live and die as Darwinian creatures of evolution, with the minimum of regulation from the state. The historian in Ferguson then comes to the fore when he draws on the work of Walter Bagehot, and here lies the weakness of Ferguson's argument. Citing the crash of Overend & Gurney, he thinks we should return to the simplicity of Bagehot's recommendations, which, if you recall, placed the Bank of England on its course as the stabiliser of banking in the UK. 'Let us go back to Bagehot's world', he says. 'A complex financial world will be made less fragile only by simplicity of regulation and strength of enforcement.' But Bagehot was arguing for the *greater* involvement of the central bank, not the lesser. He was convinced that had the Bank of England been able to oversee Overend & Gurney more closely, it could have been turned back from the brink to save it and the two hundred dependent companies that went bust.

As the title of his lecture suggests, Ferguson is big on enforcement: he would like to see errant bankers go to jail, just like Stiglitz. But he omits to mention that none of the directors of Overend & Gurney went to jail, despite being tried for fraud at the Old Bailey. And the real issue is completely ducked: if regulators and enforcers could not prevent Overend & Gurney from crashing, nor successfully bring a prosecution in 1866, in a world prior to electronic banking, derivatives, CDs and a thousand other innovations, how on earth could 'simplicity of regulation' work today, or for that matter 'strength of enforcement'? Simplicity of regulation could only work if simplicity of banking were first enforced … which would require making illegal countless financial 'innovations' that Ferguson lauds, and which in turn would require greater regulation. He is of course right to cite Bagehot's insight that banking is 'fragile' – it will always be so unless fractional reserve banking is abolished as some would argue for. But the idea that *regulation* makes it fragile is preposterous. It would be like saying that *regulation* makes automobiles more dangerous and causes car crashes, or *regulation* makes the chemical industry a danger to the environment and causes disasters like Bhopal, or *regulation* makes pharmaceuticals risky and causes tragedies like Thalidomide.

When the free market temperament encounters massive regulatory tomes that guide the automotive, chemical or pharmaceutical industries, it reacts with a longing for the 'simplicity' of a bygone age. And so, it seems, is the case in banking, perhaps all the more so, because what harm can banking do compared to a car with faulty brakes, a chemical factory that blows up, or drugs that deform babies? Ferguson's longing for simplicity in banking regulation – which he allegedly discovers in the thinking of Bagehot – is the standard right-wing response, and in it lays the appeal to the ordinary voter, to the Tea Party factions. 'Keep it simple, stupid.' But a thoughtful appraisal of the history of vehicles, chemicals, pharmaceuticals and banks shows that the accumulative effect of human innovation creates inevitable and growing complexity. The great regulatory tomes that thud on the table cannot be escaped, nor the specialist roles of those who write and enforce them, nor the tax dollars to pay for it all. As Sachs puts it: 'as economic life becomes more complex, we should expect the role of government to become more extensive.'[28]

But the longing for simplicity is matched of course with the longing for profit, so every time complexity ratchets up, the devious mind finds a new way to evade existing regulations before they evolve to cope. And banking is as dangerous to the wellbeing of society as any other industry if it goes wrong, and the near-criminal brilliance of its innovators cannot claim that their near-crimes are victimless. The Quakers regulated their own industries because, although highly profitable, they did not place profit as the ultimate value. But Crosfield's were properly prosecuted for emitting hydrogen chloride, and the directors of Overend & Gurney had to answer to the public at the Old Bailey because self-regulation failed in those instances. With the best will in the world businesspeople make mistakes and have to have their industries regulated. And where the worst will triumphs – which it does wherever profit is the sole god – calls for *less* regulation should be seen as simply perverse.

Chapter 23

QUAKERNOMICS AND ECONOMIC HISTORY

It should be clear from our historical survey that economics is a subject inextricably linked with politics. Even that most bland and technical of volumes, the academic textbook in economics, contains within it political assumptions. Economics might shrug its shoulders and declare that politics is beyond its remit or expertise, as Friedman so often does, but we are ethically bound to ask: is this broadly a left-wing or a right-wing economics? And the criteria, it seems, are fairly simple: to what extent is this economics interested in social justice? On this line of thinking it is clear that Quakernomics is an economics of the centre left. As a microcosm of the broader economic activity it is also big enough to convey a key characteristic of an economy: that it is an *ecology*. This is where the economics of the right appears weak, as it continuously demands the reduction of a vastly complex field of activity to one simple principle: the 'free' market. An ecology cannot be reduced in this way. An ecology demonstrates a key principle, that agents are free only to a certain extent, beyond which they have to recognise their interdependence on other agents. Hence the obsession with 'freedom' can prevent, as in the work of Hayek, any recognition that the liberty of economic agents has to be matched by their obligations to each other. The history of the Quakers shows that their fierce independence from convention was moderated over time – as the harsh realities of industrialisation became clear – to become effectively an advocacy for the mixed economy. Cadbury more or less initiated town planning, and conducted a large-scale social experiment in collectivism. Was there any loss of freedom entailed in this? Beyond the raw fact of human interdependence?

Ethical Capitalism: Third Assessment

Quakernomics stands in economic thinking as a rebuke to the extremists of both left and right and as an encouragement to moderates everywhere.

At its heart, Quakernomics is the enthusiastic pursuit of economic activity as a social good. It is not a grudging philosophy of scarcity, as economic theories are sometimes presented, but a positive acceptance of hard work, imagination and innovation as dignified and the source of human flourishing. Its aims are not profit but community, where profit still has a crucial role however: firstly as an index of the viability of an enterprise, secondly as an acknowledgment by the community of the social value of that enterprise, and thirdly as a means for the broader implementation of social justice within and beyond the factory gate. Profit is for redistribution. Quakernomics is always conscious of the 'bottom line' of profit, but, in a rebuke to Adam Smith, the Quaker 'butchers, brewers and bakers' were absolutely addressable in terms of the needs of others, especially when the dinner of those others was not forthcoming because in one way or another the capitalist system had 'repudiated' them. It often drew back from maximising profit where that would work against other goals; it even provided silver to the Royal Mint at below market prices. Quakernomics is about the bigger picture, therefore. It is always conscious of the four major evils of industrial capitalism: unemployment, subsistence wages, hazards to health, and harm to the environment.

We saw that the American economist Henry George, a contemporary of Marx, rejected the pessimistic Social Darwinism of Malthus. Galbraith in turn reinforced George's point, that Malthus merely spoke to the desires of the already wealthy for maintaining the status quo. Much economic thought that follows in this vein – which allows wealth to flow upwards from poor to rich – deserves Carlyle's epithet of 'dismal'; and I think I have been reasonable in applying another epithet, 'forlorn', to the thinking of Freidman. The Quaker enterprises show no reason to see economic activity as either dismal or forlorn, and especially not in the potential within it for economic justice. But that is a perennially elusive goal, and requires continued vigilance because it easily slips away, the complexity of it shown in the case of Cadbury's 'slave' cocoa, and in South Africa which seized a victory for social justice but allowed economic justice to slip away, even under black majority rule.

We saw that low or subsistence wages as an issue can be used to test the economic thinking of the masters. I have suggested that this is the central issue of economic injustice – though not the only one – and that it lives on in the extremes of inequality now shown in the huge income ratios from top to bottom in Western economies. Much public anger has been directed at bonuses paid to bankers in the wake of the

Credit Crunch, but little attention has been focussed on low wages at the bottom. Free market economics is indifferent to the question of wages at the bottom, insisting that they are set by market forces. We saw that Quaker employers often paid above average wages, resisting exactly those market forces. Most right-wing economists are against any national minimum wage. But what if wages are in fact quite unlike the prices of products? What if they reflect, not market forces, but power structures and cultural norms established through a class system that reinforces the apparent entitlement of the wealthier classes to cheap products and services? Clearly boardroom salaries and bonuses are set by peers: hence a 'race to the top'. In contrast, wages for ordinary working people are not set by their peers, beyond the pressures that unions can impose: hence a 'race to the bottom' as unions are weakened.

According to Ha-Joon Chang, prices for service goods such as taxi rides and restaurant meals are higher in a country like Sweden than in America, allowing for much better wages at the bottom and less inequality.[1] In the US it is taken as a right to eat a 99 cent hamburger, bought at the cost of low wages right across agriculture, meat-packing, catering and related service industries, never mind poor animal husbandry. I once spoke with a businessman who was proud that the ratio of wages within his company was less than ten to one from top to bottom, a very good figure when compared to the average top-to-bottom pay ratio across the FTSE 100 companies of over two hundred and fifty to one in the UK. 'What about the janitors?' I asked. 'Oh…' he said. 'Actually, we have serviced offices.' He had to concede that in reality his figure would be far worse if the wages of the janitors were taken into account, no doubt hovering around the national minimum wage. But the janitor, particularly in America, is often 'a figure of ridicule or pity', according to the Wikipedia entry on the subject – and so receives contemptuous pay. And here is the right-wing justification for it: 'In proportion to the mental energy he spent, the man who creates a new invention receives but a small percentage of his value in terms of material payment, no matter what fortune he makes, no matter what millions he earns. But the man who works as a janitor in the factory producing that invention receives an enormous payment in proportion to the mental effort that his job requires of him.' This is from Ayn Rand's *Capitalism: The Unknown Ideal*.[2] Quakernomics utterly rejects this position. The 'man who creates a new invention' – the entrepreneur – is certainly important to the modern world, but he or she is nothing without the working person, including the janitor. The factory would stop if the entrepreneurs withdrew their labour, that's true. It would also stop if the janitors and other low-paid workers withdrew their labour. It is an interdependence, and the only thing setting the wage differential is *culture*, not any 'pure' kind of market forces. How can one possibly agree with Rand that the expenditure of mental energy is what justifies huge wage differentials? It is a pleasure to think, is it not? The Swedes have less contempt for the janitor, taxi driver, or sandwich-maker, in fact for all working people, and so pay them a decent wage. In turn the workers, on their days off, can *also* afford the taxi ride and the sandwich, and so the wheels of the economy turn as well as in America, but in more equal orbits. Quakers started from a culture of equality, created a Quakernomics that built it into their businesses, and *it worked*. Quakers have never worshipped those 'at the top of the intellectual pyramid' as Rand puts it, but regards them, like Carnegie did, as trustees of surplus profits for the benefit of all. Hence Quakernomics suggests that civic virtue and economic justice lie in the following principles. Firstly, as Sachs says, pay your taxes because it buys you civilisation. Secondly, honour all workers by ending contemptuous wages at the bottom. Thirdly, let profits at the top be held in trust for all.

Non-human Energies and Theories of Value

We saw that historically almost no economists have mentioned the Quakers as an economic phenomenon. Neither, I have suggested, have they paid sufficient attention to energy, and I want to conclude this section by returning to it. In the section on Bryant & May, I asked the question: 'what price a match'? In market economies prices or values are set by market forces, and a great mystery surrounds both the values of goods and the value of labour, particularly as to whether wages will be sufficient to buy the produce of industry. In fact the *average* person's wage in the West now buys a spectacular amount of goods – many made in Eastern factories of course. It is the *below average* wage that causes concern. But the question remains: why is a match so cheap? Why has the outlay on food become such a tiny fraction of the household budget compared to a hundred years ago? The usual answer is: the division of labour makes production efficient, and this is multiplied many times by automation. But the key to automation itself is largely forgotten in economic writings: it lies in the use of non-human energies, derived from fossil fuels, nuclear and renewable energy sources. Victorian households could have continued using the traditional tinder box method of lighting their stoves and cigars, but they bought billions of matches instead. Why? Because the non-human energies used at Bryant & May – firstly coal-powered steam-engines, and then electrically driven machines run from coal-fired power stations – meant that ordinary wages could buy far more matches compared to the time and effort used in traditional fire lighting. Why spend five minutes with a tinder box, when the wages of five minutes' work buys you a dozen matches for instant lighting? When one multiplies this equation through the economy, then the real significance of non-human energies emerges. Chocolate became cheap through the steam-engine; so did countless other goods. And, given the impact of energy consumption on the environment, the significance of the use of fossil fuels in particular grows again.

Marx thought that the wealth of the capitalists existed because they extracted it from the worker – it was their 'congealed' labour. Rand thought that the wealth of the capitalists existed because they were 'at the top of the intellectual pyramid' as she puts it – and even the millions they accumulated were not, in fact, a sufficient reward. I have suggested instead that in the interdependence of entrepreneur and worker at the Bryant & May factory – or any other factory – wealth was created by both sides. Between them they had invented processes and machines, and provided the tending of those machines which churned out matches by the billion under coal power. It was the energy of sunlight, locked into compressed vegetable matter, that took the place of human exertion to create matches by the billion, and, in the reflex of the movement of matches out of the factory, cash poured in: wealth. *That wealth was largely extracted from coal.* The genius of the entrepreneur and the labour of the worker jointly enabled the extraction of wealth from non-human energies. So who then does the wealth belong to? Clearly to all of us. The wealth came neither from the entrepreneur alone, nor from the worker alone; neither did it come from their collaboration alone: it came in a very large proportion from coal. The fuel is obtained from nature, and the profits of the entrepreneurial process of extraction go to the mining companies or the oil companies or the uranium-refining companies, or whatever. But afterwards, the extraction of wealth from that non-human energy locked into these fuels is a *collective* effort. It is the phenomenon at the heart of industrial capitalism. Coalbrookdale cooking pots were extracted from coal, not from the hands of the worker or the mind of the entrepreneur. Carnegie was right: he had not himself extracted wealth by his own efforts alone – even if he did not exactly think along these lines – but from the bounty of non-human energies left as our planetary legacy. How much steel could he have made without coal? None, not even with a million workers. So his profits, after a modest return, were owed, in trust, to all of us.

This argument, the energy theory of wealth, as it were, needs to be developed to inform the ethics of capitalism. Clearly there are labour-intensive industries on the one hand, and knowledge-intensive industries on the other, where non-human energies play a smaller role than in manufacturing. But underpinning all our wealth lies the historic and continuing use on a vast scale of non-human energies, and I think its implications for economic justice are clear, if not yet well supported in theory or statistics: our wealth is a collaborative effort and no one social group should be singled out for an excessive share of it.

To conclude this section we can say that Quakers, so integral to the early development of our industrial economies, provide us with an interesting economic history. Despite Quakernomics as a phenomenon peaking in the mid-nineteenth century it clearly provides pertinent material for assessing economic thought right into the twenty-first. Religion has largely retreated from the public sphere and the family has largely retreated from boardroom control, so a contemporary ethical capitalism cannot be a direct transposition from the Quaker business world. But at the very least the history of it should inspire us to seek the modern equivalent.

Part V

CONCLUSIONS

Chapter 24

ETHICAL CAPITALISM

In the two very different major sections of this book we have explored a simple question: what is an ethical capitalism? In the first half we discovered that the business practices of the Quakers largely comprised an ethical capitalism, and through the occasional lapses from the high standards that this group set themselves we have learned about some of the difficulties along the road for such a venture. In the second half we have discovered that the works of the great economic thinkers have rarely been directly engaged with the question of ethical capitalism, and rarely proposed solutions to the inequities thrown up by unregulated industrialism. On the contrary, some of the most influential economic works have argued that any regulation of capitalism is itself unethical, a barrier to essential human freedoms.

Along the way it has become clearer what is under discussion when referring to capitalism. I started the book with the provocative assertion that economics and capitalism are much the same thing. I have narrowed 'capitalism' down to industrial capitalism, in which the Industrial Revolution triggered wealth creation on a massive new scale, mostly through the harnessing of non-human energies. The Information Revolution as we might call it is creating wealth on a different basis perhaps, but it is still underpinned by the physical infrastructure created by heavy industry. Economics as an empirical academic discipline has grown out of these phenomena, and where it deals with alternative systems is almost entirely speculative. Economics in the normal sense deals with how investments are made for a return; in the normal sense, then, economics is about capitalism. Microeconomics largely views this from the perspective of the businessman, macroeconomics largely from the perspective of society, and it is in the latter discipline that the principal ethical questions now emerge.

We have also been able to identify the key figure in modern industrial capitalism: the entrepreneur. If we believe that economic activity is in itself a good thing, and that the goods so produced actually lead to human flourishing, then the entrepreneur is a figure rightly elevated by some, though perhaps not sufficiently well regarded by the many. Few novels paint a positive portrait of this figure, perhaps because, as both Schumpeter and George Cadbury's biographer point out, they are obsessive workaholics with few interests outside their work.

If the economic activity behind industrial capitalism, and the entrepreneur who lies behind that activity, are the basis of our wealth and flourishing, then is not capitalism itself already an ethic? This is the belief of Ayn Rand and Milton Friedman, and is the essence of what I am calling Friedmanism. I have shown that this is mistaken. Industrial capitalism, regardless of how many goods it produces, and what general human flourishing it engenders, also engenders specific ills. I have summed these up in my four evils of industrial capitalism.

Those evils were clear to the Quakers and to some of the early political economists, though the latter group on the whole showed little interest in correcting them. It is obvious why: they belonged to the social class that most benefited from those evils, the principal one of which is inequality. We have seen that low wages at the bottom of the scale drive individuals and families into despair, while those at the top are so able to isolate themselves from the poor that they effectively live a fantasy. Perhaps the worst evil of industrial capitalism is unemployment, but that at least has received attention from economists of both left and right. Indeed if one were to make an argument for the recent political convergence of left and right, it might well be over unemployment. No politician now dare say that unemployment is a price well worth paying for improving the economy.

Dangerous industrial processes and products are now well regulated, at least in the developed world. Here the left and right still show disagreement however, as we saw in the instinctive assumption by Niall Ferguson that regulation of industry is a bad thing.

An ethical capitalism is therefore quite simply a capitalism that takes these evils seriously, and strives to avoid them. An unethical capitalism either fails to acknowledge these evils; recognises them but declares them inevitable; or recognises them and celebrates them as necessary for the proper working of capitalism.

Quakernomics was an ethical capitalism. But it was religious, voluntarist and paternalistic. Such a capitalism no longer fits the modern world, though contemporary philanthropists whose outlook is similar have an important role to play in the moderation of industrial capitalism. Instead we have seen that the state must inexorably play a key role in the construction of an ethics for reining in raw capitalism. Only a partnership between the entrepreneur and the state can do that. The rise of the corporation means the advent of big capitalism; only big government is a player of sufficient means to keep the evils of big capitalism in check, while allowing for its delivery of wealth and human flourishing. On this argument we can see that the advocates of small government are, perhaps unwittingly, the advocates of unethical capitalism.

The key insight offered by Quakernomics is that an ethical capitalism does not have to be a peripheral phenomenon in a dynamic economy. The 'total capitalism' of the Quaker enterprises, and the sheer scale of them, demands a radically new look at the whole question. Quakernomics was at the centre of the dramatic rise in industry and finance in the eighteenth and nineteenth centuries, and, far from being a brake on development, was at its dynamic core. Individual industrial philanthropists can perhaps be dismissed as isolated exceptions that prove the norm of aggressive, indifferent capitalism. But a group as large and coherent as the Quakers, which helped shape the very industrial base of the modern world, cannot be ignored. However, as Sir Adrian Cadbury points out in the Foreword, the specific ethical capitalism of Quakernomics has no place in the modern world, not, at least, if we attempt to resurrect it in its original form. As he says the 'publicly quoted shareholder-owned company model' makes that impossible. I have further identified factors, such as Meeting oversight, that are no longer viable moderating influences in the twenty-first century. Religion is now quite properly a matter for the private sphere. But Quakernomics is conceived here as only one possible ethical capitalism out of many. We have to forge a new one, appropriate to our era, inspired by this real historical example.

It is beyond the scope of this book to speculate much on the shape of this new ethical capitalism. We know what it must achieve: the amelioration of the four evils of unemployment, low wages at the bottom, industrial hazards and environmental harm. We also know what intellectual forces mitigate against the very idea of an ethical capitalism: Friedmanism. Here perhaps is where the initial work in forging a new ethical capitalism needs to be done. While elevating the entrepreneur, we need to carefully dismantle the mirage of the Friedmanite intellectual legacy. Here is a 'defunct economist' as Keynes put it, whose ideas we are apparently all still slaves to.

Finally, was Maggie Foster right? Should we, as some green economists appear to demand, metaphorically time-travel to Coalbrookdale in the eighteenth century and sabotage the Iron Bridge in order to undo the environmental ravages of industrial capitalism? Should we undo everything that Quakernomics achieved, from low-cost cooking pans through passenger railways to cheap chocolate bars? Even if we could I would argue that we should not. Industrial capitalism has brought us an infinity of blessings, and the austere Quakers were among the first to see that. But the road-kill along the way, the collateral damage, on people and the planet is far too high. I blame no single economist for this, but rather identify Friedmanism as the key regressive philosophy – with its roots in Hayek and further back in Malthusian pessimism – that makes capitalism unethical. To reverse Friedmanite inequity will be the first major step in creating a new ethical capitalism. To reverse Friedmanite inequity involves both a celebration of the entrepreneur and the recognition that – far from equality as a threat to freedom – the enfranchisement of all in the dignities of freedom is intimately dependent on the economic justice of ethical capitalism. And unless this economic justice is extended to the planet itself, the Maggie Fosters of the real world *will* have been proved right.

NOTES

Introduction

1 Mark's Musings, 'Danny Boyle's Olympic Programme Notes: Full Text', http://mark.goodge.co.uk/2012/07/danny-boyles-olympic-programme-notes-full-text/ (accessed 16 December 2013).
2 David Morse, *The Iron Bridge* (New York: Harcourt Brace, 1998).
3 Note, however, that Elizabeth Fry will likely be replaced with Winston Churchill on the £5 note in 2016.
4 Melvyn Bragg, 'Quakers', *In Our Time*, broadcast 5 April 2012, http://www.bbc.co.uk/podcasts/series/iot.mp (accessed 5 April 2012).
5 Zoe Williams, 'Saturday Sketch', *Guardian*, 31 March 2012.
6 Andy McSmith, 'The Father of a New Generation', *Independent*, 7 September 2010.
7 Paul H. Emden, *Quakers in Commerce* (London: Sampson Low, Marston & Co, 1939), vii.

Chapter 1: Quakers and Commerce

1 James Walvin, *The Quakers: Money and Morals* (London: John Murray, 1997), 30.
2 Ibid., 41.
3 Thomas Paine, *Agrarian Justice* (Start Publishing LLC, 2012), Kindle edition, 115.
4 Ibid., 128.
5 Ibid., 143.
6 Ibid., 146.
7 Arthur Raistrick, *Quakers in Science and Industry* (York: Sessions Book Trust, 1993), 37.
8 Max Weber, *The Protestant Ethic and the Spirit of Capitalism*, trans. Talcott Parsons (New York: Dover, 2003), 17.
9 Ibid., 27.
10 Emden, *Quakers in Commerce*, 13.
11 Noble Foster Hoggson, *Banking through the Ages: From the Romans to the Medicis – From the Dutch to the Rothschilds* (New York: Cosimo Classics, 2007), 96.
12 Weber, *Protestant Ethic*, 44.
13 Ibid., 81.
14 Ibid., 111–12.
15 Ibid., 141.
16 David Burns Windsor, *The Quaker Enterprise* (London: Frederick Muller, 1980), 70.

17 Raistrick, *Quakers in Science and Industry*, 46.

18 R. H. Tawney, *Religion and the Rise of Capitalism* (Harmondsworth: Penguin, 1961), 271.

19 Ibid., 270.

20 Balwant Nevaskar, *Capitalism without Capitalists: The Jains of India and the Quakers of the West* (Westport: Greenwood Press, 1971).

21 Atul K. Shah, 'Jain Business Ethics', *Accountancy Business and the Public Interest* 6 (2) (2007), 122.

22 Geoffrey Elliott, *The Mystery of Overend and Gurney: Adventures in the Victorian Financial Underworld* (London: Methuen, 2006), 60.

23 Emden, *Quakers in Commerce*, 21.

24 Joseph Stalin, *Leninism* (London: Lawrence and Wishart, 1940), 324.

25 Walvin, *Money and Morals*, 145.

Chapter 2: Industrial Capitalism

1 Parliament.uk, 'House of Commons: Thursday 16 May 1991', http://www.publications.parliament.uk/pa/cm199091/cmhansrd/1991-05-16/Orals-1.html#Orals-1_spnew24 (accessed 28 December 2012).

2 Bartleby.com, 'The Organization of Labour', http://www.bartleby.com/71/1612.html (accessed 16 December 2013).

3 Tawney, *Rise of Capitalism*, 270.

Chapter 3: Contrasting Cultures in 1845

1 Walvin, *Money and Morals*, 188.

2 Friedrich Engels, *The Condition of the Working Class in England* (Oxford: Oxford University Press, 2009), 103.

3 Ibid., 105.

4 Ibid., 91.

5 Ibid., xvii.

6 Benjamin Disraeli, *Sybil, or the Two Nations*, Kindle edition, B004TOUY5E, 1031–2.

Chapter 4: The Darbys of Coalbrookdale

1 Walvin, *Money and Morals*, 110.

2 Windsor, *Quaker Enterprise*, 42.

3 Ibid., 47.

4 Peter Mathias, *The First Industrial Nation: The Economic History of Britain 1700–1914* (London: Routledge, 1983), 113.

5 William Rosen, *The Most Powerful Idea in the World: A Story of Steam, Industry, and Invention* (Chicago: University of Chicago Press, 2012), 146.

6 Emden, *Quakers in Commerce*, 29.

7 Raistrick, *Quakers in Science and Industry*, 89.

NOTES

NOTES   259

8 Windsor, *Quaker Enterprise*, 45.
9 Arthur Raistrick, *Dynasty of Ironfounders: Darbys and Coalbrookdale* (Newton Abbot: David and Charles, 1970), 67.
10 Emden, *Quakers in Commerce*, 33.
11 Walvin, *Money and Morals*, 109.
12 Emden, *Quakers in Commerce*, 33.
13 Windsor, *Quaker Enterprise*, 49.
14 Mathias, *First Industrial Nation*, 3.
15 Raistrick, *Dynasty of Ironfounders*, 65.
16 Windsor, *Quaker Enterprise*, 52.
17 Ibid., 49.
18 Ibid., 48.
19 Raistrick, *Dynasty of Ironfounders*, 89.
20 Emden, *Quakers in Commerce*, 35.
21 Raistrick, *Dynasty of Ironfounders*, 207.
22 Windsor, *Quaker Enterprise*, 57.
23 Raistrick, *Dynasty of Ironfounders*, 222.
24 Windsor, *Quaker Enterprise*, 58.
25 Ibid., 60.
26 Raistrick, *Dynasty of Ironfounders*, 261.
27 Windsor, *Quaker Enterprise*, 61.
28 Walvin, *Money and Morals*, 107.
29 See www.peterkingsculptor.org (accessed 27 January 2013).
30 Raistrick, *Dynasty of Ironfounders*, 46.
31 Ibid., 4.
32 Walvin, *Money and Morals*, 112.
33 Raistrick, *Dynasty of Ironfounders*, 224.
34 Ibid., 211.
35 Ibid., 260.
36 Ibid., 264.
37 Ibid., 80.
38 Ibid., 221.
39 Ibid., 271.

Chapter 5: Quakers in Light and Heavy Industry

1 Emden, *Quakers in Commerce*, 29.
2 Walvin, *Money and Morals*, 105.
3 Raistrick, *Quakers in Science and Industry*, 61.
4 Ibid., 59.
5 Raistrick, *Dynasty of Ironfounders*, 13.
6 Walvin, *Money and Morals*, 111.
7 Humprey Lloyd, *The Quaker Lloyds in the Industrial Revolution* (London: Hutchinson, 1975), 37.
8 Ibid., 44.
9 Ibid., 59.
10 Ibid., 92.

11 Mathias, *First Industrial Nation*, 113.

12 Lloyd, *Quaker Lloyds*, 159.

13 Ibid., 256.

14 Ibid., 257.

15 Disraeli, *Sybil*, 2111–49.

16 Lloyd, *Quaker Lloyds*, 258.

17 Raistrick, *Quakers in Science and Industry*, 146.

18 Ibid., 149.

19 Emden, *Quakers in Commerce*, 39.

20 Raistrick, *Quakers in Science and Industry*, 202.

21 Emden, *Quakers in Commerce*, 39.

22 Raistrick, *Quakers in Science and Industry*, 161.

23 Margaret Ackrill and Leslie Hannah, *Barclays: The Business of Banking, 1690–1996* (Cambridge: Cambridge University Press, 2001), 10.

24 Raistrick, *Quakers in Science and Industry*, 172.

25 Ibid., 174.

26 Raistrick, *Dynasty of Ironfounders*, 80.

27 Raistrick, *Quakers in Science and Industry*, 181.

28 Ibid.

29 Ibid., 184.

30 Ackrill and Hannah, *Barclays*, 11.

31 Ibid., 14.

32 Raistrick, *Quakers in Science and Industry*, 211.

33 Emden, *Quakers in Commerce*, 65.

34 Windsor, *Quaker Enterprise*, 20.

35 Ibid.

36 Ibid., 49.

37 Raistrick, *Dynasty of Ironfounders*, 181.

38 Windsor, *Quaker Enterprise*, 19.

39 Emden, *Quakers in Commerce*, 45.

40 Raistrick, *Quakers in Science and Industry*, 217.

41 Raistrick, *Dynasty of Ironfounders*, 187.

42 Elliott, *Mystery of Overend and Gurney*, 58.

43 Raistrick, *Quakers in Science and Industry*, 76.

44 Emden, *Quakers in Commerce*, 81.

45 Karl Marx, *Capital*, trans. Ben Fowkes (London: Penguin, 1990), I: 352n22.

46 Emden, *Quakers in Commerce*, 176.

47 Ibid., 178.

48 Walvin, *Money and Morals*, 181.

49 Beaver, Patrick, *The Match Makers: The Story of Bryant and May* (London: Henry Melland, 1985), 61.

50 Emden, *Quakers in Commerce*, 167.

51 'Dangerous Lucifer Matches', *West Coast Times*, 18 July 1874, 2750: 4.

52 Beaver, *Match Makers*, 64.

53 Ibid., 69.

54 Ibid., 72.

Chapter 6: Quakers in Science, Chemicals and Pharmaceuticals

1 Mathias, *First Industrial Nation*, 124.
2 Ibid., 125.
3 Jocelyn Bell: The True Star', *Belfast Telegraph*, 13 June 2007.
4 Ormerod Greenwood, *The Quaker Tapestry* (London: Impact Books, 1990), 144.
5 Raistrick, *Quakers in Science and Industry*, 247.
6 Ibid., 267.
7 Greenwood, *Quaker Tapestry*, 117.
8 Ibid., 152.
9 Emden, *Quakers in Commerce*, 120.
10 Walvin, *Money and Morals*, 94.
11 Raistrick, *Quakers in Science and Industry*, 292.
12 Mathias, *First Industrial Nation*, 127.
13 Wikipedia, 'George Graham', http://en.wikipedia.org/wiki/George_Graham_(clockmaker) (accessed 27 May 2012).
14 Raistrick, *Quakers in Science and Industry*, 229.
15 Windsor, *Quaker Enterprise*, 20.
16 Raistrick, *Quakers in Science and Industry*, 202.
17 Geoffrey Tweedale, *At the Sign of the Plough: Allen and Hanburys and the British Pharmaceutical Industry, 1715–1990* (London: John Murray, 1993), 15.
18 Emden, *Quakers in Commerce*, 72.
19 Walvin, *Money and Morals*, 115.
20 Windsor, *Quaker Enterprise*, 71.
21 A. E. Musson, *Enterprise in Soap and Chemicals: Joseph Crosfield & Sons Limited, 1815–1965* (Manchester: Manchester University Press, 1965), 17.
22 Windsor, *Quaker Enterprise*, 70.
23 Ibid., 67.
24 Musson, *Enterprise in Soap and Chemicals*, 81.
25 Windsor, *Quaker Enterprise*, 74.
26 Musson, *Enterprise in Soap and Chemicals*, 43.
27 Ibid., 102.
28 Tweedale, *Sign of the Plough*, Preface.
29 Emden, *Quakers in Commerce*, 124.
30 Tweedale, *Sign of the Plough*, 35.
31 Ibid., 39.
32 Emden, *Quakers in Commerce*, 130.
33 Tweedale, *Sign of the Plough*, 42.
34 Emden, *Quakers in Commerce*, 135.
35 George Fox, *The Journal of George Fox*, ed. John L. Nickalls (London: Religious Society of Friends, 1975), 199.
36 American Friends Service Committee, *Speak Truth to Power: A Quaker Search for an Alternative to Violence*, https://afsc.org/sites/afsc.civicactions.net/files/documents/Speak_Truth_to_Power.pdf (accessed 16 December 2013).
37 Tweedale, *Sign of the Plough*, 49.
38 Ibid., 15.

39 Richard Palmer, 'Thomas Corbyn: Quaker Merchant', *Medical History* 33 (1989): 371–6.
40 Walvin, *Money and Morals*, 84.
41 Ibid., 181.
42 Emden, *Quakers in Commerce*, 183.
43 Ibid., 184.

Chapter 7: Quakers in Foodstuffs and Luxuries

1 Adam Smith, *An Inquiry into the Nature and Causes of the Wealth of Nations: A Selected Edition*, ed. Kathryn Sutherland (Oxford: Oxford University Press, 2008), 325.
2 Emden, *Quakers in Commerce*, 189.
3 Ibid., 190.
4 Raistrick, *Quakers in Science and Industry*, 215.
5 Deborah Cadbury, *Chocolate Wars: From Cadbury to Kraft: 200 years of Sweet Success and Bitter Rivalry* (London: HarperPress, 2010), 57.
6 Ibid., 59.
7 Ibid., 60.
8 Lowell Joseph Satre, *Chocolate on Trial: Slavery, Politics, and the Ethics of Business* (Ohio: Ohio University Press, 2005), 212.
9 Cadbury, *Chocolate Wars*, 16.
10 Ibid., 25.
11 Emden, *Quakers in Commerce*, 218.
12 Cadbury, *Chocolate Wars*, 299.
13 Walvin, *Money and Morals*, 171.
14 Ibid., 172.
15 Cadbury, *Chocolate Wars*, 255.
16 Emden, *Quakers in Commerce*, 181.
17 Ibid., 185.
18 Ibid., 199.
19 Musson, *Enterprise in Soap and Chemicals*, 5.
20 Emden, *Quakers in Commerce*, 153.
21 Ibid., 150.

Chapter 8: Quakers in Trading, Banking and Finance

1 Emden, *Quakers in Commerce*, 7.
2 Walvin, *Money and Morals*, 63.
3 J. M. Keynes, *A Treatise on Money: The Pure Theory of Money and the Applied Theory of Money* (Mansfield: Martino Publishing, 2011), 30.
4 Emden, *Quakers in Commerce*, 16.
5 Ibid., 171.
6 Walvin, *Money and Morals*, 30.
7 Ann Pettifor, *The Coming First World Debt Crisis* (Basingstoke: Palgrave Macmillan, 2006), 14.

8 Pettifor, *First World Debt Crisis*, 130.

9 Niall Ferguson, *The Ascent of Money: A Financial History of the World* (London: Penguin, 2009), 40.

10 Ackrill and Hannah, *Barclays*, 5.

11 Ibid., 6.

12 Ibid., 10.

13 Walter Bagehot, *Lombard Street: A Description of the Money Market* (New York: Cosimo Classics, 2006), 95.

14 Walvin, *Money and Morals*, 65.

15 Raistrick, *Quakers in Science and Industry*, 328.

16 Ibid., 325.

17 Ibid.

18 Elliott, *Mystery of Overend and Gurney*, 61.

19 Ibid., 68.

20 Ibid., 70.

21 Ibid., 148.

22 Ibid., 89.

23 Ibid., 158.

24 Bagehot, *Lombard Street*, 7.

25 Ibid., 7–8.

26 Ibid., 12.

27 Ibid., 275.

28 Ibid., 19.

Chapter 9: Quakers in Culture

1 Raistrick, *Dynasty of Ironfounders*, 262.

2 Ibid., 267.

3 Emden, *Quakers in Commerce*, 175.

4 Philip Ziegler, *The Francis Frith Collection: Britain Then and Now* (London: Weidenfeld & Nicholson, 1999), 7.

5 Ibid., 8.

6 Ibid., 9.

7 Francis Frith Company, http://www.francisfrith.com/company/ (accessed 29 December 2012).

8 Emden, *Quakers in Commerce*, 172.

Chapter 10: The Quaker System

1 Cadbury, *Chocolate Wars*, 4.

2 Raistrick, *Quakers in Science and Industry*, 48.

3 Emden, *Quakers in Commerce*, 17.

4 Walvin, *Money and Morals*, 4.

5 Elliott, *Mystery of Overend and Gurney*, 54.

6 Emden, *Quakers in Commerce*, 18.

7 Walvin, *Money and Morals*, 55.

8 Ibid., 73.
9 Ibid., 77.
10 Ibid., 45.
11 Ibid., 82.
12 Ibid., 211.
13 Windsor, *Quaker Enterprise*, 73.
14 Elliott, *Mystery of Overend and Gurney*, 57.
15 Windsor, *Quaker Enterprise*, 71.
16 David J. Jeremy, ed., *Business and Religion in Britain* (Aldershot: Gower, 1988), 166–8.
17 Emden, *Quakers in Commerce*, 231.

Chapter 11: Quakers in Public Life

1 Emden, *Quakers in Commerce*, 3.
2 John Hedley Brooke and G. N. Cantor, *Reconstructing Nature: The Engagement of Science and Religion* (Oxford: Oxford University Press, 2000), 299–300.
3 Emden, *Quakers in Commerce*, 57.
4 Ibid., 183.
5 A. G. Gardiner, *Life of George Cadbury* (London: Cassell and Company, 1923), 87.
6 Windsor, *Quaker Enterprise*, 72.
7 Marx, *Capital*, I: 619n.
8 Raistrick, *Quakers in Science and Industry*, 84.
9 Walvin, *Money and Morals*, 150.
10 Ibid., 131.
11 Gardiner, *Life of George Cadbury*, 23.
12 Ibid., 26.
13 Ibid., 45.
14 Ibid., 57.
15 Ibid., 95.
16 Ibid., 87.
17 Ibid., 247.
18 Cadbury, *Chocolate Wars*, 218.
19 Leo Tolstoy, *The Kingdom of God is Within You*, trans. Constance Garnett (Mineola, New York: Dover, 2006), 1.

Chapter 12: Industrial Welfare and Quaker Lapses

1 Walvin, *Money and Morals*, 57.
2 Benjamin Seebohm Rowntree, *Poverty: A Study of Town Life* (London: Macmillan, 1901), v.
3 Ibid., 120.
4 Ibid., 296.
5 Ibid., 312.
6 Walvin, *Money and Morals*, 199.
7 Ibid., 165.
8 Satre, *Chocolate on Trial*, 162.
9 Ibid., 75.

Chapter 13: Quakers and Other Ethical Capitalists

1 Walvin, *Money and Morals*, 179
2 Ibid., 176.
3 BBC, 'When Bankers Were Good', www.bbc.co.uk/mediacentre/proginfo/2011/
   47/ian-hislop-when-bankers-were-good.html (accessed 10 July 2012).
4 Tweedale, *Sign of the Plough*, 42.
5 Elliott, *Mystery of Overend and Gurney*, 59.
6 Robert Owen, *A New View of Society and Other Writings* (London: Penguin,
   1991), 106.
7 Wikipedia, 'Milton S. Hershey', http://en.wikipedia.org/wiki/Milton_S._
   Hershey (accessed 13 July 2012).
8 Satre, *Chocolate on Trial*, 70.
9 Andrew Carnegie, *The Gospel of Wealth*, http://carnegie.org/fileadmin/Media/
   Publications/PDF/THE_GOSPEL_OF_WEALTH_01.pdf (accessed 16 December
   2013).

Chapter 14: From Mercantilism to Marshall

1 Walvin, *Money and Morals*, 29.
2 J. M. Keynes, *The General Theory of Employment, Interest and Money* (Thousand
   Oaks, CA: BN Publishing, 2008), 75.
3 Paul Krugman, *Peddling Prosperity: Economic Sense and Nonsense in the Age of Diminished
   Expectations* (New York: W. W. Norton, 1994), 10.
4 François Quesnay, 'Tableau Economique', http://www.marxists.org/reference/
   subject/economics/quesnay/1759/tableau.htm (accessed 16 December 2013).
5 Smith, *Inquiry*, 291.
6 Ibid., 22.
7 Ibid., 9.
8 Ibid., 13.
9 Ibid., 16.
10 Ibid., 305.
11 Ibid., 73.
12 Ibid., 79.
13 Ibid., 414.
14 Thomas Malthus, *An Essay on the Principle of Population* (London: J. Johnson, 1798), 2.
15 Ibid., 4.
16 John Kenneth Galbraith, *The Affluent Society* (London: Penguin, 1999), 25.
17 Smith, *Inquiry*, 156.
18 Ibid., 374.
19 Ibid., 378.
20 Ibid., 383.
21 Alfred Marshall, *Principles of Economics*, 8th edition (London: MacMillan and
   Co., 1890), 7.
22 Ibid., 9.
23 Ibid., 11.
24 Ibid.

25 Ibid., 291.
26 Ibid., 294.

Chapter 15: Karl Marx

1 Joseph A. Schumpeter, *Capitalism, Socialism and Democracy* (London: George Allen & Unwin, 1976), 22.
2 Eric Hobsbawm, *How to Change the World: Tales of Marx and Marxism* (London: Little, Brown, 2011), 202.
3 Marshall, *Principles*, 339.
4 Peter Antonioni and Sean Masaki Flynn, *Economics for Dummies*, 2nd edition (Chichester: Wiley, 2011), 348.
5 Marx, *Capital*, I: 322.
6 Karl Marx, 'Review: May–October 1850', *New Rheinische Zeitung* 5–6, http://www.marxists.org/archive/marx/works/1850/11/01.htm (accessed 16 December 2013).

Chapter 16: George, Veblen and Schumpeter

1 Henry George, *Progress and Poverty* (New York: Robert Schalkenbach Foundation, 1933), 4.
2 Ibid., 8.
3 Ibid., 13.
4 Ibid., 55.
5 Ibid., 59.
6 Ibid., 93.
7 Ibid., 107.
8 Thorstein Veblen, *The Theory of the Leisure Class: An Economic Study of Institutions* (New York: B. W. Huebsch, 1918), 6.
9 Ibid., 96.
10 Schumpeter, *Capitalism, Socialism and Democracy*, 61, 167.
11 Marx, *Capital*, I: 485.
12 Joseph A. Schumpeter, *The Theory of Economic Development* (New Brunswick: Transaction Publishers, 2008), 89.
13 Ibid., 89.
14 Schumpeter, *Capitalism, Socialism and Democracy*, 132.
15 Schumpeter, *Theory of Economic Development*, 93.
16 Ibid., 78.
17 Ibid., 73.

Chapter 17: The Austrian School

1 Ludwig von Mises, *Socialism: An Economic and Sociological Analysis* (Indianapolis: Liberty Fund, 1981), 528.
2 Ibid., 530.
3 Ibid., 531.
4 Ibid., 211.
5 Ibid., 223.

6 Ibid., 379.
7 F. A. Hayek, *The Road to Serfdom* (London: Routledge, 2008), 43.
8 Ibid., 42.
9 Ibid., 125.
10 Ibid., 63.

Chapter 18: Keynes, Tawney and Galbraith

1 Keynes, *General Theory of Employment*, 70.
2 Ibid., 85.
3 R. H. Tawney, *The Acquisitive Society* (London: G. Bell and Sons, 1921), 116.
4 Keynes, *General Theory of Employment*, 235.
5 Tawney, *Rise of Capitalism*, 270.
6 Tawney, *Acquisitive Society*, 6.
7 Ibid., 17.
8 Ibid., 32.
9 Ibid., 119.
10 Krugman, *Peddling Prosperity*, 13–14.
11 Galbraith, *Affluent Society*, xii.
12 Ibid., 1.
13 Ibid., 22.
14 Ibid., 23.
15 Ibid., 26.
16 Ibid., 47.
17 Ibid., 50.
18 Ibid., 79.
19 Ibid., 81.
20 Ibid., 114.
21 Robert Skidelsky, *Keynes: The Return of the Master* (London: Penguin, 2010), 60.

Chapter 19: Economics in Fiction

1 Von Mises, *Socialism*, 421.
2 Raistrick, *Dynasty of Ironfounders*, 263.
3 Tressell, Robert, *The Ragged Trousered Philanthropists* (London: Penguin, 2004), xxiii.
4 Ibid.
5 Upton Sinclair, *Oil!* (London: Penguin, 2008), 215.
6 John Steinbeck, *The Grapes of Wrath* (London: Penguin, 1992), xiv.
7 Ibid., 365.
8 Von Mises, *Socialism*, 420.

Chapter 20: Ayn Rand

1 Jenny Turner, 'The Rise of Rand', *Guardian*, 14 March 2009.
2 Naomi Klein, 'Thanks a Million, Ayn Rand, for Setting the Greedy Free', *Guardian*, 29 September 2007.
3 Ayn Rand, *Capitalism: The Unknown Ideal* (New York: Signet, 1966), 12.

4 Ibid., 20.

5 Tressell, *Ragged Trousered Philanthropists*, 161.

6 Ayn Rand, *Atlas Shrugged* (New York: Signet, 1992), 929.

Chapter 21: Milton Friedman

1 Milton Friedman and Rose Friedman, *Free to Choose: A Personal Statement* (New York: Harcourt Brace Jovanovich, 1980), 5.

2 Friedman, Milton, *Capitalism and Freedom* (Chicago and London: Chicago University Press, 2002), 11.

3 Ibid., 8.

4 Ibid., 9.

5 Ibid., 2.

6 Ibid., 11.

7 Ibid., 12.

8 Ibid., 120.

9 Ibid., 133.

10 Milton Friedman, 'The Social Responsibility of Business is to Increase its Profits', *New York Times Magazine*, 13 September 1970.

11 Ha-Joon Chang, *23 Things They Don't Tell You About Capitalism* (London: Allen Lane, 2010), 21.

12 Friedman, Milton, *Capitalism and Freedom* (Chicago and London: Chicago University Press, 2002), 133.

13 Jonathan Freedland, 'In the US, the Right is Eating Itself: Cameron, Take Note', *Guardian*, 10 March 2012.

14 Friedman, *Capitalism and Freedom*, 108.

15 Ibid., 110.

16 Ibid., 111.

17 Ibid., 114.

18 George Jones, 'Thatcher Praises Friedman, Her Freedom Fighter', *Telegraph*, 17 November 2006.

19 Joseph Stiglitz, *Freefall: Free Markets and the Sinking of the Global Economy* (London: Penguin, 2010), 225.

20 Francis Fukuyama, *The End of History and the Last Man* (London: Hamish Hamilton, 1992), 42.

21 Ibid., 123.

22 Ibid., 104.

23 Ibid., 124.

24 Naomi Klein, *The Shock Doctrine: The Rise of Disaster Capitalism* (London: Penguin, 2007), 209.

25 Joseph Stiglitz, 'Bleakonomics', *New York Times*, 30 September 2007.

Chapter 22: Quakernomics and the Credit Crunch

1 Skidelsky, *Keynes*, 58.

2 '£13 Trillion: Hoard Hidden from Taxman by Global Elite', *Observer*, 22 July 2012.

3 Lynsey Hanley, 'The Way We Live Now', *Guardian*, 14 March 2009.
4 Galbraith, *Affluent Society*, iix.
5 Paul Krugman, 'Free to Die', *New York Times*, 15 September 2011.
6 Paul Krugman, *The Return of Depression Economics and the Crisis of 2008* (New York: W.W Norton, 2009), 182.
7 Ibid., 131.
8 Ibid., 163.
9 Stiglitz, *Freefall*, 12.
10 Ibid., 156.
11 Ibid., 175.
12 Ibid., 165.
13 Ibid., 180.
14 Ibid., 204.
15 Ibid., 273.
16 Ibid., 208.
17 Jeffrey Sachs, *The Price of Civilization: Economics and Ethics after the Fall* (London: The Bodley Head, 2011), 34.
18 Ibid., 102.
19 Friedman, *Capitalism and Freedom*, 31–6.
20 Klein, *Shock Doctrine*, 144.
21 Sachs, *Price of Civilization*, 210.
22 Ibid., 27.
23 Ibid., 115.
24 Ibid., 219.
25 Andrew Grice, 'Voters Will Reject Tax Rises, Labour Think Tank Warns Miliband', *Independent*, 18 July 2012.
26 Sachs, *Price of Civilization*, 100.
27 Richard Murphy, *The Courageous State: Rethinking Economics, Society and the Role of Government* (London: Searching Finance, 2011).
28 Sachs, *Price of Civilization*, 45.

Chapter 23: Quakernomics and Economic History

1 Chang, *23 Things*, 106.
2 Rand, *Capitalism*, 28.

INDEX

Numbers appearing in boldface refer to figures found in the Illustrations section of the book following Part II.